YOUTH:
GROWING UP
to Change the World

Daniel C. Jessen

Copyright © 2016 by Daniel C. Jessen

YOUTH: Growing Up to Change the World
by Daniel C. Jessen

Printed in the United States of America.

ISBN 9781498469197

All rights reserved solely by the author. The author guarantees all contents are original and do not infringe upon the legal rights of any other person or work. No part of this book may be reproduced in any form without the permission of the author. The views expressed in this book are not necessarily those of the publisher.

Scripture quotations taken from the Contemporary English Version (CEV). Copyright © 1995 American Bible Society. Used by permission. All rights reserved.

Scripture quotations taken from the *Easy to read version* (ERV). Copyright © 2006 by Bible League International.

Scripture quotations taken from the English Standard Version (ESV). Copyright © 2001 by Crossway, a publishing ministry of Good News Publishers. Used by permission. All rights reserved.

Scripture quotations taken from The Message (MSG). Copyright © 1993, 1994, 1995, 1996, 2000, 2001, 2002. Used by permission of NavPress Publishing Group. Used by permission. All rights reserved.

Scripture quotations taken from the New International Version (NIV). Copyright © 1973, 1978, 1984, 2011 by Biblica, Inc.™. Used by permission. All rights reserved.

Scripture quotations taken from the New International Readers Version (NIRV). Copyright © 1995, 1996, 1998, 2014 by Biblica, Inc.™. Used by permission. All rights reserved.

Scripture quotations taken from the New King James Version (NKJV). Copyright © 1982 by Thomas Nelson, Inc. Used by permission. All rights reserved.

Scripture quotations taken from the New Living Translation (NLT). Copyright © 1996, 2004, 2007, 2013 by Tyndale House Foundation. Used by permission of Tyndale House Publishers, Inc.

Scripture quotations taken from the Voice Bible Copyright © 2012 by Thomas Nelson, Inc. The Voice™ translation © 2012 Ecclesia Bible Society. All rights reserved.

www.xulonpress.com

DEDICATION

I dedicate this book to faithful women and men from many nations across the globe whose hearts reach out to adolescents with the love of Christ and the persistence of the Apostles. I commend to them the words of St. Paul which I memorized sixty years ago and have sought to follow ever since, "And the things that you [Timothy] have heard from me among many witnesses, commit these to faithful men who will be able to teach others also" (Second Timothy 2:2, NKJV). Lest females be left out of this formula, I share the CEV version, "You have often heard me teach. Now I want you to tell these same things to followers who can be trusted to tell others."

I similarly commit the musings and conclusions of this book to *emerging-adult-children,* whether in Africa, Asia, Australia, Europe, North or South America, who in their maturing by the grace of God will bring the Light and Salt of God's Word to bear upon the people and societies of many nations. May they truly become world-changers because caring Christian parents and other women and men invested in them during their adolescent years.

ACKNOWLEDGMENTS AND APPRECIATION

Most of my adult life I have focused on discipling, with the conviction that maturing men work best with boys and young men, Christian women with girls and young women. In my early years of ministry with Christian Service Brigade, I received considerable reinforcement in my beliefs from gifted colleagues. Later, when I taught at Gordon-Conwell Theological Seminary and at international venues, I usually had women in my classes and advisee groups, nevertheless I sought to interact primarily with male students because of my persuasion of its importance. I continue to flourish in ministry to men today.

Ironically, as I look back over my life I realize that it has been godly *women* who have predominantly touched me at heart, starting with my spiritual lineage. Both of my grandmothers, Lise Marie Jessen and Mamie Blatt, prayed for me from afar. My Christian mother, Eunice B. Jessen, shepherded me for years and set a pattern for lifelong service. In graduate school, it was women professors at Wheaton Graduate School who demonstrated what Christian living and effective teaching was like: Professor Vivienne Blomquist; Drs. Lois and Mary LeBar. Last but not least, my wife Nancy has been a faithful companion and treasured inspiration for me spiritually as well as professionally.

With additional irony, God saw fit to give Nancy and me two daughters and one son. In the next generation, six granddaughters and two grandsons joined our family. My first great-grandchild is also a girl!

I felt the hand of the Lord on me to write this book at the last session of the first youth ministry class I had taught outside North America, at Alliance Biblical Seminary, Quezon City, Metro Manila, Philippines. I had asked students to reflect on what God might be asking of them now that the class was nearly over. I decided I would do likewise and it seemed that God was saying, "Something needs to be written about youth ministry that is not tied to American culture." So here is the result of that call. I thank front-row students Anne Ardina-deJesus and Randolph Velasquez and the thirty other students from that class who inspired me to pursue this topic by their class participation and encouragement.

The immediate provocation for the completion of this manuscript came from Dr. Sarah Bowers Dunlop, an international youth ministry researcher from the U.K.; I appreciate Sarah's encouragement. A number of other helpful people have contributed ideas to this book: Wes Andrews, Lloyd Burghart, Sherri Carlson, Jeff Castillo, Steve Jessen, Pete Johnson, Ian Ma, Dr. Walt Mueller, Dr. Ng Peh Cheng, Ron Rynd, Gretchen Schoon-Tanis, BJ Slinger, and Gregg Yarian. Also, many friends have prayed me through this process, from the Philippines and South Africa and throughout the United States and Canada. I also thank my friend Cody Cochrane for helping to put the manuscript into publishable form and Rochelle Colon from Xulon Press who managed the production process. May God bless each one for what they have contributed.

Dan Jessen, Waxhaw, North Carolina, USA
January 2016

FOREWORD

Can it be true that in every culture, nation, tribe and people in this globe, parents desire their children to Grow Up to be responsible, able, contributing members of society. Seems so, at least in the cultures I've experienced in traveling, observing and serving in more than two dozen countries of this world — and academic research seems to point in the same direction (see note below).

Can it be true that most parents who are followers of Jesus Christ have an above-average desire for the "success" of their offspring. Seems so — how often have I heard older Christians express with joy (and pride?) that "our grown children are serving the Lord"! How often have I heard about American families who change churches because they want their teenagers to "have a good youth program," the assumption being that this will serve as a reliable conduit to adulthood!

As the average age of the global population continues to plummet downward, both Christian national leaders and missionaries seek ways to impact youth for Christ. Can it be true that a new paradigm of youth ministry needs to be developed, to make indigenous approaches more effective than "adapted" American exports across the globe? My conviction is that "adapted" (or worse, simply "translated" or exported) youth programs fail to tap into deep, non-American cultural roots and thereby miss the more profound possibilities in youth ministry outside the American cultural stream.

So, if the purpose of childhood and adolescence is MATURATION — and I believe it is — then what are the implications for Christian parents *and* for Bible-believing congregations? What are the implications for engaging in youth ministry in non-American contexts, using maturation as a backdrop? And most importantly, how does this lend itself to cross-cultural application?

In this book the reader is challenged to think about youth ministry, not as a package of transferable concepts or methods, nor a program model to be modified to another culture, nor any other American exported product. Instead, the reader will be led to examine his or her own cultural setting and devise a model appropriate at hand, in accordance with Biblical principles. If something truly indigenous emerges which enables girls and boys to truly *grow up* to be godly women and men in various countries and cultures throughout the world, then I will be immensely gratified.

Though I am writing this for my brothers and sisters globally, I hope youth ministers in the American/Canadian milieu would face these same questions to mold or remold what is happening in youth ministry in North American congregations. Having taught youth ministry students in North America, Africa, Europe, Latin America and Asia over a span of thirty-plus years, I carry a deep burden for Christian ministries to adolescents everywhere.

> May 18, 2004, San Juan, Metro Manila, the Philippines
> (also drafted in Stellenbosch, Cape Province, South
> Africa; Harare, Zimbabwe;
> La Paz, B.C.S., Mexico;
> Waxhaw, North Carolina, USA)

NOTE: The basic exceptions to parental desires for their offspring to grow up occur in cultures that either practice some form of infanticide as in some jungle tribes, or murder by abortion as in so-called civilized countries. In either case, these children are given no chance of growing up; but their siblings who survive, if any, are subject to the principle stated above — parents desire to see their children mature.

ABOUT THIS BOOK:
Terms and Sources

- References to *boy/girl, man/woman* and their plurals are put in mixed order and irregularly as they may occur in the text. The author's attempt is to be aware of gender, but any uneven distribution of pronouns is not meant to convey superiority of one gender or over.
- *Contemporary English Bible [CEV]*. The Bible passages cited are taken from the (CEV), "Copyright © 1995 by American Bible Society," unless otherwise noted.
- E*merging-adult-child*, as a term, is most frequently used to denote adolescents because it seeks to express the need for these girls and boys to be principally growing toward adulthood, not lurching back into their childish immaturity. When designating middle adolescents (probably secondary school), the term used is E*MERGING-MAN/WOMAN-boy/girl* (or plural forms).
- *Italics*. When italics are found in quotations, they are emphases added by the author.
- *Maestro de iniciació*. (Spanish: master of initiation). When it was time for the children nearing puberty to enter into and through an initiation ceremony in traditional societies, the responsibility was put into the hands of an individual man or woman, and a team of specially-designated men (for boys) or women (for girls) under his/her direction.

The role of the *maestro de iniciación,* or overseer, is a key one in traditional society — without this mature woman or man, entry into adulthood was almost impossible. Because the traditional ceremonies involved a number of adults (for example, elders, mentors, parents), the director could be compared to the conductor of an orchestra, or in Spanish, *maestro.* [The author is indebted to a group of seminary students in Mexicali, B.C.N., Mexico, for applying this term to youth ministry.]

- *Parent* as used may denote biological or adoptive parents, a step-parent, and/or a single parent, either father or mother. If another adult such as a grandparent has custody of a child, whatever is said about *parent* can be applied to that person as well.
- *Pinoy* is an informal designation referring to the Filipino people in the Philippines and overseas Filipinos around the world. Filipinos usually refer to themselves as *Pinoy* or sometimes the feminine *Pinay.*
- The word, *teenager,* has generally been avoided in the text because puberty may begin before the teen years, especially among females, and adolescence usually extends beyond age nineteen for both young men and women. The word, *kid,* is also eschewed, as is explained in textual material.
- *Youthworker* is used generically to describe persons in youth ministry, full-time or part-time, professional (paid) or volunteer (unpaid).

NOTE: An American reader will sometimes see apparent misspellings, because British spellings, when they occur in quotations, are left intact, e.g., behaviour, Saviour, counselling.

TABLE OF CONTENTS

DEDICATION

ACKNOWLEDGEMENTS AND APPRECIATION

FOREWORD

ABOUT THIS BOOK

1 When Growing Up *Ain't Fun*

PART I — Cultural Foundations

What's to be Learned from Culture about Youth Ministry in the Twenty-first Century

2 Checking Out Indigenous Patterns
3 Traditional Paths to African Manhood
4 Other Traditional Paths to Manhood
5 Traditional Paths to Womanhood
6 Echoes of the Initiation Tradition
7 A Compendium Based on *Traditional Initiation*

INTERLOGUE

PART II — Bible Foundations

What's to be Learned from the Bible about Youth Ministry in the Twenty-first Century

8 A Biblical Search for Adolescence
9 Biblically-based Youth Ministry With The *Emerging-Adult-CHILD*
10 Biblically-based Youth Ministry With The *EMERGING-ADULT-Child*.
   The Goal—Christian Adulthood; Role of the Parent(s)
11 Biblically-based Youth Ministry With The *EMERGING-ADULT-Child* (continued...) Role of Youth
12 Biblically-based Youth Ministry With The *EMERGING-ADULT-Child* (continued...) Congregation's Role
13 Biblically-based Youth Ministry With The *EMERGING-ADULT-Child* (continued...) Youthworkers' Role

PART III — Changing the World

14 A Path Through Adolescence
15 Now Where Do We Go?
16 Developing Unique Coming-of-Age Ceremonies
17 Other Questions Considered

AFTERWORD
BIBLIOGRAPHY
APPENDICES

A Traditional Female Transitions to Adulthood
B Descriptions of Filipino *Tuli*
C Description of Filipina *Debut*
D Creating a Rite of Passage in Your Family

WHEN GROWING UP *AIN'T FUN!*
Mula Pagkabata Hanggang Pagtanda
(From Childhood to Adulthood in Filipino)

Chapter 1

Youthworker: "You want to grow up, don't you?"

Youth: *"Certainly — why do you ask?"*

Youthworker: "So you like the idea of having adult privileges, making your own decisions, and the like, eh?"

Youth: *"Of course — besides, don't all children kinda grow up?"*

Youthworker: "Sometimes. But how will you *know* if *you*'ve succeeded or not?"

Youth: *"Ah, well, it's like, kinda, well, you know what I mean...."* [Non-Americans, please pardon the use of American slang. Hopefully the reader senses the youth's imprecision of expression.]

Youthworker: "No, I don't *know* what you mean—tell me, please, what does it mean to grow up?"

Growing up! If youth is about anything, it is about "growing up." It seems simple enough at first glance, but in reality young girls and boys must universally climb a very steep mountain to reach that rocky plateau called "adulthood." In a globalized culture, the Christian community has a responsibility and opportunity to assist youth cope well with this phase of life — *as well as* equip them for the heavy burdens of becoming an adult in their respective cultures, *so that* they will become Christian change-agents in a hurting and broken world.

To minister to youth in today's world, a youthworker has to divest himself or herself of the idea that all cultures include a life journey that begins in childhood, transmutes into a possibly troubled adolescence and emerges hopefully into some level of independent (or interdependent) maturity called "adulthood." In truth, adolescence was not identified as a distinct life phase until about one hundred years ago, in the seminal work of G. Stanley Hall.[1] In traditional societies boys and girls have moved and do move directly from childhood into adulthood. The transition from girl/boy to woman/man has often been accomplished expeditiously through initiation ceremonies, testing experiences or threshold rites,[2] simply bypassing adolescence and, by extension, *youth ministry*.

For instance, a people-group called the *Wai Wai* lived as they had for centuries in the Amazon River basin in northern Brazil before encountered by Unevangelized Field[3] missionaries in the mid-twentieth century. Here's what "growing up" meant in that culture:

> ... the time came for Elka to undergo the ordeal which, if passed, *would make him strong and handsome as he grew into a man*. Belts of stinging ants were to be tied to his legs. He knew the stings would hurt, but he dared not fail the test.
>
> Chekema, who was headman of the village, supervised the ritual. First he wove two belts from reeds

and tied them on his wrists. Then he and Elka went in search of a colony of stinging ants. They found one . . . an ashen mound spewing out innumerable ants . . . carrying vicious stingers in their tails. Chekema took one of the belts from his wrists and, stretching its scores of flexible holes, handed it to Elka.

"Pick them up by their heads," he said," and stick their fat rumps into the holes. Elka filled each opening with a wriggling ant, careful not to let one sting him prematurely. They came back to the village with both belts filled. A crowd had gathered in front of the house. Elka was beginning to be afraid; he had been stung before by the ants, but never by so many as this. What if he should cry in front of all those people. Some would laugh at him. Others would say, "He's *just a boy*, what can you expect? And that would be just as bad. What if he tore off the belts, unable to bear the stings. If he did, how in the world could he go through life?

Chekema had stooped down and was beginning to tie the belts on Elka, just below his knees.

"Try to keep them on as long as you can," his brother said, not unkindly. Elka bit his lip against the coming ordeal. "Stop laughing," he wanted to say to one snickering boy, "for your time is coming."

A prickle struck the back of one leg. Instinctively Elka reached down to brush at it, then restrained himself. Soon came another prick, then another. The ants, unable to free their tails from the tightened bands, were stinging furiously in retaliation.

The stings were like arrow points scratching his skin, or like the fangs of a hundred tiny snakes. . . . He dug his nails into his palms, determined not to touch his legs!

At first he felt each stings. Soon both legs were burning. They were many stings — no, they were all one. Elka wanted to tear off the bands. . . . He must run to the river to cool his burning flesh. He wouldn't, though. The people would laugh all the more and despise him for his cowardice. He would stand fast — for a while yet. Wasn't the magic of those tiny mites getting inside him? Wasn't the strength enough to last a lifetime? He stood stiffly, holding back the tears.

. . . He wanted to grow up strong. . . .

The hurt was spreading from his legs, going up and down his whole body. . . . Maybe the ants had burrowed into his flesh, as fleas did into the soles of his feet, and were stinging him from the inside.

"Ohhhhh!" . . . He was crying. He wasn't going to cry — but he did. The tears were spilling from his eyes. . . . He still clenched his fists, but he couldn't control them. Savagely they beat at his swollen legs. He couldn't stand still. He began to dance. The villagers roared.

"Take them off!" he screamed at last.

Chekema did. As the older, wiser one stooped to remove the belts, Elka wondered if he had behaved himself so as to bring reward. He had cried, and now he was ashamed of himself.

"Oh, Little Body," his brother said, smiling broadly as he surveyed the puffy skin where the belts had been. "You can boast of many stings. They will *make you a strong and desirable man.*"

This ordeal marked *the end of Elka's boyhood.* A few days later *he became a man* . . . Chekema wrapped strings of tiny white beads around his biceps. With the armbands he bore the badge of a youth who could take one of the young girls with growing breasts as his wife, one who could enter freely into the drunken frenzies of the tribal dances.[4]

....

As a man, Elka now pulled up his stool to sit with the others when they preened and painted themselves every morning. . . . A *man's* ornamentation, though, helped hide these deficiencies of early youth. . . . He tied feathers on his loincloth and stuck brilliant plumes in his armbands. . . . The final touch was painting of his own red-and-black design on his cheeks, nose, and forehead. . . .

At field-cutting time, Elka went with *the other men*.[5]

That day, Elka became a *man*. He had accomplished the gigantic leap into adulthood![6]

> **Youth:** *"So what? Doesn't sound like much fun, in fact, not at all. Just a kid with a bunch of stinging ants! What does that prove?"*
>
> *Youthworker:* "Remember we were discussing 'growing up'? Elka just became a man!"
>
> **Youth:** *"So? My world is entirely different from his...."*
>
> *Youthworker:* "Yes, but we might learn something from Elka's culture. About how "growing up' turns out for you and me!"
>
> **Youth***: "You think so?"*
>
> *Youthworker:* "Let's find out. Are you with me?"

THE TRADITIONAL PASSAGE-TO-ADULTHOOD

Adolescence or *youth* did not exist for Elka. His journey to adulthood was very well defined by tribal custom, as it is in traditional societies. A boy had a circumscribed role as *child* in society until he reached the momentous occasion when he would pass into *manhood*, with its attendant accountability and privileges. Girls were likewise thrown into fixed female roles. In Elka's world, gender defined a child's role. Although many contemporary cultures view this as highly restrictive, the system made life much simpler for *Wai Wai* boys and girls in their growth toward manhood and womanhood. Modern gender identity issues were non-existent among the *Wai Wai* people. Gender was decisive upon the delivery of a *Wai Wai* baby. If the father was displeased with the gender of the baby, he immediately beat her or him to death with a club. [Such savagery is perhaps more easily understood in today's so-called "civilized world," in which pre-birth gender identification is common, resulting in widespread female infanticide in India, China and elsewhere.]

Different Approaches for Girls and Boys

The socialization and maturation processes in traditional societies are markedly different for males and females, growing out of the physiological issues relating to child-bearing. Elka's father and other significant men, tribal elders, older brothers, uncles and others realized that he needed to be taught the ways of the jungle, the cunning and persistence of the hunter, how to fashion a canoe and more. They shouldered that role in much the same way as their forebears had done for them. The girls in Elka's village unsurprisingly followed a distinctly-different socialization on the way to marriage and childbearing.

Elka, as a boy aspiring to grow up, submitted to his training, either willingly or under compulsion. It was clear to all in *Wai Wai* society how a boy became a man, both for those on the journey to adulthood and the community at large. Because in Elka's world parent-child relationships were unambiguous, so-called and much over-emphasized "adolescent rebellion" was non-existent.

The process worked! As a child, Elka was socialized into *Wai Wai* male society, gradually learning his roles by close association with his father and other adult male role models. He knew that at the proper time he would undergo the initiation ceremony and thus become *a man*. Passing the initiation test with the stinging ants allowed him to join the other *men*.

Therewith, Elka would enter the responsibilities and acquire the privileges of *manhood* in the *Wai Wai* tribe, such as:

- hunting and fishing for food,
- cutting forest trees for garden plots in the jungle,
- repairing his hunting gear or canoe,
- accumulating strings of beads (symbols of wealth in *Wai Wai* society),
- participating in village dances and orgies,
- taking a wife and fathering children,
- murdering any of his children at birth, as he might wish.[7]

After Elka's initiation ordeal, every man, woman and child in the tribe knew beyond doubt what was expected of him as a *man*. They clearly understood that a boy was a boy — until he was a *man*. Similarly, a girl was a girl — until she was a *woman*. Growing up for Elka was no mystery nor for his parents. Elka's parents were not confused and puzzled. Neither were they frightened of Elka's coming adulthood; in fact they probably welcomed it as a natural part of human life. This deeply contrasts with Westernizing societies in which huge uncertainties exist in the gap between childhood and adulthood known as *adolescence* or *youth*.

Consequently, in Elka's jungle world, the preparation of girls for womanhood[8] and boys for manhood took widely divergent tracks, leading to different threshold rites. Each needed to learn gender-specific tasks suited to that culture.

The timing of Elka's initiation also recognized the God-given differences between males and females. A girl's expectation of adulthood is usually triggered once a girl has experienced her first menstrual period. Her thoughts of marriage and motherhood move from fantasy to potentiality. Adolescent growth spurt research[9] shows that females, on average, enter puberty a couple years before males, though there is much variation when comparing individuals. Hence, the cohort of girls Elka's age in the village had already completed female initiation. But Elka and his friends lived carefree and unaware, continuing to play and act like boys — until that moment when the village elders called the oldest ones to undergo initiation, a year or more after their female peers.

Careful Oversight

During childhood years parents and relatives were expected to gradually introduce living skills to their children. Often this took the form of what might be termed child labor, in which children from a very young age would be assigned various tasks that would insure the survival of the family and that would concurrently train them for adult roles to contribute to their world.

When it was time for the children nearing puberty to enter into and through the initiation ceremony the responsibility is/was put into the hands of an individual man or woman, or a team of specially-designated men (for boys) or women (for girls). In Elka's case above, Chekema, headman of the village, supervised the ritual.

The overseer's role is a key one in that society — without this mature leader, entry into adulthood would be almost impossible. Because the traditional ceremonies usually involved a number of adults (for example, elders, mentors, parents) the director could be compared to the conductor of an orchestra, or in Spanish, *maestro de iniciación*.[10] The conduct of this transitional ceremony was always under the direction of mature adults.

> **Youth:** *"Old folks leading the youth? You have to be kidding! Doesn't sound like fun to me!"*
>
> **Youthworker:** *"O.K., Elka definitely lived in a different world. But I wonder if we might need to take a look at our youth ministry in light of Elka's experience?"*
>
> **Youth:** *"You think so? I'm not sure where that will take us — unless to the Amazon jungle — ha, ha! — no thanks, no piranhas, pythons or parasites for me!"*
>
> **Youthworker:** *"*I don't like the idea of reptiles and insects and man-eating fish either! But seriously, what do you think it takes to* grow up *now, not then?*
>
> **Youth:** *"Look, we live in the modern world. Can't we just forget about this ancient stuff and just start having something relevant?"*
>
> **Youthworker:** *"*Let's see by exploring a case study. Like, what might *youth ministry* look like, for example, in modern-day Philippines?"
>
> **Youth:** *"Like way out in the Pacific Ocean? Aw, O.K., if you say so. . . ."*

A CASE STUDY

Charting A Journey For Relevant *Youth Ministry* In The Philippines

An analysis of a particular ethnic group may help to show the path to growing a more-culturally-relevant youth ministry. Today urban Filipino families and youth seem to be in confusion because of extended adolescence as well as the widespread, almost-one-world culture promoted by American media and commercialism. Youth ministry without an anchor to the past may also be drifting. Hence, a woman or man who is called to minister with youth in the Republic of the Philippines can benefit from reflecting on the meaning of "adolescence" and "adulthood" in their society in which the many subcultures might exist in Westernized Metro Manila, tourist-mobbed Baguio, rural Mindanao or steamy Cebu City.

The Good Old Days

Initiation rites have been used for centuries by various people-groups in the Philippines to define a clear passage into adulthood, thereby eliminating the confusion observed today in urban Filipino families. Of course, in the Philippines these initiation experiences have been fast disappearing as global media and culture penetrate even the most remote islands of the archipelago. A good starting place is digging beneath twenty-first century cultural expectations in Philippine society to explore the historical context of transitional ceremonies, even if generations old.

Traces of these ceremonies still exist for example, *tuli* (circumcision) for young boys and *debut* (formal introduction of a debutante) for upper-class girls.[11] When examined, these vestiges of initiation do serve as a step *toward* adult status for today's Filipino children, but the recipient does not usually receive full adult respect or responsibility. The young woman or man may have achieved Pinoy *adulthood* but *only* symbolically, not in significant ways to cope with today's challenges. As a result, contemporary Filipino adolescence is filled with ambiguities in spite of practicing the vestiges of tribal initiations in *tuli* and *debut*.

Contemporary Cultural Markers

If *youth ministry* is aimed at facilitating the passage of the growing child over the bridge of adolescence to womanhood or manhood, how should it be approached? When embarking upon youth ministry, a youthworker must inquire, "What are the cultural markers a young man or woman must attain in order to reach 'adult status' within this time and place, e.g. Metro Manila in the early twenty-first century?" What signs are there which tell child and family alike that he or she is leaving childhood? Equally as important, what communicates to the young woman or man that she or he has achieved *adult status*?

So in 2016, when does a Filipino boy or girl exit childhood? At *tuli* or first menstruation? Even more puzzling, when does an adolescent pass out of the *not-quite-adult-adolescent* stage into full adulthood? At a girl's debut? A young man's degree? Parents, children, congregations and youth workers in churches and communities, seeking to survive "the adolescent journey" which for many families can be unpredictable and perilous, are often in a quandary, not knowing when adult status is achieved.

The challenge for Filipino youth ministers is charting how a girl or boy develops into the status of woman or man, while passing through the trying period of societal in-between-ness known as *adolescence*. One step toward an answer to this conundrum is delineating what constitutes "adulthood" in the Philippines. Such a definition creates a solid foundation for setting relevant objectives for an authentic culturally-relevant youth ministry, rather than *copy-catting* American music and youth ministry structures, programs and curriculum. A Filipino (or expatriate) youthworker therefore must ask, *"What constitutes Christian manhood and womanhood in the Philippines?"*

Once cultural boundaries of childhood and adulthood

have been defined, the youth minister can begin to use the building blocks of Biblical truth that will be necessary to achieve the goal of assisting families and their children grow into Christian adulthood. S/he must to ponder how youth can be effectively prepared for what they will soon face as adults. These definitions will dictate program strategy in a way that is thoroughly relevant to the youth in their culture and Biblically based.

> **Youth:** *"Whoa, you've lost me. Am I a 'kid' or not? I mean, as in 'a little kid.'"*
>
> *Youthworker:* "Do you still play with toys? Dolls? Do you play tag any more?"
>
> **Youth:** *"You think I'm a kid, don't you? Well, I'm not."*
>
> *Youthworker:* "I thought not. But are you *grown up*? Like in, what do you want to be when you've grown up — a police officer, a doctor, a missionary, a parent, a carpenter, etc.?"
>
> **Youth:** "Of course, I'm not really *grown up* — yet! But I can, well, you know, I can take care of myself."
>
> *Youthworker:* "Let's see what it takes to *grow up* in the Philippines. Then get back to us."
>
> **Youth:** *"O.K., I'll go along with you."*

BECOMING AN ADULT IN PHILIPPINE CULTURE

An American definition of adulthood usually includes the concept of *independence*: economic, familial, civic, personal, spiritual/devotional. Not so in the Philippines.

> European and American mothers encourage their children to be self-reliant and assertive. . . . The Filipino child from birth constantly receives attention and help not only from parents, but from two sets of relatives, from his father's and mother's sides. The whole neighborhood also contributes to the attention. This large kinship has conditioned the child to leisurely grow up. Often, the child would seek help and care in activities he could already carry out himself.[12]

In addition to receiving protective parenting as a child or youth, Filipinos have a reputation for being highly relational.

> They are hardly alone, quite happy being together — when they eat, sleep, work, travel, pray, create or celebrate. Having a minimal sense of privacy, they are open, trusting and easily accessible socially. Instead of a meticulous concern for safeguarding their private sphere, as in the case of Western peoples, many Filipinos actively seek a convergence of their lives with the lives of others. For example, a sharing of concern is seen in a common form of greeting . . . such as, "Where are you going?" or "Where have you been?" Sharing of tasks and responsibilities within the family and the community is a way of life. Thus, they become highly skilled and creative in interpersonal relations and social interaction. The capacity to integrate socially becomes one of the hallmarks of maturity.[13]

As a result, in the Philippines, personal independence of the individual is not so much an indicator of maturity as perhaps a *healthy interdependence*. One might expect Philippine adolescence to be even more traumatic than that of American youth, that is, it will be more difficult to achieve and evaluate personal maturity when individuals seem so enmeshed with others. But "independence" may be a distinct American value that ought *not* be imposed upon Philippine youth ministry.

In any case, a Filipino youthworker seems obliged to:
(1) Study the dimensions of adulthood as they now exist, and thereafter.
(2) Seek ways to encourage and facilitate an appropriate maturation process for Pinoy youth. The following questions are asked in order to provoke thought and discussion about the process of achieving "adulthood" in the Philippines.

Social Dimensions of Filipino Adulthood

What does it mean for a Filipino to have *social interdependence?* The custom of the *barkada* can be explored in light of the healthiness (or otherwise) of those gender-specific cliques for males and females that continue into adult years. How does an adolescent create personal space for his or her individuation?[14] The *barkada* phenomenon possibly offers a potent force for increasing maturation — or it could possibly be a retardant. Only further research can provide an answer.

The widespread use of social media among Pinoy youth offers another frontier for encouraging or hindering personal growth. How this can be harnessed for maturation needs to be studied by youthworkers in churches and parachurch organizations.

Question: *How can Filipino Christian youthworkers, as they link up with parents and congregations, assist Pinoy youth to achieve healthy social interdependence in atmosphere so filled with opportunities for socialization, healthy and otherwise?*

The Economic Dimensions of Filipino Adulthood

Young Filipinos face huge issues when it comes to being economically self-supporting or family-supporting. The Philippines has an increasing youth population and a continuing unemployment problem for youth, especially among the poorer classes. This situation stimulates much migration to cities where, it is hoped, there will be more jobs. But often there are not. Families may be forced into subsisting in "squatter" communities — rude and makeshift shacks *(barong-barong)* on vacant land. Without jobs, poor youth stay dependent on their parents and/or resort to illegal earnings. Some urban migrants come without their families and when employed may be able to find more affordable housing in an arrangement known as "bed space," in which the renter receives a bed and shares other living space with others in a dormitory arrangement. How can a squatter or bed-spacer young person come to a place of economic maturity?

One solution that has appealed to thousands of Filipinos (estimated to be about 10% of the population) is to enter the international labor market, in official government parlance, "Overseas Foreign Workers"(OFW). Much of the money (estimated to be in the billions of dollars) earned by OFW's is sent back to their families in the Philippines, demonstrating the principle of economic interdependence. Male OFW's spend long periods away from home laboring as merchant marine sailors, oil field workers and members of construction crews. Females (an estimated 75% of OFW's), in order to meet the economic needs of their families, often put themselves in danger as household maids *(katulong)*, childcare workers *(yayas)* and teachers. Sadly, many end up as sex workers in Japan, Singapore and other Asian cities.

Overseas workers work very long hours (up to 12 hours a day and often deprived of days off), are underpaid and are provided with small living spaces and inadequate food rations. Additionally, they are regularly exposed to racism and discrimination, often physically abused, raped and even killed. It is modern day slavery.[15]

In spite of the frequent abuses young women may receive, many forgo their chances at marriage and childbearing to earn money for their family.

What does it mean for Filipinos/Filipinas to have *economic independence or interdependence*. To quote one young adult Filipino,

> . . . a person is actually considered as adult by the society when he or she has a stable earnings *[sic]*. Many college graduates remain jobless and dependent on their parents financially and for a place to stay. This period of time could be prolonged for years. Considering the poor economic situation of the country, many college graduates going into their mid-twenties are not able to be economically independent from their parents. The general age of marriage also falls at this age, so some people considered getting married as a marker of adulthood. But even with the lack of ability to have their own housing, some married people stay with the parents or in-laws.[16]

Question: *How can Filipino Christian youthworkers, as they team up with parents and congregations, assist Pinoy youth to achieve financial strength now and in the future in their economically troubled environment?*

Family Dimensions of Filipino Adulthood

What does it mean for a Filipino to have healthy *family* interdependence? The high loyalty to family as illustrated in the OFW phenomenon is a mystery to Americans, but familiar to Filipinos. The family can be viewed from several perspectives.

First, what about the *family of origin*? One survey of Filipino youth found that 95% agreed with the statement, "Children should love and respect their parents, regardless of their qualities and faults."[17] The survey also showed that a majority of youth (61%) live with their parents. As the youth feel more liberated by further schooling, one might assume that the shifting sands of parental authority create some tension. The predicament for youth is asserting their increasing maturity without disrespecting their parents or other significant family figures, such as their *kuya* (older brother) and their *ate* (older sister).

Second, what's the place for the single adult in Philippine life, being *"a family of one"*? At least in many churches and social settings, singles adults often face continuing assignment to youth categories, not truly an "adult." How can the local Christian community embrace the mature unmarried person in respectful ways?

Third, what about forming *one's own separate family* in the context of growing to maturity? This raises questions about contemporary sexual moral standards, courtship practices, and marriage expectations. In an era of extended Filipino adolescence and lowered barriers to premarital sex, helping youth to maintain Biblical standards is a great challenge for youthworkers.

Question: *How can Filipino Christian youthworkers, as they team up with parents and congregations, assist young Filipinas and Filipinos to achieve mature healthy sexual and family relationships as outlined in the Bible?*

Church Dimensions of Filipino Adulthood

What does it mean for a young person to have *acceptance and opportunity in the life of the Filipino Christian community?* (both independence and interdependence) The tendency toward fragmentation in many Christian congregations (for example, separate worship services for youth) inhibits the sense of youth being part of the larger community. Another challenge for youthworkers is gaining respect for young people from the so-called adult members of the congregation in a culture which has traditionally embraced respect for age, thereby automatically placing youth and those who work with them in inferior status.

The younger generation has energy, gifts and vision to share with the rest of the congregation as they gather for worship and scatter to serve in the world. It is a tragedy for a congregation to overlook these valuable resources.

Questions: *How can Filipino Christian youthworkers, as they team up with parents and congregations, assist youth to become contributing members of the body of Christ? How can congregations consciously build in respect for younger members?*[18]

Civic Dimensions of Filipino Adulthood

What does it mean for a young Filipino to have *civic independence (or interdependence)?* Ability to vote intelligently? Realize the importance of obeying tax and other laws? Develop high regard for civil authorities, in spite of endemic corruption in civic affairs and government?

As usual, the Bible provides clear directions for believers.

> Obey the rulers who have authority over you. Only God can give authority to anyone, and he puts these rulers in their places of power. People who oppose the authorities are opposing what God has done, and they will be punished. Rulers are a threat to evil people, not to good people. There is no need to be afraid of the authorities. Just do right, and they will praise you for it. After all, they are God's servants,

and it is their duty to help you. If you do something wrong, you ought to be afraid, because these rulers have the right to punish you. They are God's servants who punish criminals to show how angry God is. But you should obey the rulers because you know it is the right thing to do, and not just because of God's anger. You must also pay your taxes. The authorities are God's servants, and it is their duty to take care of these matters. Pay all that you owe, whether it is taxes and fees or respect and honor (Romans 13:1-7).

Question: *How can Filipino Christian youthworkers, as they team up with parents and congregations, assist youth to become involved Christian citizens in the Republic of the Philippines?* No easy answer is apparent, especially when some Christians regard "politics" as unfitting for the involvement of believers.

Personal Dimensions of Filipino Adulthood

What does it mean for a person to have *personal independence or interdependence?* The interdependence aspect of growing up may be complicated by the extensive use of technology by youth in Manila and other urban centers around the world. They often prefer virtual interaction like text messaging. Cell phones, social media and the like may increase interpersonal dialogue, but to what extent is heartfelt communication taking place? Hence, youth ministers will desire to teach how to use social and other media responsibly.

Personal well-being is also defined by self-control in the use of tobacco, alcohol and illegal drugs. Adolescents are prone to look at the use of these things as proof of their maturity, but it is only illusory. The teachings of Biblical temperance are needed.

Youthworkers also have the opportunity to introduce young people to spiritual disciplines, such as church attendance, personal Bible study, devotional prayer and service within and without the church fellowship. Each of these will enhance the personal development of youth.

Question: *How can Filipino Christian youthworkers, as they team up with parents and congregations, assist youth to achieve wholesome lifestyle habits?*

> **Youth:** *"WOW! You think being grown up involves all that stuff? I mean, voting, sexual purity, making money, whatever."*
>
> *Youthworker:* "Any of those you want to abandon? Like I once heard, 'Growing up ain't fun'!"
>
> **Youth:** *"Aw, c'mon, don't be so serious. We've got plenty of time for that, later, don't we?"*
>
> *Youthworker:* "I don't think so."
>
> **Youth:** *"So where do we go from here?"*
>
> *Youthworker:* "Let's take a look at some of the issues people like Filipino youthworkers — and me — and ultimately you — face."
>
> *Youthworker:* "Any of those you want to abandon? Like I once heard, 'Growing up ain't fun'!"
>
> **Youth:** *"Aw, c'mon, don't be so serious. We've got plenty of time for that, later, don't we?"*
>
> *Youthworker:* "I don't think so."
>
> **Youth:** *"So where do we go from here?"*
>
> *Youthworker:* "Let's take a look at some of the issues people like Filipino youthworkers — and me — and ultimately you — face."

BUILDING A RELEVANT YOUTH MINISTRY IN THE PHILIPPINES

Once *adulthood* is defined, the Filipino youthworker can begin to define the building blocks of Biblical truth that will be necessary to achieve the goal of assisting Pinoy children to fully grow up. S/he must ponder how youth can be effectively prepared for what they will soon face as adults. These definitions will dictate program strategy in a way that is thoroughly relevant to the youth in their culture.

What becomes the role of a youthworker once objectives are clear? A youth minister is far more than a recreation director, a teacher or at worse, a babysitter of youth — in fact, it is even more than being a discipler of youth.

The youth minister's role can be envisioned as *maestro de iniciación*, a significant aide to the parents and the congregational leaders who look to her or him to put the finishing touches on the preparation they have given the boy or girl during childhood in their church and home. In Elka's case, the *maestro*'s task was quickly completed. However, in the Philippines as in other societies with extended adolescence, the *maestro* needs to make and fulfill a long-term commitment to the child and the family. Elka's initiation masters assumed parents had done their job during childhood, but in the confusing contemporary world, Filipino youthworkers cannot make the assumption that Christian parents have been faithful. Moreover, youth from homes without Christian training will need various types of remediation.

Here are *some questions for a Filipino youth minister* to face, particularly in the twenty-first century urban setting of Manila and other Philippine cities:

1. *Who* will identify a path to adulthood for Filipino youth? *How* will it be done?
2. *How* might Filipino youth ministers assist parents and

congregations to undertake, first, the task of preparing their children *for* and, second, aiding them *through* adolescence, then, third, *into* the formidable world of adulthood?
3. Imitations or adaptations of American youth ministries usually are inappropriate. Hence, pioneering and experimentation are much needed. *Who* will take the risk of moving above American imitations to foster a distinctly Filipino youth ministry? *Where* will she or he gain emotional and financial support for such an attempt?
4. *Why* are Filipino youth ministry activities so dominated by the coed approach, when the maturation of boys and girls are on such distinctly different tracks and headed for fairly divergent outcomes? Filipino youth ministers would do well to emulate some of the traditional patterns by arranging maturation experiences that reflect male/female differences. For example, at least during the years ten to fourteen, the teaching components of youth ministry could be gender-specific, to reflect the realities of developmental differences between males and females.

AND FINALLY . . .

FUN? To grow up. Not really. It takes a lot of work by the boy or girl, continual guidance from his or her parents and ongoing encouragement from Christian mentors to reach that plateau called *adulthood*, a maturity that leads to a life of service in the world. But it can be done, in the Philippines and elsewhere. How? By experimentation, by prayer, by courage, by the Holy Spirit, on the foundation of the Bible.

Growing up! It's the goal for boys and girls in every culture, in every nation, in every home, in every congregation. *The real needs of youth in the Philippines and around the globe call out for distinctly and culturally-relevant models of youth ministry, that will carry young persons into successful*

Christian adulthood and thence to changing the world. There's a whole wide world out there — people and cultures who need the change that only Jesus can bring! Youth and their mentors are faced with the challenge to find their niches in God's kingdom. By the grace and mercy of God, they are coming!

In succeeding chapters foundational principles of global Christian youth ministry will be proposed, first out of the study of culture, then further, out of the Bible.

NOTES

[1] G. Stanley Hall. *Adolescence: Its psychology* and its relations to physiology, anthropology, sociology, sex, crime, religion, and education (Vols. I & II). New York: D. Appleton & Co., 1904.

[2] Consult Arnold Van Gennep, Monika B. Vizedom (translator):*The Rites of Passage* (Hove, East Sussex, U.K.: Psychology Press, 1960, 1977). Also Turner, Victor, *The Ritual Process* (London: Penguin), 1969.

[3] Now known as UFM International, Bala-Cynwyd. PA.

[4] Homer E. Dowdy, *Christ's Witch-Doctor* (Gresham, OR: Vision House, 1994), 14-16. Reprinted by permission.

[5] Dowdy, *Christ's Witch-Doctor,* 18.

[6] In a similar example from South America, the Satere-Mawe people *[an indigenous tribe located in the Brazilian Amazon]* intentionally use bullet ant stings as part of their initiation rites *to become a warrior.* The ants are first rendered unconscious by submerging them in a natural sedative and then hundreds of them are woven into a glove made out of leaves (which resembles a large oven mitt), stinger facing inward. When the ants regain consciousness, a boy slips the glove onto his hand. The goal of this initiation rite is to keep the glove on for a full ten minutes. When finished, the *boy's* hand and part of his arm are temporarily paralyzed due to the ant venom, and he may shake uncontrollably for days. The only "protection" provided is a coating of charcoal on the hands, supposedly to confuse the ants and inhibit their stinging. To fully complete the initiation, however, *boys* must go through the ordeal a total of twenty times over the course of several months or even years. *Wikipedia.*

[7] See Dowdy, *Christ's Witch-Doctor.*

[8] For more details on female initiation, see Chapter 5 and Appendices A

and C.

[9] For example, Robert M Malina, Claude Bouchard, Oded Bar-Or. *Growth, Maturation and Physical Activity*. (U.K.: Human Kinetics Publishers, 2004), 3.

[10] Spanish: master of initiation. The author is indebted to a group of seminary students in Mexicali, Baja California Norte, Mexico, for coining this term.

[11] For a more complete explanation of these contemporary observances, see Appendices B and C.

[12] Preciosa Solivan, "Filipino Child-Rearing Practices Delay Maturity," *The Philippine Star*, A Point of Awareness website, October 4, 2012.

[13] Felipe M. De Leon, Jr., "Philippine Arts in Context," National Commission for Culture and the Arts, July 29, 2011.

[14] Individuation. In Jungian psychology, the process of the development of the self, achieved by resolving the conflicts arising at life's transitional stages, in particular the transition from adolescence to adulthood. *Encarta® World English Dictionary* © 1999 Microsoft Corporation. All rights reserved.

[15] Sharon Elizabeth P. McAllister, "Filipino workers deserve better protection," *Peoples World Overseas*, July 2, 2013.

[16] Tony Ong, July 12, 2001, Reflection Paper #2, "Foundations of Youth Ministry" course, Alliance Biblical Seminary, Quezon City, Philippines.

[17] Gerardo Sandoval, Mangahas, Mahar, and Guerrero, Linda Luz, "The Situation of Filipino Youth: A National Survey," paper presented at the 14th World Congress of Sociology, July 26-August 1, 1998.

[18] First Timothy 4:12. "Don't let anyone look down on you because you are young, but set an example for the believers in speech, in conduct, in love, in faith and in purity" (NIV).

PART I –

What Is To Be Learned from CULTURE About Youth Ministry in the Twenty-first Century?

Chapter 2

CHECKING OUT INDIGENOUS PATTERNS

Youth are caught in the whirlpool of change that marks the twenty-first century, as are their parents and their communities, including the people of faith. Anchors of tradition are being swept aside in favor of the latest and the greatest, as put forth by technology, the media and commercialism. Around the world uncertainty about the present and insecurity about the future overshadow the growth of children into women and men.

Yet Christians are not without hope or without anchors.
- The same Holy Spirit who guided the early apostles still is at work in the world, empowering believers with all that they need to bring change to individuals and cultures.
- The Bible, the written Word of God, provides a firm foundation of Truth to point the way forward.
- An exploration of customs that have offered stability and direction for families and individuals since the inception of human society may offer clues of how life can be managed in the present.

Men and women, girls and boys, being created in God's image yet steeped in sinful nature and their resident cultures, have developed ways of looking at the world that reflect both the virtuous and the malevolent sides of humankind. As a result, cultural mores include both good and evil attitudes and practices. From a Biblical point of view, the worthwhile ought to be nurtured, the negative discouraged or discarded.

Unfortunately, the twenty-first century world constantly looks to the novel, the fresh, and the innovative as supposed *truth*. As a result, time-honored tradition is often discounted and discarded, like some overworn clothing. Christian youth ministry faces similar temptations, by seeking to be relevant, up-to-date and *with-it [American slang* for well-informed, awake, paying attention*]*, in goals, outreach, content and methodology. In the process, important discoveries from the past may be cast aside and lost. *What guidelines might a study of the cultures of the world provide for a distinctively-Christian youth ministry?*

Youthworker: *"Now wait just one minute! Are you saying that the intensive study of, let's say, an Indonesian tribe or a Western nation, might generate some ideas for my youth ministry?"*

Author: "Well, might it be a possibility? You're forever looking for new ideas, aren't you? Maybe there's something here!"

Youthworker: *"O.K., it could be possible. But it seems the long way around."*

Author: "Whoever said it would be easy? You're brave or you wouldn't be in youth ministry, so why not?"

> **Youthworker:** *"Look, I'm trying to run a youth program and your imaginings are simply a bother."*
>
> **Author:** "But you *did* say you wanted to have a Biblically-based youth ministry, didn't you?"
>
> **Youthworker:** *"You've got me on that one. O.K., so what else do I need to consider in building a youth ministry true to the revelation of God?"*
>
> **Author:** "I think we have something to learn about effective youth ministry by studying the culture we are seeking to penetrate and influence. It's dangerous to work in a cultural vacuum, you know."
>
> **Youthworker:** *"We already work in the 'heart language' of our youth. Do you want us to do more than that?"*
>
> **Author:** "Yes, because God not only reveals himself in his Word, the Bible, but also in what is often termed 'general revelation.'"[1]
>
> **Youthworker:** *"O.K, I'm willing to give it a look, so let's do it!"*

Christian theologians agree that God communicates with humankind in two basic ways: through special revelation (the Holy Bible) and general revelation. Part II explores how God's written revelation leads to certain conclusions about Christian youth ministry. But the chapters that follow investigate the possibilities for youth ministry from the standpoint of general revelation. *What can be redeemed from traditional cultural practices that might inform contemporary Christian youth ministry?* Believing that human culture largely developed under God's common grace[2] leads to an examination of foundations of human transitioning from girlhood/boyhood to womanhood/manhood. As stated by author and pastor Dr. Timothy Keller,

> ... God ... shows common grace by revealing knowledge of himself through human culture, for human culture is simply a wise recognition and cultivation of nature.
>
> ... Every advancement in human learning, every work of art, and every scientific discovery is simply God "opening his book of creation and revealing his truth" to us. . . . This is general revelation, or as theologians call it "the doctrine of common grace." All artistic expressions, skillful farming, scientific discoveries, medical and technological advances are expressions of God's grace. . . . God's Spirit does not only function as a non-saving ennobling force in the world, but also as a non-saving restraining force in the world. This is not the Spirit working as a converting or sanctifying agent but rather working to give wisdom, courage, creativity and insight—another facet of common grace.
>
> ....
>
> ... despite the false worldviews, everyone grasps and to some degree acknowledges truths about God, creation, human nature, and so on. Paul says we "suppress the truth in unrighteousness," which means that we all initially have the truth in some way.
>
> ....
>
> ... we need to appreciate truth and wisdom wherever we find it and that studying different cultures, languages, artwork, and music expands not only our appreciation of the created world but also the God who made it.[3]

Going back to the beginning of the human race, peace and joy reigned as humans and nature connected in perfect harmony (Genesis 1 and 2). The Biblical narrative makes it clear that, as a result of Adam and Eve's sin, conflict, fear, selfishness, guilt, shame, addictions, disease and death descended on earth's reality (Genesis 3).

In spite of the God-inflicted curses, humans retained memories of the time when they knew God and each other intimately. As time passed, these memories came down through generations of oral tradition, such as, for example, the universe originating from a powerful god. Over time as peoples scattered across the globe, the original truths became muddied with faulty memories, eventually becoming shadows of the realities. Multitudes of creation myths arose, postulating fecund forces such as archetypical jaguars, for example, to explain the origins of the universe and humankind. Worship of celestial bodies such as the sun and moon also reflected in some shadowy way the truth of "in the beginning, God created the heavens and the earth (Genesis 1:1)."

Hence, the study of world cultures offers some interesting possibilities about the structures and customs of human society. For example, the passage of the children into adulthood is and has been a concern of most parents and societies. Humans do not lay eggs and abandon them, as turtles and other creatures do.

So what structures and systems have been used to bring children into adulthood with varying degrees of success? One does not need to dig too deeply into the study of cultures to uncover the use of "rites of passage," as termed by some authors, and/or the use of *initiation* rites to guide a people group, a faith-community and/or a nationality. Because the community shares common expectations, the initiation of youth into adulthood has served for centuries to stabilize families and societies. This process worked wonderfully well when the culture at large was stable.

Do these traditional practices have something in common that well may suggest that God's general revelation is at the root of them? For example, traditional initiations into adulthood usually include a time of separation from society, even individual seclusion for the initiates? Might this be prefigured by humankind's ejection from the Garden of Eden in Genesis 3:23-24?

> So the Lord God *sent them out* of the Garden of Eden, where they would have to work the ground from which the man had been made. Then God put winged creatures at the entrance to the garden and a flaming, flashing sword to guard the way to the life-giving tree.

The time Jesus spent alone in the wilderness (St. Matthew 4:1-11; St. Mark 4:12-13, St. Luke 4:1-13) as a phase of his preparation for public ministry might also be identified as an example of being away from the rural village in which he lived, in order to focus on more significant issues.

Thus, to be human, one must be able to handle times of isolation, being sent out of one's comfort zone, one's society for a time. What might Christian youthworkers learn from cultural practices? Of course, today's world is marked by momentous cultural shifting and as a result the old ways are becoming ineffective.

One way to examine world cultures is through a study of "people groups." These groups may be defined by language, language/dialect/ethnicity, etc., depending on the researcher's intent. In most cultures and situations, definition by language seems appropriate for this investigation. *Ethnologue*[4] estimates there are approximately 7,000 plus linguistic peoples on earth today. Seeking answers via general revelation from this multitude of cultures is impossible, so illustrative examples are presented in an attempt to point out the possibilities. *That is, how have boys traditionally attained manhood in Africa, South America, Asia, Australia, Oceania, North America and Europe? Similarly, how have*

girls become women in traditional settings around the world?
A cursory look at the relationship between youth ministry and traditional culture issues produces the following *hypotheses:*

- The assimilation of the children into the wider society is a universal concern, so that they, as able, become productive members of that society.
- The transition of a child into adulthood tended to be quite clear-cut, in contrast to uncomfortable ambiguity existing in the twenty-first century modern world.
- The path to adulthood is undeniably gender-specific in most, if not all, cultures. Girls are prepared for women's roles; boys made ready to assume men's roles.
- Transmitting the values and beliefs of the community is a key element in transitional experiences.
- The transition for males is less specific in terms of maturation of their bodies, and usually involves a group process in which mature males instill appropriate values and skills into young men.
- The passage for females from childhood to adulthood is more an individual matter, depending on the onset of menses, with a mother and/or other female relatives providing the coaching. However, some people-groups also have communal initiation for females.
- A boy or girl gains more self-confidence as a result of being mentored by adults respected in and by the community.

The following chapters examine rites of passage, traditional paths to manhood and womanhood, criteria for contemporary transitional experiences and the role of the Christian community, including youth and their parents, in building or rebuilding a strong Biblical and culturally-relevant ministry to, among, and with youth: traditional, modern or caught between these two worlds. The result expected? Mature Christian women and men ready to impact the world for Christ and his kingdom.

In succeeding chapters an attempt is made to explore the deeper meanings of various ceremonies around the world, trying to distill the essence of the rite(s). This, then, arouses possibilities for wider application in Christian youth ministry, that is, using the same essence and purpose as part of building a suitable structure for that culture.

Specifically:
1. Explore culture from a historical perspective, examining the so-called "adolescent passage," or, more accurately, how children become adults in specific cultures.
2. Seek to discover what purposes and essence lie behind the various forms used in rites of passage ceremonies. For example, what was/is the purpose(s) behind bodily scarification as practiced in Africa and Papua New Guinea?
3. See what gaps exist between what the home and the existing Christian community offer and an ideal path to Christian adulthood.
4. Propose possible contemporary cultural equivalents to encourage the growth of children into adulthood, as guided by the Bible.
5. Suggest specific program possibilities as thought-starters.

NOTES

[1] "General revelation rests on the basis of creation, is addressed to all intelligent creatures as such and is therefore accessible to all men; though as the result of sin they are no more able to read and interpret it aright." Henry Berkhof, *Systematic Theology* (Grand Rapids: Wm. B. Eerdmans, 1996), 128.

[2] "…grace that applies to mankind in general and to every member of the human race…." Berkhof, p. 432.//
[3] "What is Common Grace," by Dr. Timothy Keller. This article is adapted from a leadership training session at Redeemer Presbyterian Church in 2003. Copyright © 2003 by Timothy Keller, © 2010 by Redeemer City to City.//
[4] M. Paul Lewis, Gary F. Simons, and Charles D. Fennig (eds.) 2015. *Ethnologue: Languages of the World*. 18th edition. Dallas, TX: SIL International. Online version: http://www.ethnologue.com.

Chapter 3

TRADITIONAL PATHS TO AFRICAN MANHOOD

The journey from childhood to maturity varies around the globe, depending on the history and culture of an ethnic group or nationality. A sampling of some traditional paths provides a broad answer to the question, *"When does a boy become a man?"* Traditional cultures across the world display unique patterns for the rite of passage known as coming of age. Rites of passage play a central role in a person's life, delineating different stages in an individual's development, as well as that person's relationship to the broader community. The journey a boy must take to manhood in traditional Africa is described below. The passage of boys elsewhere in the world is traced in Chapter 4.

A major stage in African life is the *initiation*, the transition from being a boy to becoming fully established as a man in tribal life. In a thoroughly fascinating first-person account, Nelson Mandela, a member of a South Africa Xhosa tribe, describes his own initiation experiences.

> When I was sixteen, the regent decided that it was time that *I became a man*. In Xhosa tradition, this is achieved

through one means only: circumcision. In my tradition, an uncircumcised male cannot be heir to his father's wealth, cannot marry or officiate in tribal rituals. An uncircumcised Xhosa man is a contradiction in terms, for he is not considered a man at all, but a boy. For the Xhosa people, circumcision represents the form of incorporation of males into society. It is not just a surgical procedure, but a lengthy and elaborate ritual in preparation for manhood. As a Xhosa, I count my years as a man from the date of my circumcision.

The traditional ceremony of the circumcision school was arranged for . . . twenty-six [of us boys]. . . . Early in the new year, we journeyed to two grass huts in a secluded valley . . . the traditional place of circumcision for Thembu kings. The huts were seclusion lodges, where we were to live isolated from society. It was a sacred time; I felt happy and fulfilled taking part in my people's customs and ready to make the transition from boyhood to manhood.

. . . These last few days before the actual circumcision were spent with the other initiates, and I found the camaraderie enjoyable. . . .

A custom of the circumcision school is that one must perform a daring exploit before the ceremony. In days of old, this might have involved a cattle raid or even a battle, but in our time the deed were more mischievous than martial. . . . we decided to steal a pig. . . .

The night before the circumcision, there was a ceremony near our huts with singing and dancing. Women came from the nearby villages, and we danced to their singing and chapping. As the music became faster and louder, our dance turned more frenzied and we forgot for a moment what lay ahead.

At dawn . . . we began our preparations. We were

escorted to the river to bathe in its cold waters, a ritual that signified our purification before the ceremony. The ceremony was at midday, and we were commanded to stand in a row in a clearing some distance from the river where a crowd of parents and relatives . . . as well as a handful of chiefs and counselors, had gathered. We were clad only in our blankets, and as the ceremony began, with drums pounding, we were ordered to sit on a blanket on the ground with our legs spread out in front of us. I was tense and anxious, uncertain of how I would react when the critical moment came. Flinching or crying out was a sign of weakness and stigmatized *one's manhood*. I was determined not to disgrace myself, the group, or my guardian. Circumcision is a trial of bravery and stoicism; no anesthetic is used; *a man* must suffer in silence.

To the right . . . I could see a thin, elderly man emerge from a tent and kneel in front of the first boy. There was excitement in the crowd, and I shuddered slightly knowing that the ritual was about to begin. The old man was a . . . circumcision expert *[ingcibi]*. . . who would use his *assegai [spear]* to change us from boys to men with a single blow.

Suddenly I heard the first boy cry out, *"Ndiyindoda" (I am a man!),* which we were trained to say in the moment of circumcision. . . . There were now two boys before the *ingcibi* reached me, and my mind must have gone blank because before I knew it, the old man was kneeling in front of me. I looked directly into his eyes. He was pale, and though the day was cold, his face was shining with perspiration. His hands moved so fast they seemed to be controlled by an otherworldly force. Without a word, he took my foreskin, pulled it forward, and then, in a single motion, brought down his *assegai*. I felt as it fire was shooting through my veins; the pain was so intense that I buried my chin into my chest. Many seconds seemed to pass before I remembered the cry, and then I recovered and called out, *"Ndiyindoda!"*

I looked down and saw a perfect cut, clean and round like a ring. But I felt ashamed because the other boys seemed much stronger and braver than I had been; they had called out more promptly than I had. I was distressed that I had been disabled, however briefly, by the pain, and I did my best to hide my agony. A boy may cry; a man conceals his pain.

I had now taken the essential step in the life of *every Xhosa man*. Now, I might marry, set up my own home, and plow my own field. I could now be admitted to the councils of the community; my words would be taken seriously. At the ceremony, I was given my circumcision name, *Dalibunga*, meaning "Founder of the Bunga," the traditional ruling body of the Transkei.[1] To Xhosa traditionalists this name is more acceptable than either of my two previous given names, Rolihlahla or Nelson, and I was proud to hear *my new name* pronounced: Dalibunga.

Immediately after the blow had been delivered, an assistant who follows the circumcision master takes the foreskin that is on the ground and ties it to a corner of your blanket. Our wounds were then dressed with a healing plant, the leaves of which were thorny on the outside, but smooth on the inside, which absorbed the blood and other secretions.

At the conclusion of the ceremony, we returned to our huts, where a fire was burning with wet wood that cast off clouds of smoke, which was thought to promote healing. We were ordered to lie on our backs in the smoky huts, with one leg flat, and one led bent. We were now *abakhwetha*, initiates into *the world of manhood*. We were looked after by an *amakhankatha*, or guardian, who explained the rules we must follow if we were to enter manhood properly. The first chore of the *amakhankatha* was to paint our naked and shaved bodies from head to foot in white ocher, turning us into ghosts. The white chalk symbolized our purity, and I still recall how stiff the dried clay felt on my body.

That first night, at midnight, an attendant, or ikhankatha, crept around the hut, gently waking each of us. We were then instructed to leave the hut and go tramping through the night to bury our foreskins. The traditional reason for this practice was so that our foreskins would be hidden before wizards could use them for evil purposes, but symbolically, we were also burying our youth. I did not want to leave the warm hut and wander through the bush in the darkness, but I walked into the trees and, after a few minutes, untied my foreskin and buried it in the earth. I felt as though I had now discarded the last remnant of my childhood.

We lived in our two huts —thirteen in each—while our wounds healed. When outside the huts, we were covered in blankets, for we were not allowed to be seen by women. It was a period of quietude, a kind of spiritual preparation for the trials of manhood that lay ahead. On the day of our reemergence, we went down to the river early in the morning to wash away the white ocher in the waters of the Mbashe [river]. Once we were clean and dry, we were coated in red ocher. The tradition was that one should sleep with a woman, who later may become one's wife, and she rubs off the pigment with her body. In my case, however, the ocher was removed with a mixture of fat and lard.

At the end of our seclusion, the lodges and all their contents were burned, destroying our last links to childhood, and a great ceremony was held to welcome us as men to society. Our families, friends, and local chiefs gathered for speeches, songs and gift-giving. I was given two heifers and four sheep,, and felt far richer than I ever had before. I who had never owned anything suddenly possessed property. It was a heady feeling . . . I felt strong and proud that day. *I remember walking differently on that day, straighter, taller, firmer.* I was hopeful and thinking that I might someday have wealth, property and status.

YOUTH: Growing Up

....

It was almost sunset and I hurried on to where our seclusion lodges had been. Though I was forbidden to look back while the lodges were burning, I could not resist. When I reached the area, all that remained were two pyramids of ash by a large mimosa tree. In those ash heaps lay a lost and delightful world, the world of my childhood. . . . *Now I was a man*, and I would never again play. . . . I was already in mourning for my own youth. Looking back, I know that I was not a man that day and would not truly become one for many years.[2]

> Youthworker: *"Wow, what a story! I never knew African boys had to go through such a rigorous process to become a man!"*
>
> **Maestro de iniciación** *[Initiation master, Maître de iniciación, Master erhalten]:* "You've got that right. Sometime you may wish to read the whole of Mandela's story, but for now. . . ."
>
> Youthworker: *"Yeah, what I'm interested in is NOW. So what is new and now?"*
>
> **Maestro de iniciación:** "Whoa! Let's look at some other African traditions first. You go along with that?"

Mandela's experience illustrates just one of the estimated 3500 ethnic groups in Africa,[3] most of which practice or have practiced some form of initiation as a means of bringing a boy into manhood. Mandela's initiation embodies widespread traditional practices across Africa yet each one is unique in its expression. Certain practices symbolize the transition of leaving childhood behind, then undergoing an

experience isolated from his community, which is followed by a reentry into society as a man.
- An initiate is called a *parapool,* "one who has stopped milking." Initiation means he *no longer does a boy's work* of milking, tethering the cattle, and carting dung. (Dinka, South Sudan)[4]
- The ritualistic death and rebirth process signifies *the dying of old habits and ways of thinking,* living in the spirit world (thus being in isolation, as in a woman's womb), and *being reborn again [sic]* into the corporate community. Initiates now can wear certain clothing and symbols that were not accessible to them before. They learn symbolic dances, handshakes. . . . Initiates are often given new names. . . .[5]

The first step toward manhood is a boy's departure from childhood as shown by various emblems. Boys from the Tswara nation (southern Africa) " . . . shave their heads when they first enter the initiation school as a symbol of their transitional status. . . ."[6] The Jola people in West Africa observe departure for initiation as follows:

> . . . the initiates with shaved heads and bare torsos go into the sacred forest. Mothers, sisters and aunts accompany them to the edge of the forest. Unaccompanied by the females who have supervised their childhood upbringing, the boys go on into the sacred wood.[7]

Masai boys in East Africa undergo *Eunoto*:

> . . . . an elaborate ceremony that marks *the end* of a relatively carefree life and *the beginning* of greater responsibilities. The initiates are then expected to watch over the community's cattle (. . . highly regarded as God's unique gift . . .), participate in cattle raids, and kill a lion. At the end . . . the young man's hair is shaved, *thus formally indicating the passage to manhood.* . . . they also have their skin painted with ochre in preparation for marriage.[8]

Physical Appearance: The transformation process from African boyhood to manhood usually involved visual symbols such as distinctive dress and/or scarification. A few additional examples suffice.
- Ndebele youths [wear] . . . clothing marking symbolic moments in the journey between the carefree world of the past and the responsibility they must embrace in the future.
- After circumcision, ". . . each boy is covered with a special leather 'skirt' called *motsabelo*. These are worn in order to protect the wound against flies and heat from the sun that may cause pain."[10]
- Novices are stripped, shaved, bathed, and sometimes marked with ashes or white earth, all to denude them of their previous status and to place them in a liminal[11] state, neither minor nor adult.[12]

Clothing (or lack thereof) is also used in initiation rituals to interpret what is happening. "All male . . . initiation rites involve the adoption of hairstyles and clothing that underline the *transitional status* of the initiates."[13]
- Xhosa initiates build temporary dwellings and *make hats from ephemeral materials*. Their transitional status is underlined by the wearing of blankets and other *makeshift garments* during this period in which they denounce contact with the outside world.[1] *[emphasis added]*
- . . . initiates elsewhere . . . smear themselves with substances like fat or ochre . . . in their rite of passage . . . Xhosa youths cover their bodies with white clay.[15]

Scarification is also a common practice associated with initiation. Among the Dinka people, "Initiation is marked by mutilation — tribal marks of several parallel lines or V-shaped marks are scarified onto the youth's foreheads."[16]
. . . As the initiator comes to each boy . . . he calls out the names of his ancestors. The initiator clasps the crown of

the boy's head firmly and spins it past the blade of an extremely sharp knife. After the first cut, the initiator makes . . . whatever the clan pattern . . . might be. The cuts are deep. . . . The initiate, psyched up by a night of clan song-singing, looks straight ahead and continues to recite the names of his ancestors. . . .[17]

Leading the Initiation. Young boy-candidates for initiation are guided by experienced male elders who are best equipped to pass on tribal traditions, survival skills and life wisdom in general.
- Like initiates elsewhere, Pedi boys are overseen by an initiation master. . . . He is responsible for educating and disciplining the initiates.[1]
- Before Masai boys are circumcised, they must have a *liabon*, a leader with the power to . . . guide them in their decisions.[19]
- Young boys must conform to the demands of the initiation master, who is also responsible for circumcising them.[20]

Content of Initiation Experiences. Initiation is often the time that boys receive instruction regarding marriage, sex, family life, and procreation. For example:
- Elders and spiritual leaders teach Jolo initiates *ancestral secret knowledge as well as practical knowledge* while secluded in the sacred forest.[21]
- We teach the young . . . *how they must respect their parents and behave well with others.*"[22]

The boys are also taught traditional songs and dances. Adult survival skills useful for hunting and fighting are highly emphasized. In South Africa, boys are taught to fight with sticks.

They all receive fighting sticks as a symbol of their virility. . . . these sticks are supposed to remain with them for the rest of their lives. Historically adult men carried fighting sticks both to protect themselves and their families from danger, and to hunt small game . . . on their journeys to and from home.[23]

Additionally, physical and mental tests are assigned to the boys to harden them and to teach interpersonal skills such as loyalty, honor, work ethic and sense of solidarity.

Circumcision and Other Ordeals. Often the adversity includes a period of total isolation, when boys are encouraged to reflect on life and the new meaning that it has for them as they undergo initiation.

In certain East African ethnic groups, a naked youth must successfully pass a test of agility and bravery by the "jumping of the bull."

> They [tribal members] gather the 7-10 bulls at sunset, line them up in a row and the 'bull jumper' is to run across their backs 4 times. If he falls through the row of bulls he is to start again until he completes the running 4 times without falling.[24]

If the boy completes the task, he earns the right to be called a man and bear children who will be considered legitimate heirs!

Before missionary influences entered Africa, initiates were often treated cruelly and brutally. In some tribes, it was expected that some boys would fail the tests and die in the process. If all survived, the weakest boy would be killed to reinforce the idea that manhood must be earned. When the initiates left the village, their mothers knew that one of their sons might not return! American and British missionaries tried to stamp out initiations as heathenish and sadistic, with varied degrees of success.[25] Sadly, what the well-meaning Christian missionaries did not realize was that terminating initiations effectively prevented boys from achieving adult status.

Among many African ethnic groups, as illustrated by Mandela's story, circumcision is regarded highly as a mark of distinction and a symbol of valor and/or manhood.
- A boy who cries out during the procedure is branded a coward and shunned for a long time and his mother is disgraced, whereas a boy who is brave and who has led an exemplary life becomes the leader of his age group.[26]
- In their isolated quarters, the novices —vulnerable and impressionable because of the wounds, fasting, and exposure that they have suffered are subjected to intensive instructions. . . . Circumcision marks *their ritual death as minors and their rebirth as responsible adults.*[27]

When boys living in these ethnic groups desire to become men, though terrorized, they endure whatever it takes to become a man.

Celebration: Returning Home: Initiation is concluded with lavish and exuberant rejoicing to welcome the new men as they return to the realities of adult life. A large crowd gathers for feasting, drinking (e.g., millet beer), dancing, gift-giving and singing to honor the successful initiates.[28] The "graduates" may wear distinctive clothing, possibly blankets and/or extravagant beadwork.

Traditional African rites of passage demonstrate how important the peoples of that continent viewed the achievement of manhood. It was certainly not a haphazard process but a carefully-worked-out regimen to assure that the group's solidarity and continuity were not threatened.

Is it possible that boys' African initiations hearken back to issues presented in Genesis 1-3? Perhaps boyhood is symbolic of the Edenic state of males, and if so, then the hardships of initiation might echo the life he is about to enter as an adult male. One might view boys' initiation at least in part as an introduction to the hardships men have faced since

Adam received his curse from God.
"Cursed is the ground because of you; through painful toil you will eat food from it all the days of your life. It will produce thorns and thistles for you, and you will eat the plants of the field. By the sweat of your brow you will eat your food until you return to the ground. . .. (Genesis 3:17B-19, CEV).

> Youthworker: *"O.K., so down through the centuries African boys have achieved manhood in some fascinating ways. But that's all behind us now, isn't it?"*
>
> **Maestro de iniciación:** "Yes, and no. Traditional initiation for boys is alive and well in some places in Africa and many other places in the world, too."
>
> Youthworker: *"Yeah, but it has to be passing from the scene. The boys I know want to be contemporary — no scars for them (unless it would be tattoos)."*
>
> **Maestro de iniciación:** "But what do they think will make them into men? How about their families, perhaps back in the village, what do they think about their sons imitating Western customs?"
>
> Youthworker: *"Those are not easy to answer in today's world."*
>
> **Maestro de iniciación:** "Before we face those questions, let's look beyond Africa to see how boys become men in other places. Oh, and check the questions below."

➤ QUESTIONS FOR YOUTHWORKERS ◄
To Ponder Regarding Boys Becoming Men

Some questions beg to be answered before investigating how boys have come to manhood traditionally in Asia, Australia, Oceania, Europe and the Americas.

- What benefits did Nelson Mandela and other African youth down through the centuries gain out of the pain and suffering of traditional initiation?
- What symbols, celebrations, tests or ceremonies mark entry into manhood in my culture?
- What roles might youthworkers play in smoothing the way for boys to become authentic maturing men in the here-and-now?

NOTES

[1] Local province or state in southeastern Republic of South Africa.

[2] Nelson Mandela, *Long Walk to Freedom* (New York/Boston: Little, Brown and Company, 1994), 25-31. Reprinted by permission.

[3] Copyright © 2015 Joshua Project, a ministry of Frontier Ventures.

[4] Martin Wugol, July 8, 2015, https://martinwugol.wordpress.com/2015/07/08/42/.

[5] Molifi Kete Asante and Ama Mazama (eds.), *Encyclopedia of African Religion* (Los Angeles: SAGE Publications, 2009), 1730.

[6] Sandra Klopper, *Ceremonies* [African Heritage series] (Cape Town: Struik Publishers, 2001), 49.

[7] Molefi Kete Asante and Ama Mazama (eds.), 354.

[8] Molefi Kete Asante and Ama Mazama (eds.), 1730.

[9] Sandra Klopper, 45.

[10] Tabone Shoko, "Komba: girls' initiation rite and inculturation among the VaRemba of Zimbabwe," Department of Religious Studies, University of Zimbabwe, Harare, Zimbabwe, n.d.

[11] Definition: "of, relating to, or being an intermediate state, phase, or

condition.. *Miriam-Webster Dictionary.*
12. Mircea Eliade (ed.), *The Encyclopedia of Religion,* Book 3, (Macmillan Publishing Company, 1987), 511-514.
13. Sandra Klopper, *Ceremonies* [African Heritage series] (Cape Town: Struik Publishers, 2001), page 13.
14. Sandra Klopper, 52.
15. Sandra Klopper, 55.
16. "The Dinka of Sudan, *Oxford Humanities,* "National Geographic Television International, DVD.
17. www.ezakwantu.com/Gallery.
18. Sandra Klopper. 25.
19. Molefi Kete Asante and Ama Mazama, 619.
20. Sandra Klopper, 25.
21. Molefi Kete Asante and Ama Mazama (eds.), 1168.
22. Molefi Kete Asante and Ama Mazama (eds.), 354-355.
23. Sandra Klopper, 24.
24. Bull Jumping Ceremony, https://newflowerethipia.wordpress.com/2013/02/10bull-jumping-ceremony.
25. "Successive missionaries . . . attacked African culture and required a complete abandonment of African culture and practices. . . Initiation ceremonies were vehemently condemned.. *Traditionalists, Muslims, and Christians in Africa: Interreligious,* by Prince Sorie Conteh, 114-115.
26. Molefi Kete Asante and Ama Mazama (eds.), 618.
27. *The Encyclopedia Of Religion,* 511-514.
28. *Tribal Odyssey: The Woodaabe of the Sahara,* National Geographic Documentary film, 2006.

Chapter 4

OTHER TRADITIONAL PATHS TO MANHOOD

"When does a boy become a man?" or more precisely, "When did boys become men in traditional settings?" Moving beyond Africa, what traditions are to be found in Asia, Australia, Oceania, Europe and the Americas? What can be learned historically about the growing-up process by exploring other traditional cultures around the globe?

ASIA

An estimated 60% of the world's population resides in Asia. What does coming-of-age look like there? A plethora of cultures exist, traditional and modern-day, sometimes side-by-side in the great Asian metropolises. For the sake of brevity, a few examples of traditional rites of passage must suffice, though they only represent a fraction of Asian people groups. Specifically, the Joshua Project lists 8,853 people-groups in Asia, with about 30% of them in China and India.[1]

China. Over five hundred people groups are reported in China and no doubt there are as many different forms of initiation into adulthood! One widely-used approach is known

as the "capping ceremony." Traditionally, perhaps as far back as two thousand years, Chinese boys have become adults at the age of twenty through the capping ceremony:
> Three days before the ceremony the man [initiate] chose an honoured guest whose duty was to perform the ceremony. . . . The man first got his inner cap, then a cap and finally a scarf. After these three steps the man's hair was combed into a bun. Symbolically this meant that he became an adult. The guest of honour then gave a speech congratulating the new adult man. After the speech the *new adult man* would take a bow to his mother. Then the guest of honour would give him a *new name.*

Now he would be eligible for marriage and could participate as an adult in societal activities. In other recognitions of a boy's movement into adulthood, thirteen has been the magical age, as with the Pumi/Primi people of southwest China. In this case, a change in clothing is used to signify the new status of the person. A distinctive component of this ceremony is "kowtowing" to the cooking stove" [kneeling and bowing so low as to have one's head touching the ground]!

India. Vastly different from China, India includes over 2,000 people groups. Because India is predominantly Hindu in religious belief, the coming of age ceremony called *upanayanam* applies to many Indian boys. Also known as the *Sacred Thread Ceremony*, it marks the transition to manhood at eight, twelve or sixteen years of age, depending on caste, when a boy leaves childhood and becomes a serious learner of Hinduism. However, only boys from the three upper castes may participate. *Dalit* boys (untouchables) are thereby denied entry into the Indian religious community. The ceremony may be performed with older boys as well.

Upanayanam gives the boy entrance to a school of Hinduism. Included in the curriculum are reading, writing, mathematics,

arts and other skills such as sculpting, weaving, dancing and music. *Upanayanam* is considered an intellectual birth.
> In the presence of a . . . holy teacher, the young man shaves his head and dons a saffron robe. Taking up a simple walking stick, he renounces all material possessions and then receives the sacred thread. The unadorned Thread *[yajñopaveetam]* is symbolic of the interconnectedness of all things. It consists of seven strands, each of which represents a different virtue or quality . . . power of speech, memory, intelligence, forgiveness, steadfastness, prosperity, good reputation. The boy promises to embody these qualities and for the rest of his life he wears the sacred thread. . . . The ceremony concludes with a fire sacrifice. . . . The initiate would follow his teacher into a faraway dwelling to study scriptures and to lead a life of spiritual practice and austerity. Afterwards, he would reenter society, marry and raise a family.[4]

Japan. Japan has rather homogeneous culture, compared with China or India, listing only thirty-six ethnic groups nationally. The country of Japan has had coming-of-age ceremonies going back centuries. It has been described as follows:
> . . . the ritual once initiated youth into manhood as early as age 13 with rigorous tests of physical endurance, such as climbing mountains. The ceremony also involved days of spiritual preparation during which initiates ate simple foods, purified themselves in the river and meditated with a Shinto priest. And after the initiation, the new adults would leave their families and begin independent lives living communally with other young men.

SOUTH AMERICA

Chapter 1 includes a report of the initiation of a tribal boy named Elka growing up in the Amazon jungle. Another example from history comes down from the ancient civilization of Peru.[4] The ancient Inca approach for emerging

YOUTH: Growing Up

manhood is revealed as follows:
- Before the ceremonies, the youth [a *guarachicui*] had to "undergo a physical ordeal and an examination in soldierly and athletic prowess."
- "... the Peruvian youth's 'nanny'.... was expected to initiate him, by demonstration, into the facts of life, to be his first mistress, and to be subsequently supported by him when he set up house for himself."
- The *guarachicui* had a temporary name from weaning until puberty. His man-name would have a spiritual power attached to it.
- "The *guara* was a garment and *guarachicui* means 'the putting on of the *guara*.' ... just as the toga was worn by all adult Roman citizens, so the *guara* was worn by all adult Incas."
- After the exam, "there followed a six-day fast during which candidates received nothing but raw maize and water sufficient to keep them alive.."
- "Having taken the *guarachicui* and [his name] ... put on the *usutas*, sandals made for the occasion by members of his family of fine gold reed and llama sinews."
- "... a male ... was not adult in law until he reached twenty-five, a woman was adult at eighteen. . . the majority married and led the life which their mothers had led. . . . Women were permanent minors, if not chattels."

> Youthworker: *"Let's slow down a minute. I get the point — traditionally, boys in Africa, Asia, South America, wherever, have made the jump from childhood to manhood successfully."*
>
> *Maestro de iniciación:* "Yes, but in culturally-validated initiation experiences, not in self-designed hodge-podge."

> Youthworker: *"But I work in a context that shoves all those ceremonies into irrelevance. The boys I know want the latest and greatest, the newest evidences of 'civilization' like cell/mobile phones. Who cares about the past?"*
>
> *Maestro de iniciación:* "Before you make that judgment, don't you think we should complete our round-the-world tour? Let's move forward a little farther."
>
> Youthworker: "O.K., but only if you include Western and urban settings, you know, the U.K., the cities of Latin America, Canada, Australia and the like."
>
> *Maestro de iniciación:* "Fair enough.... Meanwhile, let's think about these questions:
>
> - "Why not seek out *mature respected Christian mentors* to be available to help individual boys become fully grown as persons and as Christians?"
>
> - "Why not provide boys a growth marker or markers through some *shared group experiences* to signify their progress toward Christian adulthood?"
>
> - "If the path to adulthood is undeniably gender-specific in most cultures, why not move toward *gender-specific* directions in contemporary Christian youth ministry?"

AUSTRALIA

The cultures of *aborigines,* first peoples of Australia, have long ago been overwhelmed by immigrants from Europe and Asia, hence aboriginal traditions are fading into history. However, material about male initiation is not so far distant in time as to be inaccessible. The word, "walkabout," has been popularized in modern media, with attendant misunderstandings.

In reality, *walkabout* refers to a rite of passage during which male Australian Aboriginals, about the age of thirteen, would undergo a journey during adolescence and live in the wilderness for a period as long as six months. They may travel as far as a thousand miles, or situate themselves in an isolated verdant valley as a travel base. The goal is for them to learn how to survive on their own.

> . . . this involved them in learning the skills of living successfully in the natural environment, learning about their religion, and learning about kinship. This included learning the appropriate ways of behaving with family members and understanding their obligations to one another."[5]

The objective of the *walkabout* was deeper than sheer physical survival.

> The aborigines . . . say it is a time of reflection, a deeply spiritual time of your life and a time you can think how can you improve in your life and what you did wrong during it. Another part of the goal is to make you reflect about everything. . . .[6]

In short, the tribal expectations were that the boy returning from *walkabout* would understand his community and desire to fulfill his role in it.

This account of one Aborigine boy's passage into manhood is illustrative.

> . . . Jimmie's initiation tooth had been knocked out of Jimmie's mouth by Mungindi elders when the boy was thirteen, in 1891. So, too, he had circumcised with stone, the incision poulticed over with chalk-clay. . . . When Jimmie was taken from camp for his initiation, Dulcie Blacksmith *[his mother]* presumed him dead for the time

being. The epoch-old agenda of ceremonies was kept a secret from all the women. As far as Dulcie knew, the great Lizard had mashed and swallowed him and would now give birth to him as *a completed Mungindi man*. He was gone for weeks. . . . Grown Mungindi men . . . knew that Jimmie was hiding in the scrub. . . . Here he waited for the wound to heal and lived on possum meat. He was full of the *exhilaration of tribal manhood* and the relief of finding that the lizard story was not true to the extent of his being actually chewed or swallowed. . . .[7]

According to *Wikipedia* sources,
A Bora is the name both to an initiation ceremony . . . and to the site on which the initiation is performed. At such a site, *boys achieve the status of men*. The initiation ceremony . . . often involves scarification and may also involve the removal of a tooth [evulsion] . . . . The ceremony . . . involves the learning of sacred songs, stories, dances, and traditional lore. Bora rings are mandala-like formations . . . comprised of circles of foot-hardened earth surrounded by raised embankments. . . . Women are generally prohibited from entering a bora.
Sometimes the boys would have to pass along a path . . . representing the *transition from childhood to manhood*, and this path might be marked by a stone arrangement or by footsteps, or *mundoes*, cut into the rock. . . .

Another source reveals that "boys were closely scrutinized by elders, and those who showed signs of special talents or powers were encouraged to pursue their callings in tribal culture."[9]

OCEANIA

To explore an Oceanic culture, an examination of traditional life on the world's second largest island, *New Guinea*, is warranted. At least nine hundred different ethnic groups exist there, each one with its various customs, such as the age at which initiation takes place. A sampling of initiation practices provides the following detail:[10]

- *Purpose:* Initiation,
    . . . intended to mark the end of the lad's former close association with his mothers and other female members of the household, cleanse him of the polluting effects of such contact, and make him grow strong into a strong and healthy adult. . .
    In so doing, it cemented the boy's relationship with other men as he entered the world of male secrets.
- *Program:* Boys are made to endure painful, harsh and cruel physical ordeals such as loss of sleep, beatings and/or drinking filthy water. Hoaxes and bullying of novices is not unusual. Additionally, instruction is given about traditions of the tribe and kinship/tribal responsibilities of men. The boys might learn how to play a bullroarer (a "magic flute" similar to an Australian *didgeridoo*), reserved for men only.
- *Location:* Some kind of seclusion seems to have been the norm. No contact was permitted with women, in some cases, the initiates could not even eat food cooked by women. Associated with this secrecy is keeping male knowledge away from women. Mythical tales were ". . . invented for the express purpose of deceiving the women and keeping them in a position of inferiority."
- *Bleeding rituals:* Boys' rituals often include blood-letting of some kind, for example, circumcision, scarification, tongue-cutting and/or intentional nose-bleeds. Possibly this grew out of an underlying resentment males may have had about menstrual bleeding which is the distinct physical maturation marker for females.
- *Leadership.* Males were definitively divided during initiation between "initiators" and "initiads." Mature men guided and directed the training experiences.

- *Celebration.* At the end of the initiation retreat, the tribe observed a grand festival with the slaughter of a pig, feasting, dancing and a parade of the newly-minted men attired in full regalia. This represented a "form return of the youths to everyday life."

EUROPE

Initiation experiences such as observed in traditional tribal settings in Africa, New Guinea and elsewhere disappeared centuries ago on the European continent as medieval life and nation-states emerged. However, the need for children to find a way into adulthood did not fade away. Across Europe a system of on-the-job training arose. In short, ". . . a few hundred years ago [parents in] northern Europe took a particularly harsh line, sending children away to live and work in someone else's home," according to one contemporary observer.[12]

His remarks shine a light on a system of child-rearing that operated across northern Europe from medieval into modern times. Back then, many parents of all classes sent their children away from home to work as servants or apprentices — only a small minority, usually from upper class families, went into religious vocations or to a university. Most parents farmed children out at about age fourteen, an appropriate time for passage into adulthood.

This seemingly repugnant system grew out of economic need.
> Since most families needed their children to contribute to their own support, the young nearly always worked alongside their parents in the home and on the land. . . . they acquired their parents' vocational skills, learned responsibility, and internalized the values of their society. The practice of apprenticeship extended this family-

centered model of work and learning. . . . It transferred children or adolescents . . . to interim, external ones . . . — typically four to seven years.[13]

Thus poor parents could at the same time have one less child to feed and at the same time arrange for a possible career for her or him. At least there was the possibility for a boy to learn a trade if he was apprenticed to a craftsman, whereas a girl could prepare for domestic service. The receiving household would receive a source of cheap labor in exchange for room and board.

It was not an easy life. Some masters and housekeepers were kind whereas others were abusive. The live-in servant was at their mercy. Moreover, ". . . illiterate servants had no means of communicating with their parents, and the difficulties of travel meant that even if children were only sent 20 miles (32 km) away they could feel completely isolated."[14]

For example from the sixteenth century, a twelve-year-old apprentice ". . . wrote to his mother complaining that he wasn't being taught anything about trade or markets, but was being made to sweep the floor."[15] In another case:

> In 1396, a contract between a young apprentice named Thomas and a Northampton brazier[16] called John Hyndlee was witnessed. . . . Hyndlee took on the formal role of guardian and promised to give Thomas food, teach him his craft and not punish him too severely for mistakes. For his part, Thomas promised not to leave without permission, steal, gamble, visit prostitutes or marry. If he broke the contract, the term of his apprenticeship would be doubled to 14 years.[17]

Sometimes these apprenticeships would be primarily instructional, leading to an acceptable vocation. But others would be exploitive, with an abundance of work and a minimum of training.[18]

As a rite of passage into adulthood, the apprenticeship system potentially enabled girls and boys to learn knowledge and skills that allowed them to support themselves as they matured. Moreover, they could learn the value of hard work while imbibing the expectations of their community or, conversely, learning how to avoid drudgery by skillful avoidance maneuvers and operating on the fringes of society. Lastly, a boy could prove to himself and others that he had grown up.[19]

The European culture concurrently was chiefly built on adherence to a Christian church, Roman Catholic or Orthodox before Protestantism arose. Ecclesiastical traditions included confirmation, or something similar, as it inducted new members into their adult community. A boy realized he was becoming a man upon being confirmed.

NORTH AMERICA (Canada and United States)[20]

A study of the historic rites of passage for boys in North America must progress along two lines of investigation. First, the cultures of the First Peoples on the continent deserve attention, especially since certain native American practices of initiation ceremonies continue to exist. Second, attention must be given to the predominantly European heritage brought to the continent, originating from Spain, the Netherlands, England and France at the outset.

When the first Americans presumably ventured from Asia to the North America continent, it is estimated that there were easily more than one thousand[21] ethnic groups populating the continent, though records of that period are exceptionally sketchy. However, the introduction of European illnesses for which the First Peoples had no immunity decimated native populations. Their numbers were also measurably reduced by the ill treatment by explorers and settlers, bordering on genocide. Nevertheless, information about historic male rites of passage is still available because some of these ceremonies persist in some form or another.

Native peoples realized that a boy needed to grow up and thus provided for the entrance to manhood in some unique ways. Bravery in hardship, in isolation, and/or in danger all provided a boy with confidence in his ability to accept and succeed in the roles men engaged in tribal life.

The initiation of the Comanche Nation (presently located in Oklahoma, USA) provides one vivid example.
> As a boy approached puberty, life quickly became more serious. These were the high lonesome plains . . . and his tribe lived a hard and brutal nomadic life where nothing was guaranteed. Skill in hunting was the only real guarantee of survival and thus he was expected to perfect his skills in archery. . . . A Comanche boy had to learn to make fire. . . basic wilderness skills. . . .
> With puberty, too, came the rituals that would *transform them, in the eyes of the tribe, from boys to men.* . . . For Comanches it began with a swim in a river or stream, a form of purification. The young man then ventured out to a lonely place . . . clad only in breechclout and moccasins. With him he carried a buffalo robe, a bone pipe, tobacco, and fire-making materials. On the way to his secluded spot he stopped four times, each time smoking and praying. At night he smoked and prayed for power. He looked for signs in the animals and rocks and trees around him. He fasted. (Unlike some of the northern plains tribes, there was no self-torture involved.) Usually this lasted four days and nights, but the idea was for the young brave to remain in place until he received a vision.

> ". . . Quanah *became a full warrior* when he was fifteen years old."[22]

Sometimes native American initiates were sent on a quest for a vision. One observer described initiation by the Oglala

Lakota (Sioux), from the Great Plains of the US and Canada.
... it was the tradition for an adolescent boy to go off on his own, weaponless and wearing nothing but a loincloth and moccasins, on a dream quest. Hungry, thirsty, and bone-tired, the boy would expect to have a dream on the fourth day which would reveal to him his life's path. Returning home, he would relate his dream to the tribal elders, who would interpret it according to ancient practice. And his dream would tell him whether he was destined to be a good hunter, or a great warrior, or expert at the art of horse-stealing, or perhaps to become specialized in the making of weapons, or a spiritual leader, priest, or medicine man.[23]

The Cree of Canada also practiced vision questing.
... young men went off by themselves, without food or water, for several days, until they acquired a spirit helper. The Cree also used the conjuring lodge. This was place where a shaman, or spiritual leader, could speak to his *Manito* spirit helpers, to receive advice and to give it to others.[24]

After initiatory experiences, native Americans and first-people Canadians knew well what it was to be a man, and so did the rest of that community. A boy's manhood was never questioned after that.

Moving on to the culture of the involuntary settlers from Africa, black slavery in the Americas erased most tribal customs because Africans were scattered throughout the Western Hemisphere as individuals, not tribal groups. Hence there was little opportunity to carry on initiation traditions such as had been followed in Africa.

However, Europeans settled as ethnic groups: English, Dutch, French, Spanish and so on. They brought with them their culture of manhood development, that is, they generally followed the medieval European patterns of apprenticeship with further education reserved for boys from elite families.

As a result, no distinct initiation experiences into manhood have been observed in Euro-North-America. However, the church tradition of confirmation was used in Catholic colonies as well as in Calvinistic groups, to emphasize the movement of a boy into Christian manhood.

Finally, the traditions across the globe point to anything but ambiguity for a boy in his development. Growing up, he knew what he had to do to become a man. So did his parents and his community. The result was stability of culture and relative harmony in families and society. But that was then and perhaps where!

➤ QUESTIONS TO PONDER ◄

- What can Christian youthworkers do to help *boys* gain:

    ♦ More self-confidence as they go through the awkwardness of adolescence?

    ♦ More respect for elders as various cultures become more youth-centered?

- The transition for a boy into manhood is ambiguous compared to girls who have a definite physiological marker of their growth into puberty. Why not provide boys through some shared group experiences a marker or markers to denote their growth toward adulthood?

- How might the historic European concept of apprenticeship carry over into Christian youth ministry, with mature Christian men leading the way?

- Why be constrained with politically-correct (USA) "coeducation" expectations for youth development, if the path to adulthood is undeniably gender-specific in most cultures historically? Is it possible for contemporary Christian youth ministry to become counter-cultural in this regard? Should it?

A POSTSCRIPT, *ANCIENT PERSIA*
(for further reflection)

The Biblical record provides a hint of what might have been a model for initiation used in ancient Persia in the account of young Jewish captive Daniel and his friends. Parallels between the experience of these young men and that of various initiation models presented in this chapter are apparent.

According to other ancient texts, Iranian fathers prayed for:
. . . a child of innate wisdom who would bring help to his community, . . . who would be well-formed, strong and respectable, who would relieve distress, and who would add to the glory of his house, to the glory of his clan, to the glory of his city and to the glory of his country. . . . who would [also] be sensible, virtuous and wise, who would take an active part in the deliberations of the general assembly, who would be brilliant and clear-eyed . . . and who possess great intelligence."[25]

Does this not sound like the end-purposes of the training program Daniel and his companions received?

In Daniel's case, the preparation for manhood looked like this, according to the Book of Daniel 1:3ff. (CEV). The task of training the young men was given to King Nebuchadnezzar's "highest palace official" because it was regarded as of the utmost importance. The Bible reports, "One day the king ordered Ashpenaz, his highest palace official, to choose some *young men* from the royal family of Judah and from other leading Jewish families."

- *Qualifications:* royal lineage, healthy, smart, wise, educated and fit to serve in the civil service. "The king said, 'They must be healthy, handsome, smart, wise, educated, and fit to serve in the royal palace.'"
- *A Three-year Program:* A special diet, writing/reading the Persian language and other training for officialdom. "Teach them how to speak and write our language and give them the same food and wine that I am served. Train them for three years, and then they can become court officials."
- *Identity Change.* "Four of the young Jews chosen were Daniel, Hananiah, Mishael, and Azariah. . . . But the king's chief official gave them Babylonian names. . . ."

The narrative continues.

Daniel made up his mind to eat and drink only what God had approved for his people to eat. And he asked the king's chief official for permission not to eat the food and wine served in the royal palace. God had made the official friendly and kind to Daniel. But the man still told him, "The king has decided what you must eat and drink. And I am afraid he will kill me, if you eat something else and end up looking worse than the other young men."

The king's official had put a guard in charge of Daniel and his three friends. So Daniel said to the guard, "For the next ten days, let us have only vegetables and water at mealtime. When the ten days are up, compare how we look with the other young men, and decide what to do with us." The guard agreed to do what Daniel had asked.

Ten days later, Daniel and his friends looked healthier and better than the young men who had been served food from the royal palace. After this, the guard let them eat vegetables instead of the rich food and wine.

God made the four *young men smart and wise*. They read a lot of books and became well educated. Daniel could also tell the meaning of dreams and visions.

At the end of the three-year period set by King Nebuchadnezzar, his chief palace official brought all the young men to him. The king interviewed them and discovered that none of the others were as outstanding as Daniel, Hananiah, Mishael, and Azariah.

- *Recognition upon successful completion of the training experience.* "So they were given positions in the royal court. From then on, whenever the king asked for advice, he found their wisdom was ten times better than that of any of his other advisors and magicians" (Daniel 1:20).

Reflection. This interpretation of the Biblical account of Daniel and his companions may help to explain their maturity in face of political and spiritual opposition. They were acting as *young men*, not as *emerging-adult-boys*.

NOTES

[1] Joshua Project (2015), a ministry of Frontier Ventures.
[2] Mislav Popovic, http://traditionscustoms.com/coming-of-age/coming-of-age-ceremonies-china.
[3] Mislav Popovic, http://traditionscustoms.com/.
[4] Http://www.waupun.k12.wi.us/.
[5] Edward Hyams, and George Ordish, *The Last of the Incas* (New York: Barnes and Noble, 1963), 72-73, 115-116.
[6] *Australian Aboriginal Culture* (Canberra: Australian Gov't Publishing

Service, 1989), 30.

[7] Juan Matias Inchaustegui and Miguel Martin Perez, *Walkabout, The Aboriginal Rite of Passage*, Blog, https://juanmatiasblogforenglish.files.wordpress.com/2013/09/juan-matias-and-miguel-walkabout-final-template.pdf.

[8] Thomas Keneally, *Initiation. The Chan. of Jimmie Blacksmith* (New York: The Viking Press, 1972). 2-3.

[9] Asian graphic symbol of the universe.

[10] Http://www.greencauldrontours.com/flex/bora-rings/23/1#sthash.JekJzApA.dpuf.

[11] "Adventure Kokoda," *Encyclopedia of Papua and New Guinea* (Melbourne University Press, 2015).

[12] William Kremer, *What medieval Europe did with its teenagers* (BBC World Service. 23 March, 2014).

[13] *Encyclopedia of Children and Childhood in History and Society* (Advameg Inc., 2008).

[14] William Kremer.

[15] William Kremer.

[16] A worker in brass.

[17] *Encyclopedia of Children and Childhood in History and Society.*

[19] Ruth Mazo Karras, *From boys to men : formation of masculinity in late medieval Europe*, (Philadelphia: University of Pennsylvania Press, 2003), 109.

[20] Canada and the USA have European dominant cultures. The Central Amerian republics and *Estados Unidos Mexicanos* are more properly viewed as Hispanic-American with many similarities to South America cultures.

[21] Joshua Project (2015), a ministry of Frontier Ventures.

[22] S.C. Gwynne, *Empire of the Summer Moon*, (New York: Simon and Shuster, 2010). 198-199.

[23] C. George Boeree. "Erik Erikson, 1902-1994," *Personality Theorie*. (http://webspace.ship.edu/cgboer/erikson.html, 1997, 2006).

[24] "Plains Cree," *Library and Archives Canada* (Ottawa, n.d.).

[25] Jivanji Jamshedji Modi, *Education Among the Ancient Iranians* (Bombay: The Times Press, 1905), 42.

Chapter 5

TRADITIONAL PATHS TO WOMANHOOD

Quinceañera, *kinaalda, sanndanggu,* **debut,** *elima, nugbeto, komba, umemulo, chinamwari, ritu kala samskara,* **sweet-sixteen party,** *mascalero, ichisungu*[1] — whatever it is called or was called in various world cultures, the ceremony represents a monumental milestone in a female's life, when she moves from being a *girl* to being a *woman* in the eyes of her community. Ideally, she sees herself as *having been transformed into a beautiful, refined woman.* This is a special event for her, for her family, for her society!

A female knows beyond a doubt that something extraordinary is happening to her when she begins to bleed with her first menstruation, in contrast with a boy whose physical development toward maturity is less measurable. To her it is a mysterious event, even if she has been prepared in advance by her mother or an older sibling. Nevertheless, she realizes that her responsibilities will never be the same, as her body demonstrates its potentiality for new life.

Accordng to traditions of the Navajo Nation (USA), the pubescent female receives the respect accorded "Changing Woman," the Navajo's legendary creator of the universe.

The menstruating girl symbolizes the magical power of females in that culture.[2] South American indigenous peoples echo these beliefs when they deify "Mother Earth," "World Mother" or *Pachamama*. So, the forming of a *woman* is an event to be taken seriously.

Some ethnic customs have attention-grabbing components. The Akha people (Thailand, Laos, China and Myanmar) observe a girl's path to adulthood in both a sacred thanksgiving ritual and a form of ancestral worship, the "Swing Ceremony."

> It's this later component that makes the ceremony so very spectacular - the girls of the village come dressed in their finest hand-made . . . clothing/costumes. Indigo-dyed cotton cloth jackets skirts and "leg wraps" are embroidered in intricate patterns of every possible distinctive colour. The most ornate of headware made from silver & colourful beads adorn their heads. The girls laugh their heads off as they launch each other on the swing - individually, in pairs, seated, standing.[3]

To be part of such an event must be a delightful experience!

A sampling of *coming-of-age observances for girls* around the globe includes some **common components**.

THE WAKE-UP CALL

The flow of blood not only constitutes the wake-up call for a girl and her family, but it also introduces a degree of mystery into their lives.[4] This onset of puberty traditionally leads to customs and ceremonies that constitute initiation into womanhood, with considerable variance from one ethnic group to another.

Blood is often used in sacred rituals for purification or incantation. It echoes the Bible's reminder that without the shedding of blood, there is no remission for sin.[5] The issue of personal cleanliness is also addressed, because the girl must find a way or ways of coping with the flow over which she has no control. Some cultures recognize first menstruation quite directly. For example, a Nuba girl (South Sudan) traditionally undergoes scarification, from her breasts to her navel.[6] To enter womanhood, Fulani girls (West Africa), had their faces painfully tattooed with a sharpened piece of wood.

Girls in many cultures realize at first blood that they will very soon be expected to take on a woman's responsibilities, including marriage and child-bearing. In many parts of the world, the pressures are great for a married woman to get pregnant and soon bear a male child. Additionally, many females then also face hard physical labor in the home and in the fields. Hence, menses is often is a sobering event for a girl, whether she has been instructed about it in advance or not.

SECLUSION

Girls entering puberty discover that their freedom of movement and other behavior becomes subservient to tribal customs that seem to center around the concept of menstruation[7] as "impurity." Girls may be forced into seclusion in a special dwelling some distance away from the village that can last a short time or up to several years. Some examples of proscriptions placed on the girl during her first period are:[8]

- Neither touch the ground, nor see the sun (common).
- Not allowed to see any males, not even relatives (Bengal).
- Not permitted to see a cow or touch any person, tree or plant (India).
- Covers her head with a blanket (Zulu).

A specific example comes from an Asiatic Indian woman,
   The Indian coming of age ceremony [*nalanggu*] starts,

when the girl's first menstruation begins, with *a period of ritual seclusion.* The girl sits separately on a wooden plank in a corner. Neighborhood women gather for a ceremonial meal that is served on banana leaves, after which they paint the girl's feet with a mixture of red ochre, turmeric and limestone.

. . . a hut is made of fresh leaves. . . furnished with all the things needed by the girl, including toiletries, clothing and vessels. Food is brought to her, and she takes complete rest. She is helped by other women while bathing. Daily bathing alternates between 'head-bath' and 'ordinary bath.' When she goes to the toilet, she must carry neem leaves and something made of iron, to ward off evil spirits. Special foods are prescribed for this *seclusion*, which is continued for 9, 11 or 13 days (it must be an odd number of days).

During the seclusion, the girl is instructed not to look at birds on an empty stomach, not to go out alone, and especially not to go into the *pooja* [prayer] room. She is warned not to leave leftover food where dogs could get it, because she would get a stomach ache if a dog ate the leftovers. Further restrictions symbolize her ritually dangerous status: she should not touch flowering plants (they might wilt), and she should not touch stored food items such as tamarind, rice or salt, which might be spoiled by her contact.[9]

According to one late-nineteenth-century interpretation:
. . . the object of secluding women at menstruation is to neutralise the dangerous influences which are supposed to emanate from them at such times. That the danger is believed to be especially great at the first menstruation . . . . The general effect of these rules is to keep her suspended . . . between heaven and earth. Whether enveloped in her hammock and slung up to the roof as in South America . . . being shut off both from the earth and from the sun,

she can poison neither of these great sources of life by her deadly contagion. . . . But the precautions thus taken to isolate . . . the girl are dictated by a regard for her own safety as well as for the safety of others. . . . she herself would suffer if she were to neglect the prescribed regimen. . . . the girl is viewed as charged with a powerful force which . . . may prove destructive both to herself and to all with whom she comes in contact. To repress this force within the limits necessary for the safety of all concerned is the object of the taboo. . . .[1]

Whatever the interpretation of these practices, a time of seclusion seems to be a "given" in female entry to adulthood. The girl symbolically leaves childhood behind and gets ready for advancement.

FEMALE GENITAL MUTILATION

In addition to seclusion and other taboos, initiation experiences for girls often include tests of endurance and strength, such as was practiced by the Nootka tribe (Canada) in which a girl having her first period was dropped in the Pacific Ocean a long distance from shore and was expected to swim back in order to become a woman.[11]

But at the core of the suffering in some traditional cultures is female genital mutilation (FGM). This consists of painful practices that damage the female genitalia as part of the "becoming adult" ceremony. In fact, it might be the central feature of some cultural observances for females. This mutilation may also be called "female circumcision," though it is more accurately described in one of four ways: clitoridectomy, excision, infibulation or other physical violence to the genitalia. Traditionally, FGM is carried out with or without (normally) anesthsia, by a a despoiler using a knife, razor or some crude cutting instrument. Whatever the method, it is extremely painful for the victim.

Whatever the origin of these rituals, they represent a defilement of God's creation of females, as found in Genesis 1:27, 28, 31.

So God created humans to be like himself; *he made* men and *women*. God gave them his blessing and said. "Have a lot of children! Fill the earth with people. . . . God looked at what he had done. *All of it was very good!* Evening came and then morning — that was the sixth day.

Also, the natural procreation of children was part of God's plan, not to be thwarted by cruel, painful damage to female reproductive organs by well-meaning women, possibly under the pressure from male-dominated cultures, as predicted in Genesis 3:16 when God pronounced a curse on Eve, "To the woman He said, '. . . your husband . . . will rule over you.'"

Yet for centuries in many parts of the world, girls have had to face this trauma as part of their journey into adulthood, ". . . clitorectomy symbolized the death of the girl and the emergence or rebirth of a new person—the woman." [12] Belief in greater fertility for the girl also often undergirded such practices. In spite of efforts by missionaries, colonizers, health agencies, national governments and women's advocacy groups, FGM continues to exist in almost every African country, Middle Eastern countries and Muslim[13] nations such as Indonesia and Malaysia, including Philippine provinces on the island of Mindanao. Moreover, FGM is also practiced in places like the United Kingdom by families who have immigrated there from the aforementioned places. It is estimated that over 130 million girls and women worldwide have undergone FGM.[14]

INSTRUCTION

A traditional rite of passage for girls often includes instruction of what it means to be a woman in that particular society.

Hence, during the period of seclusion, girls would typically receive guidance from *older women* who share and impart their wisdom and life experiences on a variety of subjects, such as:
- Their future role as women, how to be a good mother and wife.
- The history of her people.
- Ways to cook traditional foods and other household duties. In tribal situations, a women might be expected to arise early, fetch firewood, draw water and cultivate fields.
- How to behave as a married woman. For example, "a MuRemba woman is taught the art and splendour of sex."[15] A Zimbabwe an researcher concluded, "The initiation processes and messages reduce women' role in marriage to being able to serve and sexually satisfy her husband."[16]
- How to function as a proper woman in her societal surroundings, in manners and other propriety, for example, behave properly with in-laws.
- Participating in traditional music and dancing.
- The way to spiritual maturity; sacred teachings.
- "One of the most important functions of female initiation ceremonies is to underline the need for co-operation and a sense of responsibility to the community." [17]

Youthworker: *"O.K., I think I get it. There's a lot a girl has to learn to be a woman, in every culture. Seems like it can be very frightful and painful process, physically and otherwise."*

Maestro de iniciación: *"So what can you do about it?"*

Female youthworker: *"Me? I can be the Christian woman I am called to be!"*

> Male youthworker: *"Me? Not my concern — what do I know?"*
>
> *Maestro de iniciación*: "Are you avoiding the broader issue?"
>
> Youthworkers: *"O.K., maybe as Christians we need to broaden the scope of what we teach to young females."*
>
> *Maestro de iniciación*: "Like sex education? Like female decorum? Like cooking and grooming? Like self-respect?"
>
> Youthworkers: *"Whoa, we're supposed to be teaching the Bible, about salvation, spiritual growth, outreach, you know! Your questions raise too many peripheral issues!"*
>
> *Maestro de iniciación:* "Really? Think about it, as we learn a bit more about how girls around the world have become women."

INSTRUCTION BY ADULT WOMEN

The time-honored way for a girl to learn how to live as a woman is receiving instruction from older women who serve as their *mentors*. A mentor is an individual, usually older, always more experienced, who helps and guides another individual's development. Perhaps Naomi's guidance of her daughter-in-law Ruth, as told in the Bible, provides a model of how female mentoring works. Effective mentors usually hold high social status in their communities. Sometimes the mentors may be older relatives, as in a report from a Zambian young woman, "Two of my mother's aunties were at hand to give advice and impart some wisdom on my transition into womanhood."[18] Also, in the story of Jesus (Luke 1), young pregnant Mary consults her elder cousin Elizabeth.

Mature women are well able to pass along not only women's secrets, relating to sex, marriage and childbearing, but also cultural heritage, homemaking and other skills required of women. As one reported from Zimbabwe, "In every Remba village there are some elderly women called *Mbuya Nyanye* or *Chinoni* whose role is to . . . initiate young girls. . . ."[19]

Another African example tells the story more fully.
> There are *four important leaders* in the [initiation process of Bondo/Sande girls]. . . . First there is a chief official who represents spirits of female ancestors. She has the ability to transform into a spirit being. When she dances on special occasions, her identity is concealed by a mask and a special dress. Below the chief are an assistant leader, a mother, and a supervisor. The supervisor is responsible for cooking, washing, and general domestic affairs. This *team of women* teaches young initiates myths, ethics, herbal medicine, health and hygiene, preparation of cosmetics, spinning, dancing, singing and storytelling.[20]

It appears that established and experienced women in the community do the training, not "twenty-somethings" barely in to their own womanhood.

HOMECOMING

The end of a girl's initiation is marked with great celebration. She is welcomed back into her community as a *woman*. In many parts of Latin America, young girls celebrate their *Quinceañera* when they turn 15 years old. This coming of age tradition typically begins with a Catholic mass in which the girl renews her baptismal vows and solidifies her commitment to her family and faith. Immediately following the mass is a fiesta where friends and family eat and dance. Sometimes prayer or prayers are included in the initiation ceremonies. For example, in the Navajo Nation (USA), ". . . The family prays all night long for the girl, her family and the whole tribe."[21] Then the transformation process is complete; it is an occasion for remembrance and rejoicing.

From an Asiatic Indian comes this report.

> The third and final part [of the initiation] is the *lavish public function*, where the men folk and friends are all invited. The girl's maternal uncles are supposed to gift her richly. The girl gets her first sari, which is made out of silk. . . . The girl wears the saris for the first time on this day. Gifts are also given by family friends. Elaborate *pujas* [worship events] are performed, both at home and in the public function.[22]

The phenomenon of celebration is also observable in contemporary Jewish *Bas Mitzvah* fêtes and at the completion of Christian confirmation in certain congregations. Thus a girl is recognized as being mature and conscious of her womanhood and being ready to be accepted as an adult in her community. Certain Muslim customs follow the same pattern.

> The 11th birthday is special in Malaysia for Muslim girls. They participate in a ritual called the *Khatam Al Koran*. The girls prepare arduously for this *prestigious coming of age ceremony* that allows them to show their maturity and spiritual growth. The final chapter of the Koran is memorized and recited *before their family and friends* in the mosque.[2]

Another traditional path is recorded from the country of Zimbabwe:

> The *procession* starts from *Nyanye's [initiation master]* home but she walks behind. The event is marked by singing and dancing. Upon arrival at the homestead, the

Nyanye hands over the girls to their respective parents. At this stage they stand up and recite their new names that have been adopted at the camp. The Komba tradition requires that a girl changes her name. . . . The initiates demonstrate some of their performances at the camp. This event brings with it *great joy for the girls* who have maintained virginity, their parents and would-be spouses. The girls are a source of pride. . . . This celebration marking the initiates' completion of their training is punctuated *by singing, dancing, drinking and feasting.* The ceremony concludes with the initiates taking vows not to disclose their sacred tradition and teaching . . . before they finally disperse to their homes.[24]

Male youthworker: *"The festivities sound like fun. I'm always looking for more fun stuff!"*

Maestro de iniciación: "You think this is about fun?"

Female youthworker: *"Not at all. Becoming a woman is imperative."*

Male youthworker: *"Oh, well, I guess you are right."*

Maestro de iniciación: "Definitely! Achieving womanhood never has been simply a fun experience, in fact, more the opposite."

Youthworkers: *"And they are becoming women – how fantastic is that! Wish our job was as 'simple' as having an initiation ceremony. No quick fix for girls in today's modern world."*

Maestro de iniciación: "That's true — but think how resolute Christian women changed their world. Like Mother Teresa. Like Harriet Tubman. Like Florence Nightingale. Like Rosa Parks. It's worth the effort!"

NOTES

[1] Zambia. "... the most important semipublic ceremony is the *ichisungu* initiation for young girls. When a girl begins to menstruate, she is taken into the bush by a ritual specialist . . . instructed in the duties of womanhood through songs and sacred clay figurines and paintings. . . . Men are not allowed. . . . After initiation the girl is considered ready for marriage.. David Gordon, *Encyclopedia of World Cultures Supplement, 2002,* (The Gale Group, Inc.:2002), www.encyclopedia.com/topic/Bemba.aspx.

[2] Trudy Griffin-Pierce, *Earth is My Mother, Sky is My Father* (Albuquerque: University of New Mexico Press, 1992), 63.

[3] Jeffrey Hays, *Facts and Details,* "Akha Ethnic Group," 2013. http://factsanddetails.com/asian/cat66/sub417/item2745.html.

[4] "When a girl first gets her period, doctors call it *menarche* . . . doesn't happen until all the parts of a girl's reproductive system have matured and are working together." http://kidshealth.org/teen/sexual_health/girls/menstruation.html.

[5] Hebrews 9:22, "In fact, the law requires that nearly everything be cleansed with blood, and without the shedding of blood there is no forgiveness" (NIV).

[6] Tasha Davis, *African Holocaust,* "Rites of Passage," 10-2011, http://www.africanholocaust.net/ritesofpassage.html.

[7] "When a girl first gets her period, doctors call it *menarche* . . . doesn't happen until all the parts of a girl's reproductive system have matured and are working together." http://kidshealth.org/teen/sexual_health/girls/menstruation.html.

[8] From *Wikipedia,* "Seclusion of Girls at Puberty."

[9] "The Indian Tradition Of Holding Coming Of Age Ceremony For Girls: Is It Relevant Today?" *Both Coin,* http://bothcoin.blogspot.com/2014/02/the-indian-tradition-of-holding-coming.html.

[10] James George Frazer, *The Golden Bough* (London, Macmillan Press, 3rd edition, 1926), 606.

[11] Louise Carus Mahdi, Steven Foster, Meredith Little (eds.), *Betwixt & Between: Patterns of Masculine and Feminine Initiation* (LaSalle, IL: Open Court, 1987),114.

[12] Thomas Houssou-Adin and Katherine Lukemi Bankole, *Encyclopedia of African Religion,* Molefi Kete Asante and Ama Mazama (eds.), 626.

[13] Some Muslim authorities insist FGM is not required by orthodox Islam, but apparently FGM widely continues as part of folk-Islam.

Culturalsurvival@culturalsurvival.org. Also, see *The Islamic Monthly,* "'A Tiny Cut': Female Circumcision in Southeast Asia," by Sya Taha, March 12, 2013.

[14] Website, *FORWARD*, "Safeguarding Rights and Dignity" (London: 2002-2015).

[15] Tabona Shoko, *Komba: Girls' Initiation Rite and Inculturation Among the VaRemba of Zimbabwe* (Department of Religious Studies, University of Zimbabwe, Harare, Zimbabwe), 5.

[16] Tabona Shoko, 4.

[17] Sandra Klopper, 30.

[18] Jackie Mwanza, "Ichisuingu: Teenage Mutants, Zambian's in the Diaspora Have Stopped Initiation Ceremonies," *Ukzambians Media*, January 31, 2012, 1.

[19] C. Mabuwa, C., *The Komba Ritual of the VaRemba Tribe of Mberengwa* (unpublished BA Hons. Dissertation). (Harare: University of Zimbabwe. 1993), 12-13, as quoted in Shoko, 3.

[20] Willie Cannon-Brown, *Encyclopedia of African Religion*, Molefi Kete Asante and Ama Mazama (eds.), 511.

[21] *Naya* webpage, www.miesiaczka.com

[22] "The Indian Tradition Of Holding Coming Of Age Ceremony For Girls: Is It Relevant Today?. *Both Coin Newsletter,* http://bothcoin.blogspot.com/2014/02/the-indian-tradition-of-holding-coming.html, April 2, 2014.

[23] "Coming of Age Traditions, Rituals, and Ceremonies From Around the World," *Shindigz*, March 21, 2015.

[24] Shoko, 51.

Chapter 6

ECHOES OF THE INITIATION TRADITIONS

While many traditions are dying in today's changing world and although some traditions are deadly, some refuse to die. As in any human construct, traditions often contain some elements worth preserving, as well as some harmful features best discarded. Cultures do not necessarily preserve what is helpful, and some cannot, given the tidal wave of modernity sweeping the globe. A Christian is obliged to sift through the past and uncover what seems to be of divine origin, as a part of general revelation. Whatever is discovered of various traditions that are at heart of God needs to be encouraged, revitalized, perhaps even re-created. How this might be done remains a puzzle to be solved, as godly youthworkers scrutinize their specific culture.

> Youthworker: *"Look, this initiation stuff, it's mostly passé, over! Ancient history! Who cares?"*
>
> *Maestro de iniciación:* "No one, perhaps. On the other hand, maybe *you* should?"

> Youthworker: *"Come on, admit it, as villagers migrate to the cities, traditional ways begin to vanish; youth want to be up-to-date."*
>
> **Maestro de iniciación:** "What about their parents? Are they also dumping the traditions?"
>
> Youthworker: *"I suppose not, but we are primarily trying to* reach the youth. *Many of the tradition-bound parents are not yet Christians, so. . . ."*
>
> **Maestro de iniciación:** "But aren't the youth still emotionally attached to some of the traditions — caught between two worlds?"
>
> Youthworker: *"Well, yes, but I want to be on the cutting edge, current, culturally-savvy."*
>
> **Maestro de iniciación:** "Nothing wrong with that, but in our wanting to be up-to-date, let's make sure we don't overlook anything valuable from the past."
>
> Youthworker: *"O.K., I give up. What's out there?"*

Traditions do not just "go away." They may influence present behavior in important ways, so it is imperative to get "under the skin" of a culture to understand it. This is very difficult if one has grown up in that culture, because some degree of objective perspective is needed. In any case, the tough question to be faced is this: "Is it possible that surviving traditions have some value in measuring progress toward manhood and womanhood?"

WHAT SURVIVES OF *THE TRADITIONS*?

Africa

Of all the continents where initiation of youth was and is used, Africa represents the place where traditions remain strong, in spite of the interferences of European-style school calendars that disrupt village life and customs. According to one observer, Africans . . .

> No matter where they travel, the traditional value systems, rituals and human ties are not lost but celebrated and maintained, at least in Africa . . . many African cultural traditions remain with us, though distorted today, for example, familial gatherings and respect of Elders.[1]

Some forms of tribal initiations survive in spite of the increasing urbanization of sub-Saharan Africa. Circumcision rites seem to lie at the center of the vestiges of initiation as experienced by Nelson Mandela (see Chapter 3) and others.

Meanwhile, governments such as the Republic of South Africa seek to regularize circumcision into health clinics to prevent infections caused by unsanitary surgical procedures used in traditional circumcisions. King Goodwill Zwelethini of Swaziland, as a tactic in the fight against the spread of HIV, has adapted the *Umkhosi woMhinage* ceremony as a way to encourage young Zulu girls to delay sexual activity until marriage. Meanwhile, women's rights advocates across the continent continue to press for elimination of FGM as a highlight of female initiation, with limited success against entrenched tribal traditions.

Europe

At the exact opposite of the modernization spectrum lays the continent of Europe, where tribal initiations ended centuries ago. Moreover, in the drive for higher education, apprenticeships are not nearly so widespread. However, in nominally Christian countries (e.g., Scandinavia, Germany), many adolescents are shepherded through traditional confirmation classes and celebration that may or may not mark their progress toward adulthood. Many European youth also have iconic events that seem to promise passage into adulthood. Some of the more remarkable are:

- Secularized equivalents to Christian confirmation. In Denmark, youth from secular families were coveting the lavish parties and gifts that advancing "Christian" confirmands received in mid-teen years. In response to pressure from those families, the government now issues bona fide certificates of "nonconfirmation," enabling all youth to share in the rewards of this rite of passage. The children of "free thinkers" were presumably indoctrinated with a humanistic worldview.
- Similarly, in eastern Germany in a carryover from state socialism, youth experience *Jugendweihe*. Here's one account.[2]

    Strange things happen every year in early summer in the eastern part of Germany: On the weekends, the streets are packed with 14-year-olds. The girls are wearing ball gowns and their hair is pinned up in a complicated fashion; the boys are in suits and ties. The young people seem happy to be out with their parents and grandparents, who are also decked out in their Sunday best. Strangers may scratch their heads in puzzlement but every villager knows what is going on - it is "Jugendweihe" season.

    ... The event typically takes place in a large hall or movie theater. A band plays festive music and the mayor or another local politician gives a speech in which the boys and girls are welcomed into the circle of adults. When the speech is over, the freshly minted adults go to the front of the hall to accept their ovation — and then the family celebrates together.

. . . .

The Jugendweihe Association surveyed 14-year-olds to find out why they participate in the traditional rite. The most frequent answers were that they wanted to consciously experience the beginning of their adulthood, because there would be a family party and last but not least, because they would receive presents. . . . the Jugendweihe trend is holding steady. Even kids from families that were originally from West Germany but now live in the eastern part of the country sometimes participate. No wonder —occasions that mobilize so many presents, so much attention and so many emotional parents are rare indeed.

- Norwegian students in their final semester of *videregående skole* (secondary school) participate in *russefeiring* (red caps). Originally the cap was worn for graduation, but today various colors, depending on institution and one's course of study, are reflected in clothing and specially-decorated vehicles. Most of the participants (*russ*) are age 18, thereby eligible for driving licenses and buying alcohol. Hence, the month-long event, by all accounts, is marked by considerable group revelry, rowdiness and excessive consumption of alcohol *(treukersfylla,* 3-week binge). A few students subscribe to a non-alcoholic version of *russefeiring* that has been termed *kristenruss*.
- Another example of boys-becoming-men comes from the Danish Faroe Islands. Animal rights activists find the custom offensive, but it seems to be meaningful for the islanders. Adolescent boys attack and kill dolphins as a way to show they are grown up.[3]
- In the U.K., some more affluent youth can observe their growth toward adulthood with a "gap year." After

finishing secondary school, with friends, perhaps, they plan to work or travel abroad. Less wealthy might take their "gap year" by taking unskilled jobs or doing unpaid internships in the marketplace. The expectation is that one will "discover one's self" and sometimes this is achieved. American youth may also do a "gap year" but it is less prevalent than in the U.K.

- Spanish boys used to be feted when they reached the age of 18, at which time they were subject to compulsory military service. Before the *quintos*, as they were called, had to leave their village, the group would have a feast ". . . and sometimes painted some graffiti, *Vivan los quintos del año*, as a memorial to leaving their youth."[4] Today the practice has lost its meaning and apparently ignored by most Spanish males.
- *Szecskáztatás*, a mild form of hazing (usually without physical and sexual abuse) is practiced in some Hungarian secondary schools. First-year students are publicly humiliated in various ways.

Nevertheless, across Europe youth continue to seek authentication of their adulthood through academics, for example, the *matura* or "O- and A-level exams. Youthworkers in Africa and Europe may wonder the degree to which the various cultural or academic emblems of "adulthood" are authentic passages into maturity in today's world. However, effective youthworkers seek to understand the unique features of the coming-of-age customs of their nation, or sub-culture within the nationality as a starting point in building an indigenous model of youth ministry.

Asia

Asians retain traditional ways helpful to their societies in building stable cultures that are resistant to change. The youth of China, Japan, India and elsewhere may covet Western ways culturally, but they find themselves also involved in traditions, as shown in the following examples.

- Japanese youth participate in a National Holiday known as "Coming of Age Day," *Seijin-no-hi*, the second Monday in January. When they reach the age of twenty, they are formally recognized as adults; voting, smoking and drinking are now permitted. Traditionally, young men wear new suits. Women however, are permitted to a formal kimono. The formality of Seijin-no-hi garments lends an air of importance and anticipation to the celebration. Speeches by politicians, the giving of gifts and family get-togethers are essential for proper observance of *Seijin-no-hi*.

- In China, apparently the age-old traditions of *capping* for boys and *hair-pining* for girls goes on (see Chapter 5) among the Han people. Also, the various minority groups within China have unique traditions. For example, among the Blang or Buland people-group, a black teeth kiss is featured in the ceremony called *baoji*. While young people are sit around a fire, every person dyes the teeth of the one sitting next to him or her in black. After that, they receive gifts from their parents and are allowed to start a relationship.[5]

- Indian young women, at least from the upper classes, can be expected to learn an intricate dance, *byarathnatyam*, and pass into womanhood by means of their debut performance, the *arangetram*. Girls start training for this dance in preschool years and it takes years to master.
For Indian families, the arangetram is a major event in a daughter's life, and they spare no expense in the planning of the occasion. The most elaborate *arangetrams* rival weddings — with stylish invitations, expensive wardrobe and jewelry, hundreds of guests, catered meals, gifts and plum venues that

are booked, in some cases, years in advance.

....

Perhaps one of the most endearing features of this ancient dance form is the relationship between the teacher — or guru — and her student. Bharathnatyam teachers are revered and held in the esteem of parents or elders. In keeping with the Indian tradition, students never call their teachers by their given name, but refer to them by an affectionate term — usually "auntie."[6]

The elements of the dance patterns are imbedded in Hinduism and Indian tradition.

- Korean youth also celebrate a "coming-of-age" day, on the Monday of the third week of May. Inductees into "adulthood" receive gifts: flowers, perfume and a kiss.
- See Chapter 1 and Appendices B & C for descriptions of current coming-of-age ceremonies in the Philippines.

Latino Cultures

In Latino communities, fifteen-year-old girls celebrate their entry into presumed-adultood through the *quineañera*, as described in Chapter 5, as part of the dominant Latin culture. In many places, however, traditional initiation may coexist among minority sub-cultural communities, especially those isolated geographically or linguistically, beneath the veneer of Western cosmopolitan ways.

Elsewhere

In North America, some smaller ethnic groups retain various customs of initiation. The Apache Nation, for example, requires children to undergo a ritual lasting several days. Girls are indoctrinated into womanhood through dances, singing, praying, cooking special meals, and a feast for and with the community.

Religious Customs Recognizing Entry to Adulthood

Remnants of traditional initiation exist in some religious groups. In some national settings, these ceremonies are more important in defining adulthood than underlying tribal ways, though at times they are combined in a syncretistic folk version of the religion, as can be observed in Latin America where Roman Catholicism enfolds beliefs in "mother earth." This is clearly shown in the gardens of the Basilica of Our Lady of Guadalupe in Mexico City, a popular site for tourists and pilgrims. They include two waterfalls, uniting as one stream at the bottom of the hill Tepeyac. One stream avowedly represents Aztec culture, the second Roman Catholicism.

Folk versions of Islam are found in Africa, hence definitions of adulthood may rest more on Muslim beliefs than tribal. Muslim doctrine requires a person beginning puberty to perform *salat* [prayer] and other obligations of Islam. When a Muslim boy or girl turns fifteen in lunar years, they are considered adult. The evidence for this is the testimony of Ibn 'Umar:

> Allah's Apostle called me to present myself in front of him on the day of the battle of Uhud. I was fourteen years of age at that time and he did not allow me to take part in that battle. But he called me in front of him on the day of the battle of the Trench when I was fifteen years old, and he allowed me to join the battle." Upon hearing this, Umar Ibn Abdul Aziz [emperor] made this age the evidence to differentiate between a mature and an immature person.[7]

Youthworkers in Islamic environments are already aware of such observances.

> Youthworker: *"Cultural awareness? Historic awareness? Religious awareness? I get it!"*

> *Maestro de iniciación:* "You really sound enthusiastic! You are probably ready to dig deeper into your own cultural milieu to see what you can discover about the growing-up process."
>
> Youthworker: *"Yes, but you need to know — I'm not in relationships with Muslim youth, or Buddhist, or Confucian, or Hindu, or Jewish, or Shinto youth."*
>
> *Maestro de iniciación:* "Ever hear of secular youth? Or non-Christian youth? Or nominally-Christian youth? Whatever the case, a knowledge of historic and religious rootage is going to help you shape a youth ministry that is relevant to them."
>
> Youthworker: *"But all this seems so far from actually reaching youth? My guess is that many youth go through the traditional stuff without much thought — and does getting circumcised, for example, really enable them to become mature adults?"*

HOW IRRELEVANT — or RELEVANT — ARE *THE TRADITIONS* NOW?

If anything can be said about contemporary youth, it is that they live in a time of great ambiguity. Cultural roots run strong and deep, with modernity perhaps only skin deep. So the question, "Who am I" is relevant. To increase the strain and stress, the life-stage known as *adolescence* is getting longer and longer. In one poignant example, in Italy, young men are referred to as *bamboccioni,* meaning overgrown babies. As far as cultural expectations are concerned, they have until age 30 to "grow up."

They don't want to grow up and assume responsibilities. They live at home, mamma cooks for them and does their laundry. . . . many don't even have jobs, but even if they do, they don't contribute to the home expenses, and they work and have fun. That's it.[8]

The apparent demand for further education pushes some young adults into several years more of dependence upon parents, as these neophytes realize an undergraduate degree is insufficient for many professional positions.

Adolescence is also lengthened at the other end of the age scale. The availability of mass media to children often bumps them into over-early adulthood through their premature knowledge of sexual matters. It certainly becomes a tragedy for them, to be given, symbolically, the keys to a powerful car but with little ability to drive it. Societal messages may also give them understandings of adulthood that have little relationship with reality. As one African writer put it:

> So a young African male in townships/inner city believes that the definition of being a man is to be a criminal, shooting people, being incarcerated, denigrating women and bastardizing children . . . young African women believe that the definition of being a woman is to be a single mother who 'doesn't need a man' and uses sex instead of her God-given ingenuity to gain power.[9]

A struggle exists, then, between traditional values and otherwise. One clash that becomes apparent is the shift in understanding of the fundamental unit of society. Traditional social focus is often upon the community and family being; modernity spotlights the individual. The Western (and Christian) ideas of the value of the individual person grow out of Biblical sources. However, modernity often overwhelms the equally Biblical obligation of concern for others, as Jesus expressed it, "Love your neighbor as yourself." That struggle is also fundamentally expressed in Galatians 6:2-5,

> "You obey the law of Christ when *you offer each other a helping hand*. If you think you are better than others,

when you really aren't, you are wrong. Do your own work well, and then you will have something to be proud of. But don't compare yourself with others. *We each must carry our own load.*"

A Biblical perspective includes both individual growth *and* a social conscience that also considers family, clan, tribe and nation. Moreover, the matter of family stability can be undermined by laxity in Biblical standards of morality, as ideas of sexual freedom are presented in secular media. Hence, individuals may not have a strong foundation for achieving their mission or support systems to focus them. Also, families may find it difficult to cultivate a Christian ambiance for the rearing of their children.

Another victim of the loss of traditions seems to be respect for the wisdom and guidance of elders. A culture of youth wrestles with the ancient (and Biblical) concept of looking to past generations for direction. Unfortunately, extended adolescence may lead to increasingly immature and individualistic adults who lack self-control, motivation and purpose, except the quest of happiness. As a result, fewer role models of maturity may exist in modern society. Christian *elders,* as models for youth, need to demonstrate a life of purpose and gravity to gain a hearing.

QUESTIONS TO PONDER

- What do boys and girls have available to them in the twenty-first century to mark their progress toward adulthood?
- Has anything meaningful from traditional ways survived in urban/suburban locales? If so, what is it?
- To what extent do cultural hangovers still wield power in helping girls and boys come to womanhood or manhood?

> - How do present-day congregations encourage boys' and girls' growth toward Christian adulthood?
> - *Think about* — "Progress should not be at the expense of custom but an intermingled part, interweaving the old wisdom with the new" *(source unknown).*

NOTES

[1] Tasha Davis, "African Cultural Initiation Rites," *Rites of Passage*, October 2011, blog.
[2] *The German Times, for Europe*, October 2009.
[3] http://greenplanetethics.com/wordpress/dolphin-killing-in-denmark-faroe-islands/#ixzz3sv9Uh33I
[4] *Wikipedia.*
[5] Alena Rasi, "Ancient coming-of-age ceremonies: Chinese Traditions,. *gbtimes*, October 29, 2011.
[6] Ivey DeJesus, idejesus@pennlive.co. September 05, 2011.
[7] 'Abd al-'Azīm ibn 'Abd al-Qawī Mundhirī and Muslim ibn al-Ḥajjāj al-Qushayrī, *The Translation of the Meanings of Summarized Sahih Muslim* (Riyadh, Saudi Arabia: Darussalam Publishers & Distributors, 2000).
[8] Personal letter from Sherri Carlson, missionary to Italy, December 9, 2015.
[9] Tasha Davis, "African Cultural Initiation Rites," *Rites of Passage*, October 2011, blog.

Chapter 7
A COMPENDIUM BASED ON *TRADITIONAL INITIATION*

A survey of traditional paths to adulthood, both for boys and girls, reveals their inadequacy for helping a man or woman live in the modern world. Life in urbanized, globalized communities bears little relationship to the ways of the rural village, so traditional rites seem irrelevant. Likewise, the vestiges of the old ceremonies for passing into adulthood, like the *debut* or *bar mitzvah*, seem to carry little value for living as a woman or man. Moreover, within the Christian community, formulae such as *confirmation* may be quite inadequate for facing life as a believing adult.

> **Youthworker:** *"Ah, ha, I knew it! Looking at the past isn't so valuable after all!"*
>
> **Maestro de iniciación:** *"Whoa, my friend! Shouldn't we try to refine the raw material to seek gold that may be there?"*

> Youthworker: *"I remember that you did speak of God's general revelation. Do you really think we could examine the data further to discover principles for godly youth ministry?"*
>
> **Maestro de iniciación:** "Yes, I do. Let's keep an open mind and wade into the thicket of cultural data available to us."
>
> Youthworker: *"Here we go again. I AM willing. . . ."*

AN ANALYTICAL MODEL

One way to attack the mountain of cultural data accumulated over the centuries across the globe is to separate out the specifics from the underlying principles, like distilling various aromatic substances into perfume. It is helpful to identify what is purely external in the process as compared to what is at its heart. Additionally, knowing the purposes will enable the observer to assess the validity of each for today's world.

Forms

What does initiation to adulthood look like, on the outside? What shape do the ceremonies for girls and boys take? What are the external forms that present themselves to the observer?

The possibilities seem endless, depending on the cultural, geographical and religious settings. Some features of some initiation experiences seem gruesome and cruel — and they indeed may be so, like filing of the initiate's teeth, FGM, starvation, beatings, being tortured by spears, facial scarification and the like. Few of the forms of initiation report any sports and/or recreation. Other than the building of *esprit de corps* among the youths being initiated, little falls into the category of light-hearted playfulness. Instead, an atmosphere of earnestness pervades.

Other aspects of initiations seem appropriate to the future faced by the boy or girl, such as instruction in sexual and other family matters, spirituality, hunting for wildlife, tribal songs, history and dances. Also, the time and duration of the initiation may vary, from a one-time painful torture (as with Elka in Chapter 1) to several weeks in the bush (as with Nelson Mandela in Chapter 3).

Purpose

The underlying intention of each initiation experience is quite clear: assisting boys to be transformed into men, girls to become women, as defined by that society. Some subsidiary aims grow out of that overall objective. Boys and girls who leave the village as children to be initiated are expected to return as adults, ready to undertake the physical, mental, social/civic, economic, familial and spiritual/devotional responsibilities of adulthood appropriate to that community (as illustrated in Chapter 1).

Living up to the expectations of tribal life requires a variety of skills to be developed before passing into the world of adulthood. For instance, a woman is usually expected to be adept at preparing food for her family; a man is assumed to be ready to take part in masculine tribal parleys. Sexual mores for the tribe are also communicated and the anticipation is that she and he will accept accordingly to insure family and social stability.

The Bible teaches that children are expected to grow up, to become mature in faith and life, to act responsibly before God and fellow humankind. St. Paul expresses this belief clearly in First Corinthians 13:11, "When we were children,

we thought and reasoned as children do. But when we *grew up*, we *quit our childish ways*." The apostle also states in Ephesians 4:14-16,
> *We are not meant to remain as children* at the mercy of every chance wind of teaching and the jockeying of men who are expert in the crafty presentation of lies. But we are meant to hold firmly to the truth in love, *and to grow up in every way* into Christ, the head (JBP).

Furthermore, the writer of Hebrews indicates that parenting embraces the responsibility of guiding children into maturity (12:7-9).
> ... No true son ever *grows up* uncorrected by his father. For if you had no experience of the correction which all sons have to bear you might well doubt the legitimacy of your sonship. After all, when we were children we had fathers who corrected us, and we respected them for it. (JBP).

And again, in Colossians 3:21, St. Paul writes, "Fathers, don't overcorrect your children, or they will *grow up* feeling inferior and frustrated" (JBP).

Jewish beliefs about maturity are shown in the narrative about the man born blind in the Gospel of St. John (9:20-21).
> "We know that this is our son, and we know that he was born blind," returned his parents, "but how he can see now, or who made him able to see, we have no idea. Why don't you ask him? *He is a grown-up man; he can speak for himself*" (JBP).

Hence, the goal of traditional initiation was indeed similar in intention to God's plan for children, to assist boys and girls to *grow up*.

Essence

Looking at the elements that lay beneath both outward forms and vital purpose is where the distillation process bears fruit. It is in the realm of *essence* that God's general revelation may best be seen. The Bible underscores the validity of these core elements of traditional initiations, seemingly vindicating the source as divine truth. Some of the fundamental elements found in traditional rites of passage into adulthood are:

- *Readiness for adulthood*
  The *maestros de iniciación* realize that getting girls or boys equipped for adult responsibility is a grave one. These boys, the male *maestro* will reason, will shortly become husbands, workers, members of the adult world. None of these will be easy transitions for young boys to make, yet make it they must. So the curriculum becomes intensely practical and realistic. Little time is/was allowed for sports and other play. Initiation, as far as the girls and boys are concerned, is not a recreational outing, but a solemn learning experience. The leaders likewise have the same commitment.

The Bible places directly on parents the responsibility to *guide their children into adulthood*. Founder of the Israeli nation Moses put it this way,
> [Parents,]... tell ... [God's laws] to your children over and over again. Talk about them all the time, whether you're at home or walking along the road or going to bed at night, or getting up in the morning (Deuteronomy 6:7).

Additionally, from the wisdom of Proverbs (22:6), "Teach your children right from wrong, and *when they are grown* they will still do right." It is unthinkable in God's plan for children to be abandoned to wander through juvenile years on their own. Over the centuries, Christian congregations have sought to assist parents in the complicated process known as *growing up*. This practice is entirely in line with the exhortations in Hebrews 10.

> And let us consider how we may spur one another on toward love and good deeds, not giving up meeting together, as some are in the habit of doing, but encouraging one another... (Hebrews 10:24-25, NIV).

Seeking to get children ready for the challenges of modern life ought to drive every parent and congregation to prayer and vigilant action.

- *Gender-specific preparation.* As implied in the previous point, boys and girls are on separate paths in their journey toward manhood and girlhood. Even though gender-blurring seems to be a characteristic of "modern society," the fact is that simple biology charts different paths for girls and boys. To whatever degree gender roles exist in any society, to that degree the youth must be trained to take up those functions as adults.

Examples of discipleship in the Bible demonstrate the value of same-gender relationships. The grounding of new leaders such as Moses with Joshua, Elijah with Elisha, Jesus with the disciples, Barnabas with Saul and Paul with Timothy illustrates the process. On the female side, the Bible includes a few, such as Naomi with Ruth, Elizabeth with Mary, plus the admonition to Titus by St. Paul.

> ... teach *the older women* to be reverent in the way they live, not to be slanderers or addicted to much wine, but to teach what is good. Then *they can urge*

the younger women to love their husbands and children (2:3-4, NIV).

- *Older, mature men and women in leadership of youth.* Almost without exception, seasoned elders serve as the doyens and gurus in the initiation experiences. It is believed that insight comes with life experience, opening the vast storehouse of accumulated wisdom to young people. A West African proverb reveals why, "When an elder dies, a library is lost forever." In no case were the responsibilities placed into the hands of young adults just finding their own ways on the paths of adulthood.

In the words of St. Peter,
> Now may I who am *myself an elder* say a word to you *my fellow-elders*? . . . I urge you then to see that your "flock of God" is properly fed and cared for. Accept the responsibility of looking after them willingly and not because you feel you can't get out of it, doing your work not for what you can make, but because you are really concerned for their well-being. You should aim not at being "little tin gods" but as examples of Christian living in the eyes of the flock committed to your charge (First Peter 5:1-4, JBP).

St. Paul reiterates the need for mature qualified persons to be in leadership in his letter to Titus (1:5-9).
> . . . *leaders for the churches* . . . must *have a good reputation* and be *faithful in marriage. Their children* must be followers of the Lord and not have a reputation for being wild and disobedient. Church officials *[youthworkers]* are in charge of God's work, and so they must also *have a good reputation.* They must not be bossy, quick-tempered, heavy drinkers, bullies, or dishonest in business. Instead, they must be friendly to strangers and enjoy doing

good things. They must also be sensible, fair, pure, and *self-controlled*. They must stick to the true message they were taught, so that their good teaching can help others and correct everyone who opposes it.

Again, from St. Paul, ". . . children are placed in the care of guardians and teachers until the time their parents have set" (Galatians 4:2).

- *Learning respect, for others, for one's elders, for the community.* Respect among youth for "the wisdom of the aged" seems to be a scarce quantity in the modern world. The media and commercialism convey messages of how important it is to be young, to be carefree (that is, irresponsible), to be individualistic and crass, perhaps to become elderly adolescents. Tribal traditions realized that older adults owned a vast storehouse of experiences and accumulated wisdom that younger folks would and could benefit from. Tradition points to the stability of the past to guide present and future action, personally and with others in family and society.

When declaring judgment on Jerusalem and Judah, the prophet Isaiah (3:5b) possibly describes contemporary youth, "Young people will insult their elders; no one will show respect to those who deserve it." The concept of respect for God and others has divine origin. Hence, in the words of St. Peter (First Peter 5:5-7a),
> You younger members must also *submit to the elders*. Indeed all of you should defer to one another and wear the "overall" of humility in serving each other. "God resists the proud, but gives grace to the humble." So, humble yourselves under God's strong hand, and in his own good time he will lift you up. . . (JBP).

St. Paul echoes this teaching in First Timothy 5:17, "Elders with a gift of leadership should be considered *worthy of respect"* (JBP). King David spells out the wonderful opportunity for older Christians, "Don't leave me when I am old and my hair turns gray. [instead] Let me tell future generations about your mighty power" (Psalm 71:18).

- *Acknowledgement of a Creator.* In the traditional context, becoming adult means knowing about a Supreme Being and how to live in harmony with He/She/It. Religious customs, behaviors and standards are carefully taught to the initiates, so that they will be able to participate in community religious celebrations such as dances and prayers. Girls and boys are taught how to live their lives in harmony with a divine being or idea.

The Bible affirms the communication value of natural creation, in pointing to a Creator, as in the following passages.

➤ The wrath of God is being *revealed from heaven* against all the godlessness and wickedness of people, who suppress the truth by their wickedness, since *what may be known about God is plain to them*, because God has made it plain to them. For since the creation of the world God's invisible qualities — his eternal power and divine nature — *have been clearly seen*, being understood from what has been made, so that people are without excuse (Romans 1:18-20).

➤ *The heavens declare the glory of God; the skies proclaim* the work of his hands. Day after day they pour forth speech; night after night *they reveal knowledge*. They have no speech, they use no words; no sound is heard from them. Yet their voice goes out into all the earth, their words to the ends of the world (Psalm 19:1-4).

➤ Remember your Creator in the days of your youth, before the days of trouble come and the years approach when you will say, "I find no pleasure in them" (Eccclesiastes 12:1, NIV).

Traditionalists want their boys and girls to know a Creator early on.

- *Family life education.* Underlying tribal customs is a respect for sexual mores that reign in and direct the instinctual urges of women and men. *Maestros de iniciación* realize intuitively through general revelation that sex drives must be channeled to prevent societal chaos. Whatever the culture expects, whether polyandy, levirate marriage, patriarchal, polygyny or monogamy, initiates receive careful instruction.

Three of the Ten Commandments (Exodus 20), the core of Christian ethics, disclose God's priorities for orderly family life. God expects human beings to follow rules that will build family solidarity and set boundaries on community misbehavior, as follows (verses 12, 14, 17).

➤ *Respect your father and your mother,* and you will live a long time in the land I am giving you.

➤ Be *faithful in marriage.*

➤ Do not want anything that belongs to someone else. *Don't want anyone's* house, *wife or husband,* slaves, oxen, donkeys or anything else.

Traditional initiations seek to instruct youth how to live sexually wholesome lives, according to their cultural norms. These norms might or might not correspond to the Bible, but they insure tribal harmony.

> Youthworker: *"I'm impressed. Traditional peoples and their customs certainly incorporate kernels of God's truth, however twisted their ceremonies might be."*
>
> Maestro de iniciación: "Seems so! I wonder how we can flesh out valuable elements of the essence and purpose of traditional initiations to suit a youth ministry for our time and place. What ideas do you have?"
>
> Youthworker: *"I'll tell you this, we are not going to do hazing under any circumstances. Or facial scarification."*
>
> Maestro de iniciación: "Speaking of scars, you haven't forgotten about tattoos, have you? How about a logo for your ministry on everyone's ankle? No, I'm just joking."
>
> Youthworker: *"But your point is for us to work out our own externals, our own unique program, built on Biblical essence and purposes. Sorry I started at the form stage. My blunder. . . ."*
>
> Maestro de iniciación: "Oh, we'll all make some of those before we are through. It seems like uncharted territory to me."
>
> Youthworker: *"Me, too, but I'll take the risk to rethink what we are doing or might do in youth ministry, IF it will get us to our goals."*
>
> Maestro de iniciación: "Let's do this together! I predict this is going to be a remarkable journey. Shall we give it a try?"

LEARNING FROM CULTURAL UNIVERSALS

A Biblical youth ministry would be well-advised to bring together observations from human culture to begin development of its own unique approach. The gleanings from Chapters 2-6 yield the following model.

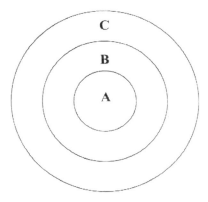

Figure 1—Into the Core

C = Forms, an almost infinite number of outward expressions.

Forms vary as a result of religious, geographical, ethnic and/or national beliefs and influences. Whatever is done (or not done) in terms of "the program," it must proceed out of the essence (A) and fulfill the purpose (B) or purposes that are being sought. Too often Christian youth ministry seems to focus on "what to do" (forms) with insufficient regard for essence or purpose. Essence and purpose(s) must be defined *before* thinking about the "how" to reach, disciple and develop youth. Thus, it is best left for last in the development of a unique youth ministry.

B = Purpose(s).

The overriding goal is to assist parents in facilitating their boys and girls to become responsible adults. In terms of Biblical youth ministry, the objective is development of Christian *women and men,* adults who are ready to undertake appropriate physical, mental, social/civic, economic, familial and spiritual/devotional responsibilities of life.

A = Essence.

At the core, God, as expressed through His Word, the Holy Spirit and the created universe, guides parents, youthworkers and other Christian adults in the process of furthering girls and boys in their journeys toward maturity. This seems best done in the context of Christian community.

INTERLOGUE
a pause for thinking

> **Before going on . . .**
>
> Youthworker: *"But coming back to the twenty-first century, what do we know now about God's will as it has been shown in world cultures? I got lost in all the details."*
>
> **Maestro de iniciación:** *"*Good point. Where has our frenetic global journey taken us? What Truth has God shown us through all of this?*"*
>
> Youthworker: *"Let me try. First, we have seen that in God's established order, children are to be cared for by parents as well as by the community. God loves them all and desires the children to grow up to be responsible adults."*
>
> **Maestro de iniciación:** *"*Well said! When communities show concern for the next generation, that's a godly practice, isn't it? Every culture we've surveyed looks after their children, except unborn babies are often regarded tragically as throw-aways in the Western world, China and elsewhere.*"*
>
> Youthworker: *"How sad that is! We're seeking to bring the Gospel to every person because they are precious in God's sight."*

Maestro de iniciación: "So true. Every youth is so deeply valued by God! What other signs of God at work do you see in world cultures?"

Youthworker: *"The importance of a girl's and a boy's family and clan. I knew that instinctively, but probably I can do much more to engage with these folks."*

Maestro de iniciación: "Most of us too easily forget that youth are members of families. Glad you've grasped that. Anything else you've observed as we've trekked along?"

Youthworker: *"A god of creation seems to be featured time after time. The traditions teach girls and boys to have an awesome respect for creation, God's handiwork."*

Maestro de iniciación: "This reminds me of St. Paul's experience on Mars Hill, when he pointed Athenian intellectuals of that time to the 'Unknown God' (Acts 17:23-24). Maybe that's a way we can connect with youth who are under the influence of a traditional religion!"

Youthworker: *"I can relate to that, in fact, it gives me hope to create suitable approaches to youth."*

Maestro de iniciación: "Anything else?"

Youthworker: *"One more observation. Through culture God differentiates between female and male, especially in the family. Not about who washes the clothes and/or cooks meals, but dealing with what it means to be a godly father or a mother."*

Maestro de iniciación: "You've unscrambled that one well. I wonder how we seem to have so often failed to see that. You want to disciple youth? Then you must deal with boys and girls as unique gender creatures."

Youthworker: *"Yeah, but I'm only one person. Both godly men AND women need to be called and involved in youth ministry, like in a team, don't you think?"*

Maestro de iniciación: "Amen to that! You've learned a lot so far. Are you now ready to search the Bible for some insights on youth ministry?"

Youthworker: *"Definitely. Let me turn the page!"*

NOTE re: *Interlogue*: "Novels on occasion have a prologue, which happens at the beginning of the book. There's also the epilogue, which happens at the very end.... The *interlogue* is something similar, except that it happens about in the MIDDLE of the book.... This will be a random, one-off chapter which ... has significance to the SERIES... It'll serve as an intermission and provide clues, make you think about what's to come; as well as the significance of other events that are happening 'behind the scenes.'" Blog. Jeffrey Hawboldt, October 6, 2012.

PART II

WHAT DOES THE BIBLE SAY ABOUT YOUTH MINISTRY?

Chapter 8

A BIBLICAL SEARCH FOR *ADOLESCENCE*

God's plan for life is always the best one. God designs the human race, beginning with helpless infancy, continuing with year-by-year growth through childhood until a mature woman or a full-grown man appears on the scene, ready to repeat the cycle of life all over again as marriage and childbearing take place. So it has been since time began.

Through the ages, much of humankind has come to realize that the Bible charts well the path to maturity, to *life* in all its fullness through faith in Jesus Christ and dependence upon God and the Bible on life's journey. A study of the Bible's teaching becomes foundational in order to understand youth ministry in its Christian context.

So then what does the Bible say about "youth ministry," specifically about "Christian youth ministry"?

THE SEARCH

Hebrew society, as we know it from the Bible and Jewish tradition, followed the traditional, two-step system illustrated in Elka's story in Chapter 1, but with some significant modifications. In traditional cultures boys and girls passed from childhood to adulthood with a brief transitional experience, often expressed in various cultures as "initiation."

The Jewish mind-set for "growing up," as it has come down through centuries of tradition and possibly functioned in Bible times, is easier to understand in light of the "initiation ceremonies" described in Chapters 1-5. Recognizing the Bible-times pattern of growth to adulthood helps to lay a firm foundation for an effective youth ministry that will motivate young Christian adults to be world-changers.

GROWTH TO MANHOOD

The following pages explain what catapulted a Hebrew boy into manhood, subsequently by what seems to have been the culturally prescribed journey a Hebrew girl experienced.

Stage 1: Hebrew Boyhood (birth to approximately age 12 or 13)

The Bible recognizes the dependence children have on parents from the moment of birth, as in Psalm 22:9, "You, Lord, brought me safely through birth, and you protected me when I was a baby at my mother's breast." The special relationship mothers have with their infants is revealed in Isaiah 49:15, "The Lord answered, 'Could a mother forget a child who nurses at her breast? Could she fail to love an infant who came from her own body...?' This concern is echoed by St. Paul when writing to one of his congregations, "We chose to be ... *like a mother nursing her baby. We cared so much for you, and you became so dear to us, that we were willing to give our lives for you...*" (First Thessalonians 2:7b-8).

The early childhood of Moses reveals a Hebrew mother's profound concern for her infant's welfare in the familiar story in Exodus 2.

At once the baby's older sister came up and asked, "Do you want me to get a Hebrew woman to take care of the baby for you?

"Yes," the king's daughter answered. So the girl brought the baby's mother, and the king's daughter told her, "Take care of this child, and I will pay you."

The baby's mother carried him home and took care of him. And when he was old enough, she took him to the king's daughter, who adopted him (verses 7-10).

Once a baby was weaned, the Bible depicts childhood as a time of *play*. These Biblical depictions of children tell the story for girls and boys.

- "*. . . boys and girls play in the streets* (Zechariah 8:4-6).

- "Their *children play and dance* safely by themselves" (Job 21:11).

- "*Little children will play* near snake holes. . ." (Isaiah 11:8).

- ". . . death . . . even struck down *children at play*. . ." (Jeremiah 9:21).

- " Can it [a sea monster] be tied by the leg like a *pet bird for little girls*" (Job 41:5)?

- "You are like *children* sitting in the market and shouting to each other, 'We played the flute, but you would not dance! We sang a funeral song, but you would not cry'" (Luke 7:32)!

In short, boys and girls were expected to play! No doubt they also began to help with household and/or work-related tasks as part of typical child socialization, with little girls following their mother around and with little boys aping their fathers.

The Bible recognizes that boys' and girls' reasoning powers were still developing, as St. Paul described it.

It's like this: *when I was a child I spoke and thought and reasoned as a child does.* But when I became a man my thoughts grew far beyond those of my childhood, and now I have put away the childish things (First Corinthians 13:11, TLB).

In every respect, all children, male and female, were clearly under the authority and guidance of their parents.

God's authority structure for the family was spelled out early in Israel's history. As Moses revealed what God had told him on Mount Sinai, parents learned from the *Ten Commandments* that they had explicit authority over their children. As a result, boys and girls needed to be taught the commandment in Exodus 20:12 (NIV): "Honor your father and your mother. . . ."

Later, Moses' recounting of the Law made it crystal clear to parents that God expected parents to be the chief educators of their daughters and sons. The familiar passage from Deuteronomy well captures the principle.

So love the Lord your God with all your heart, soul, and strength. *Memorize His laws and tell them to your children over and over again.* Talk about them all the time, whether you're at home or walking along the road or going to bed at night, or getting up in the morning (6:5-7).

Several implications grow out of this commandment to parents.
- It is God's pattern, not Moses.'"These are the commands, decrees and laws *the Lord your God directed me to teach you* to observe. . ." (Deuteronomy 6:1, NIV).

- The foundation upon which a Biblical family is built is the parents' love for and obedience to God.

- Daily life provides the context for the training of children. Moses presumes that the parents' *example* in life will match the teachings of the Law.

- Parents must necessarily *articulate* their faith in God and His Word to their daughters and sons.

- Parents are to become so familiar with God's Word that they can *talk about it* freely.

The pattern of parental training for children continued as a pattern throughout the Bible. The writer of Proverbs underscores the Deuteronomy passage. "My child, obey the teachings of your parents" (1:8). "Obey the teaching of your parents" (6:20).

St. Luke records that Jesus, the Son of God, lived under this principle. "Jesus went back to Nazareth with *his parents and obeyed them*" (Luke 2:51). The Apostle Paul reiterated these teachings when he wrote in his letters to the children in the Colossian and Ephesian churches.

- "Children must always obey their parents. This pleases the Lord" (Colossians 3:20. Cf. Ephesians 6:1.).

- Parents, don't be hard on your children. Raise them properly. Teach them and instruct them about the Lord (Ephesians 6:4, Colossians 3:21).

Jewish children, therefore, looked to their parents for moral guidance and spiritual training. However, the parents were not abandoned in an educational vacuum. St. Paul reported that he had received religious instruction from Rabbi Gamaliel in Acts 22:3, "I am a Jew, born in Tarsus of Cilicia, but brought up in this city. I studied under Gamaliel and was thoroughly trained in the law of our ancestors. . . ." He did not relate the timing of this rabbinical training except to say that he was "brought up" (or "reared") in Jerusalem. It is impossible to know if this happened in St. Paul's boyhood years. It may have happened later. However, in future centuries, boys, and boys only, would receive extensive rabbinical education.

In summary, Moses had ordained parents to be the chief educators of their girls and boys *within* the context of the Hebrew community, or congregation. Moses was the spiritual overseer of all the Hebrew people, assisted by tribal elders. Moreover, the Levite tribe was dedicated to leading the people in periodic worship festivals, for example, Passover, the Feast of Tabernacles or Pentecost. Here children observed and shared, as they were able, in events that pointed toward God and his ways. As a result, children were socialized into the life of the faith community by participation in community worship and celebration.

Moses also decreed that an unmanageable son or daughter should be brought to civic leaders for punishment, and a severe one, death by stoning! One can assume the community would preventively succor parents to avoid this extreme measure. In short, parents knew that they could depend on others to help them in their guiding their offspring. The parents were not alone!

From puberty onward, the paths to Jewish adulthood diverge distinctively into male and female streams, as is true in many cultures. The Pentateuch did prescribe different values according to gender, reflecting the patriarchal society of Old Testament times with males valued more than females.

> If anyone makes a special vow to dedicate a person to the Lord by giving the equivalent value, *set the value of a male between the ages of twenty and sixty at fifty shekels of silver* . . . for a *female, set her value at thirty shekels*. . . (Leviticus 27:2-4, 7).

In Hebrew culture, gender mattered!

In the following sections, a male's progression through life is outlined, then succeeded by the stages in life for females in the Jewish community.

Stage 2: The Rite of Passage into Jewish Manhood; The Emerging Adult Male (from *Bar-Mitzvah* **at perhaps age 12 or 13 through age 19)**

In Jewish tradition, a boy passes from childhood directly to adulthood through the *bar mitzvah* at which time he becomes a participating adult male in the affairs of the local congregation. He was expected to be able to read Hebrew script, so that he could take his turn reading from the Torah in synagogue services, as Jesus did in Luke 4:16. "Jesus went back to Nazareth, where he had been brought up, and as usual he went to the meeting place on the Sabbath. When he stood up to read from the Scriptures [i.e., the *Torah* scroll]. . . ."

Historically, a synagogue could not be formed without a minimum of ten adult males (a *minyan*). Thirteen-year-old boys who had been through *bar mitzvah* counted toward this minimum number in Jewish tradition. They were judged no longer boys, but legally and religiously *men*. The transition from childhood to adulthood was thus accomplished in short order. The transformation was clear and forthright for boys by the rite of passage, the *bar mitzvah*.

The *bar mitzvah* tradition is not found explicitly in the Bible, but its roots are hinted at in the Bible's account of Jesus accompanying his parents to the feast in Jerusalem at age 12 (see Luke 2:41-50[1]). Jesus may have interpreted his being invited to go with his parents to the Jerusalem feast as his entry point into some stage of manhood. Hence, he started to interact with the teachers (verse 46), not as a precocious child, but as if he had now been admitted to adult status, almost as a young colleague chatting with his elders! Perhaps this could be viewed as Jesus' proto-*bar-mitzvah*.

In traditional Judaism, post-*bar-mitzvah* young men are expected to participate in all aspects of Jewish community life, including the responsibility for religious observances and, more importantly, obeying God's Law voluntarily instead of being under parental supervision. In Biblical times, marriage might have been an expected event for a man following the *bar mitzvah* rite.

Also some or many of these emerging men would probably be learning a trade as well as possibly being newly-married, perhaps with very young children at home, certainly not a good time to leave for military service. God in His wisdom did not intend to send thirteen-to-nineteen-year-olds to wage war — perhaps they would not be entirely capable physically in battle.

Other relevant Biblical references are found in Deuteronomy.

- When you are about to go into battle... the officers shall say to the army, "... Has anyone planted a vineyard and not begun to enjoy it? Let him go home, or he may die in battle and someone else enjoy it. Has anyone become pledged to a woman and not married her? Let him go home, or he may die in battle and someone else marry her" (20:2a, 5-7).
- When a man takes a new wife, he is *not to go out with the army* or be given any business or work duties. He gets one year off simply to be at home making his wife happy" (24:5, MSG).

God's concern for the emerging adult male's family and livelihood are clearly seen here. God also showed special mercy for those people under twenty years of age when God cursed disobedient Israelis twenty and older as recorded in Numbers.

YOUTH: Growing Up

- In this wilderness your bodies will fall — every one of you *twenty* years old or more who was counted in the census and who has grumbled against me (Numbers 14:29).
- "Because they have not followed me wholeheartedly, not one of those who were *twenty* years old or more when they came up out of Egypt will see the land I promised on oath to Abraham, Isaac and Jacob" (Numbers 32:11).

Stage 3: Enhanced Hebrew Manhood, age twenty and older

Twenty then is the next point of demarcation in the progress toward a man's maturity. According to developmental studies, many adolescent males do not achieve full physical stature and strength until they are nearing twenty. Perhaps this is also why this age marker is differentiated in the Old Testament as a growth marker.

Twenty-year-old and older men had the following expectations placed upon them by God through Moses.

▶ *Military service.* Hebrew fighting men were tabulated in military censuses according to their age. At twenty, men had to be ready for mobilization into fighting units.
- The people of Israel . . . were living in the Sinai Desert. . Moses was in the sacred tent when the Lord said: "I want you and Aaron to . . . make a list of all the men *twenty years* and older who are *able to fight in battle*" (Numbers 1:1-3).
- . . . . the Lord . . . said to Moses and Eleazar, . ."I want you to . . . list every man *twenty years* and older who is able to *serve in Israel's army*" (Numbers 26:1, 2, 4).
- David . . . mustered those twenty years old or more and found that there were three hundred thousand men *fit for military service* (Second Chronicles 25:5).

▶ *Taxation.* Able adult males in Israel were expected to contribute to the needs of the Hebrew community. God expected payments of money (taxes) for certain societal needs, for example, funding the building expenses of the sacred tent.² The apparently newly-married and/or newly-employed men under twenty were exempt from these adult-years' assessments, possibly to allow them to establish financial footing.

▶ *Devotion.* The Pentateuch speaks of believers who want to make special promises to God and it also assesses the amounts to be paid by the person's age and gender.
> If anyone makes a special vow to dedicate a person to the Lord by giving the equivalent value, *set the value of a male between the ages of twenty and sixty at fifty shekels of silver* . . . for a female, set her value at thirty shekels. . . (Leviticus 27:2-4, NIV).

Additionally, twenty-year-old and older male Levites were expected to give ceremonial assistance at the temple.
- . . . the descendants of Levi . . . counted individually, that is, the workers *twenty years old or more* who *served in the temple of the LORD* (First Chronicles 23:24).
- From now on, *all Levites at least twenty years old will serve the Lord by helping Aaron's descendants do* their work at the temple. . . (First Chronicles 23:27-29).

Later, during the time of the rebuilding of the post-exilic temple, Levite men twenty years and older supervised the construction process.
> In the second month of the second year after their arrival . . . in Jerusalem, Zerubbabel . . . (the priests and the Levites and all who had returned from the

captivity to Jerusalem) began the work, *appointing Levites twenty years of age and older to supervise the building of the house of the LORD* (Ezra 3:8).

Twenty, therefore, intensified adult responsibilites for males.

Stage 4: Generative Manhood (30 until "old age")

Noted student of adult development in Western culture, Erik Erikson,[3] and others speak of generativity[4] coming to the fore in mid-life. Similarly, according to the Bible, certain privileges opened up to Hebrew men at or about age thirty, so perhaps this could be considered the period of Jewish "generativity." For example, Abraham's great-grandson Joseph became governor of Egypt at age thirty. Later, at age thirty, Kings Saul and David took the throne. Jesus himself assumed his ministry at the same age.[5] The Bible also notes age thirty as a qualification for certain religious ceremonial tasks for the community.

- The Lord told Moses and Aaron, "Find out how many *men between the ages of thirty and fifty* are in the four Levite clans of Kohath. Count only those who are able to work at the sacred tent" (Numbers 4:1-3).
- He then counted the Levite men who *were at least thirty years old*... (First Chronicles 23:3).

Responsibilities of leadership and service seem, therefore, to have been conferred on men thirty years of age and older, as compared to those expected of men at age twenty.

> **QUESTIONS TO PONDER** ◄

- An interesting inquiry for any local congregation is, "How many of our youthworkers are in the *generative stage* of life (mid-life or beyond)?"
- If youth are to achieve *maturity* (however it might be defined culturally), how can adulthood be accomplished unless there are suitable models of Christian womanhood and manhood to follow?

Stage 5: Life-Review (older manhood, 50+)

By Biblical reckoning, religious workers who reached fifty years old entered another stage of adulthood. Levites were allowed to step back from temple duties at age fifty. The Lord said to Moses, "This applies to the Levites: Men twenty-five years old or more shall come to take part in the work . . . but *at the age of fifty, they must retire from their regular service and work no longer* (Numbers 8:25).

But why the change of role at age fifty? Possibly they were expected to step down because of the strenuous physical exertion needed in slaughtering animals for the sacrifices.

Another possible rationale underlying a change of role at age fifty would be the life expectancy in Biblical times. An undocumented but educated guess is that for a male peasant to live beyond forty would have been unusual in Bible times, and females had even lower life expectancies. St. Luke, as a physician often fascinated by medical data, states that the parents of John the Baptist were ". . . not able to conceive and they were *both very old"* (Luke 1:7). Yet the text also tells the reader that Zechariah was "on duty" at the temple, serving as an active priest (Luke 1:8). One would assume therefore that Zechariah was not yet age fifty, yet at that time and place Luke considered him to be "very old." In any case, it appears that God's expectations for the fifty-plus males changed, at least for the Levites and possibly for the population in general.

The age *sixty* also is mentioned in the Pentateuch with regard to sacred vows in Leviticus 27: 7, "For a person *sixty* years old or more, set the value of a male at fifteen shekels and of a female at ten shekels." Moses gives no reason for this age marker. Possibly some very old people might have fewer financial resources, as might be corrobated by St. Paul's words to Timothy regarding church charity, "For a widow to be put on the list of widows, she must be at least *sixty* years old, and she must have been faithful in marriage" (First Timothy 5:9).

Looking at today's world, humans may have opportunity to look back on their lives as they approach the end of life, at least those fifty percent living above survival status. Erik Erikson[7] defined the later years of life in the Western world as possibly a time of "ego integrity." As described in a medical dictionary, ideally this last stage of life is ". . . an acceptance of self, both successes and failure. It implies a healthy psychologic *[sic]* state."[8] Erikson proposed despair as the unhealthy alternative of life-review for those in the twilight years.

Whether Erikson's stages are applicable or not, an aged St. Paul wrote a glowing review of his life of integrity to Timothy, "I have fought the good fight, I have finished the race, I have kept the faith" (Second Timothy 4:7). By contrast, in Ecclesiastes King Solomon illustrates the despair dimension of an older man as he looks back on life. "'Meaningless! Meaningless!' says the Teacher. 'Everything is meaningless!'" (Ecclesiastes 12:8). King Solomon probably penned the following end-of-life reflections.

> Skilled living gets its start in the Fear-of-God, insight into life from knowing a Holy God. It's through me, Lady Wisdom, that your life deepens, and the years of your

life ripen. Live wisely and wisdom will permeate your life; mock life and life will mock you (Proverbs 9:10-12, MSG).

At the very least, King Solomon and Saint Paul did some kind of mature reflection in their later years.

Thus, a presumed *Biblical route to manhood* can be summarized as follows:

Stage 1 — Childhood (up to a proto-*bar mitzvah*, ages 12-13)
Stage 2 — Emerging manhood (from proto-*bar mitzvah* to age 19)
Stage 3 — Enhanced manhood (age 20 and older)
Stage 4 — Generative manhood (age 30 until "old age")
Stage 5 — Life-review manhood (older adults, ages 50+, the "survivors")

GROWTH TO WOMANHOOD

Stage 1: Hebrew Girlhood (birth to puberty)

The section on boyhood above includes some matters applicable to females. For example, no doubt young women were expected, as boys were, to participate in all aspects of Jewish community life and, more importantly, obeying God's Law voluntarily instead of being under parental control.

Few gender distinctions seem to be made in the Bible during childhood years, except for the religious vows as seen in Leviticus 27.

The Lord told Moses to say to the community of Israel:
"If you ever want to free someone who has been promised to me, you may do so by paying . . . *five pieces of silver for boys* ages one month to five years, *and three pieces for girls*" (verses 1-3, 7).

Thereafter, the path to adulthood for Hebrew girls apparently grew out of the future roles of females in the home, primarily in bearing and rearing children.

Stage 2: Entrance to Jewish Womanhood; The Pubertal Emerging-Adult (eligible for marriage)

The Bible does not suggest anything like the *bar mitzvah* for females. In fact, the *bat mitzvah* for girls was not introduced until the twentieth century in the U.S.A. and it is only practiced in some Jewish congregations. It is not recognized in orthodox Judaism.

Quite possibly Jewish girls entered their adult roles at approximately the same time as their male counterparts, that is, at the arrival of physical puberty (ages 11-14?) in connection with first menstruation. Christian Scriptures suggest that the physical changes of puberty were recognized by the Israeli community, as in the following verses.

- We have a little sister whose *breasts are not yet formed*. If someone asks to marry her, what should we do. (Song of Solomon 8:8. One inference — No child marriages allowed.)
- The Lord said: ". . . I took care of you [the people of Jerusalem]. . . . You *grew up to be a beautiful young woman with perfect breasts and long hair*, but you were still naked." (Ezekiel 16:6-7. Another inference — Breast development was synonymous with womanhood.)

Apparently in Biblical times, marriage was an expected event for girls sometime after the onset of puberty, when the female body is ready for childbearing. Some Bible scholars believe that Jesus' mother Mary conceived and gave birth to Jesus as a teenager, possibly as young as fifteen. But the Bible does not give specifics on this matter.

Stage 3: Enhanced Jewish Womanhood (getting married)

To be married set apart an emerging-adult woman from her unmarried contemporaries. Her marriage communicated to the community that she was *grown up*. She could now focus her attention on homemaking and her husband's needs. As St. Paul stated it, "... a married woman is concerned about the affairs of this world—how she can please her husband" (First Corinthians 7:34, NIV). He was even more specific in his letter to Titus regarding proper conduct of wives.

> ... to live quietly, to love their husbands and their children, and to be sensible and clean minded, spending their time in their own homes, being kind and obedient to their husbands so that the Christian faith can't be spoken against by those who know them (2:4-5).

Stage 4: Superior Jewish Womanhood (becoming a mother)

The Bible is silent on any transition point for women at a specific age, but the birth of a child certainly enhanced the status of a young woman. The birth of a child was cause for rejoicing, whereas barrenness was experienced as a curse on a woman in Biblical times.[9]

Note the elation that came with pregnancy and childbirth and the distress that accompanied barrenness.

- Later, when Hagar knew she was going to have a *baby*, she became *proud*... (Genesis 16:4).
- Jesus said, "A woman giving birth to a child has pain because her time has come; but when her baby is born she forgets the anguish because of *her joy that a child is born* into the world" (John 16:31).
- [Leah, patriarch Jacob's first wife] Leah became pregnant and gave birth to a son. She named him Reuben, for she said, "It is because *the Lord has seen my misery. ...*"

Leah's servant Zilpah bore Jacob [and Leah legally] a second son. Then Leah said, *"How happy I am!* The women will call me *happy."* ...
God listened to Leah, and she became pregnant and bore Jacob a fifth son. Then Leah said, *"God has rewarded me.* ...

Leah conceived again and bore Jacob a sixth son. Then Leah said, "God has presented me with *a precious gift.* This time my husband will treat me with honor, because I have borne him six sons." ... She became pregnant and gave birth to a son and said, "God has taken away *my disgrace"* (Genesis 30:12-13, 17-20, 23).

- Rachel was very jealous of Leah for having *children*, and she said to Jacob, "I'll die if you don't give me some *children"* (Genesis 30:1)!
- Sidon, you are a mighty fortress. ... But you will be *disgraced like a married woman who never had children* (Isaiah 23:4).

Without medical knowledge about conception or of birth control, it was culturally expected that a baby would soon be born to a young married couple. If no child was expeditiously produced, the woman faced increasing anxiety about her childlessness. As in many societies, having a child was therefore a female's ticket to authentic adulthood. The inference is that motherhood gave the young female new status, in terms of the local community's acceptance of her as a woman.

Stage 5: Life-Review Womanhood
(older women, possibly 50+)

St. Paul instructed Titus, his representative on the island of Crete, to equip older women as mentors of the young.

And here's what I want you to teach the older women: Be respectful. Steer clear of gossip or drinking too much *so that you can teach what is good to young women. Be a positive example,* showing them what it is to love their husbands and children, and teaching them to control themselves *in every way* and to be pure. *Train them* to manage the household, to be kind, and to be submissive to their husbands, all of which honor the word of God (2:3-5, VOICE).

The older woman thus had an important role to fulfill in New Testament communities. In the midst of their passing on of life's wisdom, did older women have the good fortune to look back on their lives as they approached the end of life? An old saying puts it this way, "A woman's work is never done."[1] Perhaps this was the case for older Hebrew women. But at least two older women in the Bible had the opportunity to reflect back on life with delight.

- "The prophet *Anna* was also there in the temple.... and she was *very old*.... And now she was *eighty-four years old*.... At that time Anna came in and *praised God*. She spoke about the child Jesus to everyone who hoped for Jerusalem to be set free (Luke 2:36-38).
- *Naomi* said, "You must go back home, because I am too old to marry again.... Life is harder for me than it is for you, because the Lord has turned against me.... Don't call me Naomi any longer! Call me Mara, because God has made my life bitter. I had everything when I left, but the Lord has brought me back with nothing. How can you still call me Naomi, when God has turned against me and made my life so hard?" (Ruth 1:11-13, 20-21)

....

Boaz married Ruth, and *the Lord blessed her* with a son. After his birth, the women said to Naomi: "Praise the Lord! Today he has given you a grandson to take care of you.... He will *make you happy and take care of you in your old age*, because he is the son of your daughter-in-law. And she loves you more than seven sons of your own would love you.. Naomi loved the boy and took good care of him... they called him "Naomi's Boy" (Ruth 4:13-17).

Both Naomi and Anna had reason to look back over their lives without despair, as God gave them pleasant experiences in their mature years.

CONTEMPORARY *ADOLESCENCE?*

So what is the next stage of life for the growing Hebrew boy or girl? A youthworker who is familiar with Westernized or Westernizing culture might anticipate that *adolescence* would be the natural life stage subsequent to Hebrew childhood, but it was *not*!

Because cultural structures in Biblical times had no ambiguous gap between *childhood* and *adulthood* as observed in contemporary world cultures, any Biblical illustrations that may be cited become irrelevant. Adolescence simply did not exist either as a psychological concept or as a cultural reality. Hence, *youth ministry* cannot be found as a category in the Bible. Surprised?

A Hebrew male seldom experienced, if at all, an extended period of ambiguity and uncertainty in his life. First he was "a boy," then he became "a man." During adulthood, he underwent a movement through several stages, though not adolescence as it is commonly defined in the twenty-first century. For females, the ability to bear children defined their maturity. In Hebrew society, the leap from childhood to adulthood proceeded by graduated stages. But nowhere is there any indication of an in-between step such as adolescence that was neither "fish nor fowl."

It is, therefore, a vain search for Biblical principles of youth ministry when the quest is based on a concept of *adolescence* in which some individuals in a community will be in suspended animation, as it were, between childhood and adulthood. Any culture that has a phase that postpones adulthood until the ambiguity of *youth* is past, as is the case with Western and Westernizing societies worldwide, calls for another model from which to derive Biblical principles. Consequently, what principles applicable to contemporary youth ministry, if any, are to be found in the pages of the Bible?

A STARTING POINT

Professor Dr. J. Grant Howard (1929-2004) proposed an intriguing model for building a Biblical youth ministry.[1] He set forth several theses for developing a Biblical basis for youth ministry.

First, youthworkers should conceptually look upon adolescents as *BOTH* children (Stage 1 above) *AND* as emerging adults (Stage 2). How this works operationally is explained later in Chapters 9-13. Briefly, for the duration of adolescence, however that may be defined in a given culture, the youth is *both* a child in the process of leaving his family of origin *and* simultaneously an "emerging adult" who is moving gradually into adult responsibilities.

In viewing the adolescent as a child subject to parental authority, youthworkers and parents must follow Biblical guidelines for appropriately rearing children through adolescence.

At the same time, youthworkers and parents must seek to enable adolescents to move into "adult" status as taught in the Bible. This requires the young man or woman to aspire to live up God's expectations of them as "adults."

Ideally this movement toward adulthood might follow

a predictable growth curve, but in real life the youth and the parents vacillate in their relationships and ability to be responsible. An adolescent's period of solid personal growth might be followed by an abrupt plunge into immaturity, followed by an amazing feat of adulthood, and so on. As St. Paul wrote to Christians in the ancient city of Corinth,

> To be perfectly frank, I'm getting exasperated with your infantile thinking. How long before you grow up and use your head—your *adult* head? It's all right to have a childlike unfamiliarity with evil; a simple *no* is all that's needed there. But there's far more to saying *yes* to something. Only mature and well-exercised intelligence can save you from falling into gullibility (First Corinthians 14:20-25, MSG).

Lastly, Howard's blueprint also includes the qualification that *adolescents are NEITHER children NOR adults in the modern world.* The ambiguity of the status of youth, as well as the unpredictability of the journey into adulthood, increases the complexity of the task. Approaching adolescents as *neither/nor* as well as *both/and* is a monumental challenge for a youthworker in the twenty-first-century where widespread culture is characterized by adolescent uncertainty.

Howard's model for Biblical youth ministry fleshes out in succeeding chapters. For purposes of clarity, a fabricated term, *"emerging-adult-CHILD"* is used to signify the youth who is still largely dependent upon parents, and yet struggling to leave childhood status. Additionally, the label, *"EMERGING-ADULT-child"* is employed to focus on the maturing person who is approaching adulthood and yet with vestiges of childhood present. The nature and length of these *overlapping* identities varies according to specific cultural expectations.

The treatment of each of Howard's principles includes:
   (1) its Biblical basis,
   (2) the role of the youth in Biblical obedience,

(3) the role of the parent(s) in Biblical parenting,
(4) the role of the congregation (as available),
(5) questions youthworkers must ponder for application.

The goal in each case is to facilitate the growth of a child into full adulthood, hopefully well-grounded in the Christian faith.

Chapter 9 explores Howard's principles for the *"EMERGING-ADULT-child,"* as his model applies to the youth, his/her parents, the local congregation and youthworkers.

Chapter 10 explores ministry goals for the *"EMERGING-ADULT-child"* in terms of a definition of Biblical maturity and how that translates to youth.

Chapter 11 explores growth expectations for the *"EMERGING-ADULT-child"* and implications for parents.

Chapter 12 explores adequate responses by the congregation for the *"EMERGING-ADULT-child."*

Chapter 13 explores the implications for those called to work directly with youth, that is, *youthworkers*.

NOTES

[1] Every year Jesus' parents went to Jerusalem for Passover. And when Jesus was *twelve years old*, they all went there as usual for the celebration. After Passover his parents left, but they did not know that Jesus had stayed on in the city. They thought he was traveling with some other people, and they went a whole day before they started looking for him. When they could not find him with their relatives and friends, they went back to Jerusalem and started looking for him there. Three days later they found Jesus sitting in the temple, listening to the teachers and *asking them questions*. Everyone who

heard him was surprised at how much he knew and at the answers He gave. When his parents found him, they were amazed. His mother said, "Son, why have you done this to us? Your father and I have been very worried, and we have been searching for you!" Jesus answered, "Why did you have to look for me? Didn't you know that I would be in my Father's house?" But they did not understand what he meant. Luke 2:41-50

[2] • Exodus 30:13-16. The Lord said to Moses, . . . *"Each man over nineteen,* whether rich or poor, must pay me the same amount of money, weighed according to the official standards. This money is to be used for *the upkeep of the sacred tent,* and because of it, I will never forget my people..

• Exodus 38:21, 25, 26. "These are the *amounts of the materials used for* . . . *the tabernacle* of the covenant law . . . The silver obtained from those of the community who were counted in the census was 100 talents and 1,775 shekels . . . one beka per person . . . from everyone who had crossed over to those counted, *twenty years old or more.* . . ."

[3] Erik Erikson (1902-1994) is best-known for his famous theory of psychosocial development and the concept of the identity crisis. His theories marked an important shift in thinking on personality; instead of focusing simply on early childhood event, his psychosocial theory looked at how social influences contribute to personality throughout the entire lifespan. *Psychology.about.com*, March 16, 2015.

[4] *Generativity* : "a concern for people besides self and family that usually develops during middle age; *especially* : a need to nurture and guide younger people and contribute to the next generation— used in the psychology of Erik Erikson." *Merriam-Webster On-line Dictionary.*

[5] • Genesis 41:46, Joseph was thirty when the king made him governor, and he went everywhere for the king.

• First Samuel 13:1, Saul was [thirty] years old when he became king. . . .

• Second Samuel 5:4, David was thirty years old when he became king. . . .

• Luke 3:23, Now Jesus himself was about thirty years old when he began his ministry.

[6] Philip J. King and Lawrence E. Stager, *Life in Ancient Israel* (Louisville: Westminster John Knox Press, 2001), 37.

[7] Erik Erikson believed if we see our lives as unproductive, feel guilt about our past, or feel that we did not accomplish our life goals, we become dissatisfied with life and develop despair, often leading to

depression and hopelessness. Success in this stage will lead to the virtue of *wisdom*. Wisdom enables a person to look back on their life with a sense of closure and completeness, and also accept death without fear. simplypsychology.org/Erik-Erikson.html.

[8] Farlex,*The Free Dictionary,* medical-dictionary.thefreedictionary.com/ego-integrity.

[9] • Sarai/Sarah. "Abram's wife Sarai had not been able to have any children" (Genesis 16:1).
  • Rebekah. "Almost twenty years later, Rebekah still had no children. So Isaac asked the Lord to let her have a child, and the Lord answered his prayer" (Genesis 25:20b-21).
  • Hannah. "Lord All-Powerful, I am your servant, but I am so miserable! Please let me have a son. I will give him to you for as long as he lives. . ." (First Samuel 1:11).
  • Elizabeth. "But they *did not have children*. Elizabeth could not have any, and both Zechariah and Elizabeth were already old" (Luke 1:7).

[10] This comes from an old rhymed couplet: "Man may work from sun to sun, But woman's work is never done." The American Heritage® New Dictionary of Cultural Literacy, Third Edition, Copyright © 2005 by Houghton Mifflin Company.

[11] "Biblical Perspectives on the Church and Home," unpublished paper by J. Grant Howard, Western Conservative Baptist Seminary, n.d. [Author's NOTE: If Dr. Howard's ideas are in print elsewhere, the author been unable to find them. Hence the expansion of his basic theses in following chapters are not to be attributed directly to Howard.]

Chapter 9

MINISTRY WITH THE
Emerging-Adult-GIRL/BOY

Examining the challenges of youth ministry from the perspective of what the Bible says about *youth in their least mature dimension* is a good starting point for youth-workers, parents and congregational leaders. This volume uses the designation, *"emerging-adult-CHILD,"* to describe those facets of personhood displayed by a "youth" who is neither a child nor as fully mature as any culture expects an "adult" to be.

The *emerging-adult-BOY/GIRL* is still largely dependent upon parents, and yet intuitively yearning to leave childhood status. As a butterfly struggles to shed its cocoon, so the neophyte youth is gradually leaving childhood behind. But the cocoon hangs on for some time. Ideally, the person shakes off childishness as an adult, but retains the ability to be childlike, for example, in matters of faith. As endorsed by Jesus,

> Let the little children come to me, and do not hinder them, for the kingdom of God belongs to such as these. Truly I tell you, anyone who will not receive the kingdom of God *like a little child*[1] will never enter it (Mark 10:13-15, NIV).

The questions to be asked with regard to advancing the growth of a child into trustworthy adulthood, grounded hopefully in the Christian faith, are, "What are the *Biblical responsibilities* of:
- "The *emerging-adult-CHILD* himself/herself?"
- "The parent(s) of an *emerging-adult-BOY/GIRL?*"
- "The Christian congregation?" That is, how do they serve their youth, their *emerging-adults-*GIRLS/BOYS. If the context is that of a parachurch organization, its leaders want to consider how to fill in the gaps in the absence of a local Christian congregation.
- "The Christian youthworker?" He/she must ponder the implications thereof.

Viewing The Adolescent Youth As *Emerging-Adult-CHILD*

As adolescent youth struggle slowly toward the goal of "growing up," their childlikeness and childishness continue to be evident. These girls and boys may be eager to seize the privileges of adulthood, but they may be unable to leave childhood behind just yet. Hence they enter these years with their childhood-past understandably clinging to their person. Up to this point in life, they have been more or less under the authority of parents, teachers, coaches, religious leaders and others. They may have left childhood pastimes behind them (for example, a girl playing with dolls), yet they are left wondering what it means to be otherwise.

Parents and youthworkers should not be surprised when youth frequently act like children—in fact, it is a recognized characteristic of the foggy world of adolescence. As former U.S. President George W. Bush aptly wrote about himself, "When I was young and irresponsible, I was young and irresponsible."[2]

A confounding factor in this understanding of "youth"

is the differential rate of maturation between males and females. This discrepancy is easily observed by comparing individuals in early puberty. On the whole, females are advancing rapidly toward physical, mental and social maturation, whereas the boys, on average, lag behind, perhaps two years or more. As baffling and troubling as this phenomenon is to the *emerging-adult-BOY/GIRL,* it is even more mystifying to parents, teachers and other youthworkers. In group settings, it has often proven to be more fruitful to separate boys and girls for better development of followers of Jesus through genuine community (boys with Christian men, girls with Christian women, as observed in traditional initiation programs). In many congregations around the world, women and men sit separately in church meetings, for whatever reasons! Perhaps youthworkers need to take note of this practice!

Nevertheless, during the years between childhood and adulthood, parents continue to exert considerable authority — and influence — over their children and rightly so, in both cases. However, in cases of unusually dysfunctional families, parents may have forfeited their impact and power by neglectful parenting.

Youth may act childishly when they want their parents' support and/or when they feel the need to be protected, figuratively, under their parents' wings. In fact, some youth act quite irresponsibly into early adulthood, or, tragically even longer, though parents realistically have little influence over puerile decisions made by someone who is legally an "adult."

Hence, even though youth are in the process of leaving childhood behind, they are still in the realm of dependency. Dr. Howard therefore asserted that within the framework of the Biblical family, adolescents are still *children* and *they should be viewed in that light, at least partially and intermittently so,* until they reach maturity. This assertion rings with validity.

Guidance From The Bible

The Bible spells out the extent of parental entitlement over the youth as an *emerging-adult- CHILD*, as follows. As stated unequivocally in the *Ten Commandments* (Exodus 20:12), God commands children to acknowledge that their parents have full authority over them.
- *"Respect your father and your mother*, and you will live a long time in the land I am giving you" (CEV).
- *"Honor your father and your mother,* so that you may live long in the land the Lord your God is giving you" (NIV).

The *Proverbs* further define what it means for children to honor and respect their parents, specifically by obedience.
- My child, *obey* the teachings of *your parents*...(Proverbs 1:8).
- Obey the teaching of *your parents* (Proverbs 6:20).
  Jesus also insisted that children follow the direction of their parents.
- "Didn't God command you to *respect* your father and mother?" (Matthew 15:4a).
- "Is this any way to show *respect* to your *parents*? You ignore God's commands. . ." (Matthew 15:6).

The Apostle Paul reiterated this principle with his letters to children in the Ephesian and Colossian congregations..
- Children,[3] you belong to the Lord, and you do the right thing when you *obey your parents*. The first commandment with a promise. . . (Ephesians 6:1).
- Children must always *obey their parents*. This pleases the Lord (Colossians 3:20).

In summary, the Bible is not obscure on this point — children are expected to respect and obey their parents. But what if the children are beginning to leave childhood behind them? The Bible implies that the emerging-adult youth must *not* try to throw off the parental yoke as she or he reaches for societally-recognized adulthood, even though the relationship will change as chronological time goes on.

THE *Emerging-Adult-CHILD's* ROLE In Moving Toward Adulthood

As a boy or girl transitions into adulthood, however, their childhood fades into the past. The focus moves from *obedience* to *respect,* as the individual achieves an increasingly mature relationship to her or his parents. Whatever the situation, an *emerging-adult-CHILD* must *listen to, learn from, and obey his or her parents* until the time in life when he or she makes their own decisions (depending on cultural expectations). From that time, the Bible teaches them to continue to respect their parents as long as they live. While this sounds like a simple formula, the *emerging-adult-CHILD* may find their natural desire for individuation pushing back against God's plan. Ideally, children will begin to appreciate God's sovereign plan to have given them these particular parents, for her or his best start in life.

The recognition of a young person's dependence on the support of his or her parents is *not* an endorsement of total parental domination. Some parents have interpreted their authority as expressed, "As long as you are under my roof, you will do as I say." Such a statement infers unbridled parental authority, unfettered by reason or mercy. Sadly, some cultures seem to embolden parents to become unloving tyrants, treating their children, often the females, as little more than slaves. Contrariwise, other cultures seem to be overtly child-centered, running counter to the Biblical model. In these milieus children seem to have the decisive say-so in everyday matters as in traditional Chinese families, some Near Eastern and some twenty-first-century-American families. This approach has been termed a *kindergarchy*, a context in which children's needs and wishes are given equal or greater status than those of adults.[4] Biblical parenting is not exemplified in either tyrannical or *kindergarchic* models. At one extreme or the other, the Bible confronts the culture and so must the people of God.

Another phenomenon observed in some families reflects gender expectations that are differential and also unbiblical. Boys may receive greater freedoms growing up, whereas girls live under restrictions. Though cultural mores may be more relaxed for males, God's plan is for both girls and boys to have parental guidance that is loving and equitable.

Nevertheless, the *emerging-adult-CHILD's* role is easily defined cross-culturally: live under the authority of your parents. The parent(s)' role is much more complex: teaching and modeling a Biblical life style, guiding the child toward personal maturity, including a vibrant relationship with God, as explained below.

THE PARENT'S ROLE in Supporting an *Emerging-Adult-CHILD* Toward Adulthood

Christian mothers and fathers may be unaware of their God-given responsibilities, yet the Bible spells them out quite clearly. In short, parents are expected to *love* their children, *teach* them God's Truth, *train* them in the importance of obedience to God's Will and, finally, *model* the Christian life before their children.

The Bible provides examples of Godliness being transmitted through the family:
- Amaziah *followed the example of his father* Joash by obeying the Lord and doing right. But he was not as faithful as his ancestor David (Second Kings 14:3).
- Jotham *followed the example of his father* by obeying

the Lord and doing right (Second Kings 15:34).
- Jehoshaphat *followed his father's example* and obeyed and worshiped the Lord (Second Chronicles 17:4).
- [St. Paul writing to Timothy] "I also remember the genuine faith of *your mother* Eunice. *Your grandmother* Lois had the same sort of faith, and I am sure that you have it as well" (Second Timothy 1:5).

God expects parents to set an example of godly living before their children, even as St. Paul admonished his followers to follow his person.
- "You must *follow my example*, as I follow the example of Christ" (First Corinthians 11:1).
- "My friends, I want you to *follow my example* and learn from others who closely follow *the example we set for you*" (Philippians 3:17).
- "But since I was worse than anyone else, God had mercy on me and let me be *an example* of the endless patience of Christ Jesus. He did this so that others would put their faith in Christ. . ." (First Timothy 1:16).

Conversely, the Bible tells in authentic fashion about other children who did not follow in the godly ways of their parents, for example, Cain (Genesis 4), Esau (Genesis 26:43-35; 27:46; 28:8-9), the prophet Samuel's sons (First Samuel 8:1-3[5]) and Solomon (First Kings 11:3-4[6]).

Bible-believing parents lay down the foundation stones for a boy or girl on the road to adulthood as follows:

➤ TEACHING.

When Moses delivered God's initial expectations for parents (Deuteronomy 6:5-9), the ultimate goal of God's agenda was beautifully summarized, "Love the Lord your God with all your heart, soul and strength" (verse 5).

Hebrew parents were expected to use all means at their disposal to bring their children to an ultimate understanding of their relationship to the heavenly Father—loving God and concurrently loving their neighbor (". . . love your neighbor as yourself." Leviticus 19:18b). Jesus reinforced this dual commandment, " Love the Lord your God with all your heart, soul, and mind" (Matthew 22:37). Also, Jesus once asked an ardent student of Hebrew Scripture about its core teachings.

> The man [a scribe] replied, "The Scriptures say, 'Love the Lord your God with all your heart, soul, strength, and mind.' They also say, 'Love your neighbors as much as you love yourself.'"
> Jesus said, "You have given the right answer. . ." (Luke 10:26-28).

Jesus thus made it apparent that the end result of the divine directives given to parents at Mount Sinai is obedience to God's Will as expressed in loving God and loving others.

The Deuteronomy 6:5-9 passage also tells parents their instruction should be carried out *within the context of the family's daily life*, not inside a classroom nor within a congregational setting (for instance, in a "youth group"). Likewise, *"Talk about them* [God's Laws] all the time, whether you're at home or walking along the road or going to bed at night, or getting up in the morning" (6:6b).

Moses additionally told parents to labor persistently in this teaching task, "Memorize His laws and tell them to your children *over and over again"* (6:5-6a). So parents have a role of explicitly and continuously teaching God's Word to their children, as best as they are able, given their gifts and opportunities.

➤ Training with Loving Discipline

Training is another aspect of the Biblical parental role, also called *discipline*. Expressed positively, exercising discipline is a coaching experience, as in the training of an athletic team or a military unit. It is not necessarily a punishment role, though it might include such as part of correction. The Bible assumes that parents take an active role in preparing their children for life through loving discipline.
- The Lord corrects everyone he loves, just as *parents correct* their favorite child (Proverbs 3:12).
- If you love your children, you will *correct* them; if you don't love them, you won't correct them (Proverbs 13:24).
- Be patient when you are being corrected! This is how God treats his children. Don't *all parents correct their children*? (Hebrews 12:7).

Sometimes punishment, corporate or otherwise, becomes a primary form of discipline in the home rather than a means of correction. Regrettably, some parents take their God-given authority and use it inappropriately in the unbridled exercise of power, sometimes to the extent of physical, mental and/or spiritual abuse. Family unity is threatened; the home will lack the warmth of Christian love. God speaking through St. Paul warns against unkindness to children.
- "Parents, don't be hard on your children. If you are, they might give up" (Colossians 3:21).
- "Fathers, do not embitter your children, or they will become discouraged" (Colossians 3:21, NIV).
- "Parents, don't be hard on your children. Raise them properly. Teach them and instruct them about the Lord" (Ephesians 6:4).
- "Fathers, do not exasperate your children; instead, bring them up in the training and instruction of the Lord" (Ephesians 6:4, NIV).

Administering discipline may not be pleasant for a parent and, not surprisingly, receiving correction is often painful for the child. The Book of Hebrews explains the natural outcomes of punishment, both divine and parental.

> ... the Scriptures say to God's children, "When the Lord punishes you, don't make light of it, and when he corrects you, don't be discouraged. The Lord corrects the people he loves and disciplines those he calls his own." Be patient when you are being corrected! This is how God treats his children.[7] *Don't all parents correct their children?* God corrects all of his children, and if he doesn't correct you, then you don't really belong to him. *Our earthly fathers correct us,* and we still respect them. Isn't it even better to be given true life by letting our spiritual Father correct us? *Our human fathers correct us for a short time, and they do it as they think best.* But God corrects us for our own good, because he wants us to be holy, as he is. It is never fun to be corrected. In fact, at the time it is always painful. *But if we learn to obey by being corrected, we will do right and live at peace* (Hebrews 12:5-11).

In some cultures, corporal punishment may be an accepted form of discipline; in others, not so much. The principle remains the same — the child needs to be corrected and trained for life by loving parents. It is not a matter to be taken lightly in any culture.

Framing the context for discipline, the Bible urges parents to be affirming of their children, genuinely accepting of them as individuals made in the image of God.

> [God said:] "Now let Us conceive *a new creation—* humanity—*made* in Our image, *fashioned* according to Our likeness. ... so God did *just that.* He created humanity in His image, created them male and female" (Genesis 1: 26-27, VOICE).

Each child has God-given individual abilities, quirks, weaknesses, intelligence and personality. Believing in

Divine Providence, Christian parents must seek to celebrate each son or daughter under their care who has been chosen and uniquely shaped by God. As parents develop their own maturity, they are able to sincerely thank God for children God has given them. As St. Paul put it, "Give thanks *to God* no matter what circumstances you find yourself in. (This is God's will for all of you in Jesus the Anointed.)" (First Thessalonians 5:18, VOICE). Thus parents enable a child to begin the lifelong process of accepting herself or himself, so important for healthy personal development.

In short, God expects godly parents to exercise discipline wisely and judiciously for the long-range benefit of their children with the expectation that these offspring will bring glory to God in a despairing world.

➤ Modeling the Christian life

Educators largely agree that the socialization approach to learning makes maximum impact on a child. Indisputably, the relational atmosphere of the home is a stronger influence on a child than any classroom or other educational approach. Moreover, the much-feared "negative influence of peers" is almost certainly not as strong as commonly believed, though it varies from child to child. Rather, the modeling of the Christian life by parents enables and motivates their children to follow their attitudes and behaviors. In this way, mothers and fathers are teaching implicitly, in conjunction with the explicit teaching outlined above.

Because imitation has such strong learning effects, the Bible urges parents to *set the proper example,* obeying and displaying God's Truth for their children in their conversation, attitudes and behavior. For instance, "My son, pay close attention and gladly follow my example" (Proverbs 23:26). Or, as may be implied for parents in First Peter 5:3, "Don't be bossy to those people who are in your care, but set an example for them." The modeling of proper Christian speech, behavior and attitudes makes an enormous imprint on the lives of children, as opposed to a "do-as-I-say, not as-I-do approach."

> ➤ QUESTIONS TO PONDER ◀
>
> What the Bible asks of parents is a high standard, regardless of their cultural setting and/or their level of education and/or their socio-economic status. It becomes even more daunting for mothers who are single or part-time, step-parents, grandparents, too.
> ➤ How will Christian parents learn about parenting according to the Bible's standards?
> ➤ How will they develop sensibilities and skills to carry out their role with excellence?
> ➤ Why should they have to "go-it-alone"?
> ➤ Where can they go for assistance?
> The next two sections seek to address these questions.

THE CONGREGATION's ROLE
in Repositioning an *Emerging-Adult-GIRL/BOY* Toward Adulthood

Christian parents may rightfully look to their spiritual family, that is, their local church congregation, for support just as Hebrew parents were assisted by the believing community in nurturing and leading their children. When a Christian congregation becomes an interlocking web of believing individuals and families, their leaders and members attend to the needs of *"emerging-adults-CHILDREN* in their midst.

The New Testament is replete with exhortations for Christians to care for one another, both young and old.
• Love must be sincere. . . . *Be devoted to one another*

in love. *Honor one another* above yourselves (Romans 12:9-10, NIV).
- Finally, brothers and sisters . . . *encourage one another,* be of one mind, live in peace (Second Corinthians 13:11-12, NIV).
- And let us consider how we may *spur one another* on toward love and good deeds, not giving up meeting together . . . but *encouraging one another* . . . (Hebrews 10:24-25, NIV).

Hence, a Christian congregation is required by the Bible not only to encourage parents in the instruction of their children but also to assist them in that task. Here are *some questions congregational leaders* in a twenty-first century setting ought to be asking themselves about supporting families who have children in their assembly:

- In what ways are we reminding parents of God's goals for parents and helping them find various healthy means to train their children and youth?
- What kind of strategized, ongoing education, both formal and informal, are we providing for parents to assist them in preparing their children for adolescence and adulthood? Realistically many parents are without the ability to teach as traditionally viewed. The Apostle Paul makes that clear in First Corinthians 12 regarding spiritual gifts, ". . . Not everyone is a teacher. . ." (verse 29). Thus, mothers and fathers may need some opportunities for parent education, for example, training in listening skills.
- What resources might we provide for parents to enable them to better fulfill God's goals for them as parents? Websites? Media resources? Books? Referrals? Seminars?
- In what ways might we help parents in their catechetical instruction, home-schooling and/or child discipline? A congregation may also want to consider

age-graded group instruction and/or intergenerational learning (as in the *messy church* approach[8]).

- By what means can our youthworkers motivate and equip parents to live up to Biblical expectations for mothers and fathers so they will in turn provide appropriate guidance and modeling for their children?

Upon answering these questions, *two difficulties* become apparent.

First, many congregations traditionally have focused almost exclusively in their adult ministries on teaching Bible content — and/or that is certainly a priority. But a congregation serious about youth ministry will need to broaden its adult-equipping-ministries to include parenting issues.

Second, to complicate matters further, some congregations assign some of the youngest of their adult members and professional staff to be the official youthworkers, usually based on the misconception that twenty-something-year-olds will be best able to relate to youth. Unfortunately, many of these young adult workers are still struggling with their own maturity issues, perhaps causing them to interact awkwardly with their parent constituency. Also, regrettably, they may be inept at setting a model of maturity for the youth under their direction.

➤ ISSUES FOR YOUTHWORKERS TO PONDER
Regarding the *Emerging-Adult-BOY/GIRL* ◄

Several important implications grow out of the conviction that adolescent youth are, in many ways, children who still need to be subject to their parents. First and foremost, youthworkers must rigorously stand with parents in affirming the Biblical principle, "Respect and obey your parents." Furthermore, youthworkers must teach it unashamedly and consistently to all youth in their charge. However, even though obedience to parents is a key element in God's plan for the family, it may not be a popular theme with youth, especially as they grow older and become less dependent. Nevertheless, right relationships with one's parents must be a prominent aspect of the teaching curriculum in any youth ministry. To whatever extent a young person is still part of a family and dependent on their family, to that extent *youthworkers need to respect the authority of parents over their offspring.* This is a clear teaching of the Bible.

Beyond that, *how can youthworkers include parents within the scope of their overall ministries? Further questions* — to be answered in culturally-appropriate ways are:

1. How can fledgling youthworkers, perhaps barely out of adolescence themselves, overcome the disadvantages that come with their own personal life inexperience? Immaturities of "twenty-somethings-youthworkers" must be faced honestly by and with congregational overseers.
2. In what ways can youthworkers help parents keep their covenantal responsibility based on the Biblical formula that recognizes children to be duty-bound by the authority of their parents?
3. What means might a youthworker use to support parents who seek to be Biblically-obedient?
4. What is the ideal relationship for a youthworker to seek to build with a parent or parents whose lives and values are seemingly non-Christian?
5. In what ways can parents be encouraged to be responsible for, yet not unreasonably overbearing, toward their adolescent children?
6. By what means will youthworkers be able to genuinely embrace and provide for the maturational differential between girls and boys, especially in cultures that are biased toward widely-favored American

coeducational approaches?
7. How can both female and male youth be affirmed as peers with each other within the body of Christ, as taught by St. Paul in Galatians 3:28, "Faith in Christ Jesus is what makes each of you equal with each other, whether you are . . . a man or a woman"?
8. How can youthworkers maintain neutrality in the normal tensions between youth and their parents? In American and similar cultures, the natural and appropriate tendency for youth to differentiate themselves from their family of origin may eventuate in some family friction. Bridging the age gap, then, becomes a difficult task. As an agent of God, a youthworker who is pursuing a Biblical approach to youth ministry seeks to (1) reinforce parental authority as well as (2) work toward a rapport with parents that facilitates communication between the generations.

On those occasions when tensions emerge between parents and their adolescent children, it is highly tempting for the youthworker to side with the youth when they are invited to do so. But it is not faithful to the Bible for a youthworker to say to a young person, "I agree with you — your parents are unfair, they're really being hardhearted." Listening to the youth's expressions of familial stress is helpful, but taking their side against the parents is simply wrong. The temptation is so great for a youthworker, because to agree with the adolescent may appear to cement a relationship, i.e., "he or she will really confide in me now." But supporting the youth against her/his parent(s) is in violation of the Bible. Rather, the youth must be urged to be true to God's Word, that is, obey their parents. Youthworkers runs the risk of being misunderstood when they seem to take the parents' side, perhaps even being cut off in a relationship with the young person, but it is the right course to take.

If the youth seems to be treated unfairly, and this may happen occasionally, the youthworker's role is to listen compassionately. Also, they may serve as a mediator in some family situations. Possibly intervention and/or confrontation with the parents might be appropriate, depending on the cultural setting. For example, "It seems your child may be making a legitimate point and he (or she) deserves to be heard. In any culture, the more mature and the older the youthworker, the more trust s/he has earned with a parent, the better this kind of intervention will be received.

How Does Generational-Neutrality Work In Culturally-Tense Societies?

In many contexts, one of the most challenging aspects of youth ministry is bridging the culture gap between traditional parental expectations and Westernizing youth, those youth who are pursuing the trends of the so-called "global youth culture." This divide is often exacerbated by the common tension found between persons of rural background and their offspring growing up in urban contexts. As worldwide mass migration from the provinces to the city continues, this cultural gap cannot be ignored nor underestimated in urban youth ministry.

It is extremely difficult in cultures where parents often follow traditional family customs, expecting unquestioning obedience from youth regardless of age. For example, in sub-Saharan-Africa, children may be seeking to express themselves in Western ways (for example, listening to trendy music, wearing NBA sports gear, carrying cell/mobile phones and/or other accoutrements of "modern life"). More thoughts on this issue are to be found later in this volume.

Summary:
Ministry To/With Youth, As *Emerging-Adults-CHILDREN*

In summary, recognition of the ongoing childlike innocence, faith and immaturity in youth is essential for effective youth ministry. The Bible makes it clear what is expected for the care of children in the Christian community, including those who are in the confusing process of becoming adults. A youthworker must tread an exceedingly difficult tightrope of neither talking down to the *emerging-adult-GIRL/BOY* nor expecting a maturity that simply has not yet developed.

> ➤ **QUESTION TO PONDER** ◄
>
> How can youthworkers undertake and also succeed on this unpopular, seemingly-impossible trail?

In the providence of Almighty God, youthworkers have *potential allies*.

(1) Parents who are committed to Christ and the Bible. Parents acutely long for the *emerging-adult-CHILD* to *grow up* to be a responsible person in their families, congregations, communities, workplaces and wider roles in society. Christian mothers and fathers do want to direct the mentoring of their *emerging-adult-BOY/GIRL* and are usually more-than-ready to support youthworkers. As one mother reported about her son, "I have one job as a mom, to get him ready for the world, to get him up to meet it and be the best he could be."

(2) The *emerging-adult-CHILD* wants to *"grow up."* Everything within her or him cries out for privilege and freedom from childhood restrictions. Eventually and hopefully, they

will learn that maturity includes a healthy component of responsibility. They are open to opportunities that will enable them to become responsible people, as guided by mature youthworkers.

(3) The Christian community is invested in seeing their younger members become *mature* Christian men and women. Moreover, young members can often be trusted to contribute gifts and energies to the overall effectiveness of the congregation (or youth organization).

Therefore, facilitating the *emerging-adult-CHILD* in moving toward an impactful adulthood involves a *tripartite alliance of youthworkers* all in close collaboration:
   (1) The youthful person himself or herself,
   (2) Parent or parents of youth,
   (3) The congregation (including volunteer and/or paid personnel assigned to youth ministry).

By the grace of God, as youth ministry flourishes, emerging-adults-GIRLS/BOYS in many cultures will prosper and grow into the persons they wish to be, into the adults that parents desire for their offspring, into the *Christian young women and men* coveted by congregations worldwide and crucial to a world dying for the salt and light that believers bring. Amen.

NOTES

[1] The Greek word for child in this case, *paidion*, refers to young boys and girls, perhaps even infants.
[2] George W. Bush, *41, A Portrait of My Father* (New York, Crown Publishers, 2014), 81.
[3] The Greek word for child in this case, *teknon*, refers to the name transferred to that intimate and reciprocal relationship formed by the bonds of love, friendship, trust, as between parents and children in affectionate address.
[4] Joseph Epstein, "The Kindergarchy," *The Weekly Standard*, 6/9/2008, The Herald©, The Individual vs. the State.
[5] "Samuel had two sons. . . . But *they were not like their father*. They were dishonest and accepted bribes to give unfair decisions."
[6] "As Solomon got older, some of his wives led him to worship their gods. He *wasn't like his father* David, who had worshiped only the Lord God."
[7] The Greek word used here infers a legitimate son or daughter.
[8] Ross Parsley, *Messy Church: A Multigenerational Mission for God's Family* (Colorado Springs: David C. Cook, 2012).

Chapter 10

Biblical Youth Ministry To/With The "EMERGING-ADULT-Child"

The youth of the world, their parents, their home Christian congregations and wider community as well as their youthworkers — all have a vested interest in discovering what lies ahead as the maturing process continues. Particularly significant to Christian believers is discerning what the Bible teaches about the appropriate objectives, activities and processes of youth ministry.

The Bible's teaching on youth ministry in its the *emerging-adult-CHILD* dimension has been developed in the previous chapter. As youthworkers thoughtfully look at individuals in their care, they see childhood immaturities. These glimpses remind them of Biblical expectations for the *emerging-adult-CHILD*. But adolescents inhabit a multi-dimensional reality, in that they simultaneously reflect aspects of their own adulthood coming into focus, termed in this chapter as the *"EMERGING-WOMAN/MAN-child."*

Before entering the thickets of middle adolescence, a study of God's expectations for maturing adults is necessary, in order to identify the unresolved arenas of life that are ahead for youth. Appropriate objectives and processes for youth ministry will emerge from an examination of the Bible, *in terms of its EMERGING-ADULT-child dimension*, in this chapter and the chapters following.

Viewing Youth As *EMERGING-ADULT-Child*

As childhood slowly disappears and an adult begins to appear, the role of the adolescent as an *"EMERGING ADULT . . ."* comes into focus, even though youth continue to manifest childish immaturity. Teachers, counselors and coaches of youth as well as successful business leaders have discovered that high expectations often produce better results. The mission here is for parents and others to come to believe that the *EMERGING-MAN/WOMAN-child* truly wishes to grow up, in spite of the frequently-frustrating ambivalence of these youth. A corollary conviction is that adult-level teaching, responsibility and opportunity appropriate to the *EMERGING-ADULT-child* should be available for them.

This chapter presents the ultimate goal of youth ministry and the role parents have in seeing it happen. Chapter 11 then highlights the responsibilities of the *EMERGING-ADULT-child* himself or herself in light of Biblical goals for maturity. Chapter 12 raises questions that congregational leaders need to face with the *EMERGING-ADULT-girl/boy*. Chapter 13 follows with issues for youthworkers to ponder.

THE BIBLE'S EXPECTATIONS OF ADULT BELIEVERS

If the goal of Christian youth ministry is to enable youth to *grow up*, then what the Bible teaches about personal maturity comes to the fore. Helpfully, most of the Bible is directed to full-fledged adults, not to children. Hence, it is not too difficult to outline *God's standards for Christian growth*, thereby setting goals not only for ministry with the *EMERGING-ADULT-child* but also for parents seeking to continue to grow in their faith and life.

God's objective for believers is nothing less than personal maturity, making the Bible's expectations for a *self-responsible Christian adult* and *emerging-adults* very high! The Apostle Paul admonished adult believers basically to, "Grow up!"

- Brothers and sisters, don't think like children. In evil things be like babies, but in your thinking *you should be like full-grown adults* (First Corinthians 14:20, ERV).
- ... speaking the truth in love, *we will grow to become in every respect the mature body* of him who is the head, that is, Christ (Ephesians 4:15, NIV).
- When we were children, we thought and reasoned as children do. But *when we grew up, we quit our childish ways* (First Corinthians 13:11).

Growth toward Christian maturity is understandably the desired outcome for both adults *and* emerging-adults. The ultimate goal for youth ministry, consequently, is captured by St. Paul's declaration in Colossians 1:28, "He is the one we proclaim, admonishing and teaching everyone with all wisdom, *so that we may present everyone fully mature in Christ*" (NIV).

In Hebrew society now and in all probability in Bible times, the newly-designated young men (via *bar mitzvah* or its antecedent) were expected to undertake adult-level religious responsibilities immediately under the authority of Jewish Scriptures; for example, reading *Torah* in a synagogue service.

"Before Bar Mitzvah age, the boy was not considered accountable for any religious shortcomings on his part (rather, his father was considered to be responsible for his conduct), but from Bar Mitzvah onwards *the boy is considered accountable for his own actions*."

Doubtless this leap into adulthood jolted some of these newly-minted adults into higher levels of maturity as God-followers, family members and citizens. Might this also be a possibility for today's youth who find themselves under *Emerging-Adult-child* expectations?

In the twenty-first century, what does it mean across the globe to be "fully mature in Christ"? *The Bible presents a five-fold pathway to Christian maturity*, a vision that shows adult believers how to love God and their neighbors. Each of these is important in its own right and establishes step-by-step goals not only for Christian adult ministries but also for Biblical youth ministry, that is, encouraging and assisting the *Emerging-Adult-child* to *grow up*.

The five components are:
- Building and maintaining healthy family relationships.
- Serving God and neighbor in daily work.
- Honoring God through community service and in the world.
- Ministering in and among a Christian congregation.
- Caring for one's self.

A Maturing Adult Christian:

➤ **Builds and Maintains Responsible Relationships With Family** (Component 1).

The family was created by God to provide personal well-being, societal stability and perpetuation of the human race. In Genesis 2:18-25, the Bible prescribes heterosexual monogamous marriage as the proper base for human families.

> The Lord God said, "It isn't good for *the man* to live alone. I need to *make a suitable partner* for him. . . . None of these [animals] was the right kind of partner for the man. So the

Lord God made him fall into a deep sleep, and he took out one of the man's ribs. . . . the *Lord made a woman* out of the rib. The Lord God brought her to the man, and the man exclaimed, "Here is someone like me! She is part of my body, my own flesh and bones. . . !" That's why a man will leave his own father and mother. He marries a woman, and *the two of them become like one person.*

Passages such as Ephesians 5:21 through 6:4 make clear what responsible husband-wife relationships are to be, as well as healthy parent-child interactions. Family estrangements may be inevitable in life,[2] but the admonition throughout the Bible "to love others" definitely applies to Christian family relationships, quoting Jesus, "You must *love* each other, just as I have *loved* you. If you *love* each other, everyone will know that you are my disciples" (John 13:34-35).

St. Paul asserts that love is closely tied to forgiveness, "When people sin, you should forgive and comfort them, so they won't give up in despair. You should make them sure of your love for them" (Second Corinthians 2:7-8). Likewise Jesus taught in the *Lord's Prayer,* ". . . forgive us our sins, as we have forgiven those who sin against us" (Matthew 6:11-12, NLT). The ability to forgive one another is a significant element of Christian maturity.

The greatest enemy to steadfast marriages down through the centuries and across world cultures has been sexual immorality. "God wants you to be holy, so don't be immoral in matters of sex," declares St. Paul in First Thessalonians 4:3. God desires women and men of God to be pure in their deeds, words and thoughts. A Christian, therefore, must walk a careful line between the moral decadence of any culture in which she or he lives and the standards of the Bible. He or she should be careful to avoid all practices that fall short of Biblical standards, yet may be culturally acceptable, as often rationalized, "Everybody does it." Mature Christians in the same culture can help to define what is or is not morally wrong as they interpret Biblical truth about sexual sin.

The Bible repeatedly warns about the dangers of sexual self-indulgence. St. Paul's warning from First Corinthians 6 suffices.

> But you can't say that our bodies were made for sexual immorality. They were made for the Lord, and the Lord cares about our bodies. . . . Don't you realize that your bodies are actually parts of Christ? Should a man take his body, which is part of Christ, and join it to a prostitute? Never! And don't you realize that if a man joins himself to a prostitute, he becomes one body with her? . . . But the person who is joined to the Lord is one spirit with him. *Run from sexual sin!* No other sin so clearly affects the body as this one does. For sexual immorality is a sin against your own body. Don't you realize that your body is the temple of the Holy Spirit, who lives in you and was given to you by God? You do not belong to yourself, for God bought you with a high price. So you must *honor God with your body* (First Corinthians 6:13, 15-20, NLT).

A Christian who is committed to moral purity is assured happiness and peace of mind, "God blesses those people whose hearts are pure. They will see him!" (Matthew 5:8). This promise applies to single and married, heterosexual and homosexual, though not without significant moral struggle for those who would remain chaste.

Sexual innocence is more than avoiding the excitements and heartaches of adultery and/or prostitution (see Proverbs 6:24-35), "Be faithful in marriage" (Exodus 20:14). Also, in Hebrews, "Have respect for marriage. Always be faithful to your partner, because God will punish anyone who is immoral or unfaithful in marriage" (13:4). Moral purity calls for sanctity of all physical expressions of sex and also for chastity in thinking. But Western culture is highly polluted by both sexual innuendo and pornographic expressions, especially in the mass media, above all in certain domains of the Internet. Christian men are subject to sexual temptation all around them. They must realize they are called as men, husbands and fathers to keep high standards.

The Christian who is moving toward maturity, young or old, needs spiritual discernment, therefore, in matters of morality. Every aspect of life must be examined to keep an exemplary life especially in human cultures that lack defined standards such as in the morally-deteriorating Western world. The Bible does provide guidelines for those who desire to be uncorrupted.

- But solid food is for *the mature*, who by constant use have *trained themselves* to distinguish good from evil (Hebrews 5:14, NIV).
- With wisdom you will learn what is *right and honest and fair*. Wisdom will control your mind, and you will be pleased with knowledge (Proverbs 2:9-10).
- If any of you *need wisdom*, you should *ask God*, and it will be given to you. God is generous and won't correct you for asking (James 1:5).

Sex is not just for procreation, but procreation is one of its purposes. Genesis 1:27-28 records, "So God created . . . men and women. God gave them his blessing and said: 'Have a lot of children! . . .'" Having children is hereby defined as the normative experience for married couples. As the Bible story unfolds, God continues to reveal his basic, wonderful plan for families with children. "Behold, children are a heritage from the Lord, the fruit of the womb a reward," as in Psalm 127:3-5.

A maturing person also becomes comfortable with existing family relationships; for example, honoring one's parents. Moreover, a responsible Christian adult seeks to promote loving and forgiving interactions among family members. For those who become parents, one's maturity is reflected in the degree to which the nurture described earlier is fulfilled.

Thus, the Bible's prescription for maturing in Christ

is developing responsible relationships with one's family. Moving forward, being mature involves responsible action in wider society, as follows.

A Maturing Christian:

➤ **Loves God and Neighbor Through The Service of Daily Work** (Component 2).[3]

The Bible speaks out forcefully on ways Christians glorify God through a life given to the service of humankind. As Jesus articulated it,". . . the second [commandment] is . . . 'Love your neighbor as yourself" (Matthew 22:39). Responsibly loving others as much as you love yourself is shown in productive work.

In Genesis 1 and 2, the father of all humankind was given a mandate to care for his world; Eve subsequently joined Adam in that work.

> So God created humans to be like himself. . . . God gave them his blessing and said: ". . . Fill the earth with people and bring it under your control. Rule over the fish in the ocean, the birds in the sky, and every animal on the earth." Genesis 1:27-28

Furthermore, God gave Adam a specific job, "The Lord God placed the man in the Garden of Eden to tend and watch over it" (Genesis 2:15, NLB). God thereby blessed daily work and, in spite of the curse Adam was given that turned honest work into tiring toil (see Genesis 3:17-19), God's approbation continued, as illustrated from these Proverbs:
- "Four things on earth are small, yet they are extremely wise: Ants are creatures of little strength, yet they store up their food in the summer. . ." (Proverbs 30:24-25).
- "Go to the ant, you sluggard; consider its ways and be wise! It has no commander, no overseer or ruler, yet it stores its provisions in summer and gathers its food at

harvest" (Prov. 6:6-8, NIV).

Consequently, throughout the Bible humankind is called to *a life of service through productive labor.* New Testament writers spell out how Christian adults are to behave on the job.
- *Serve wholeheartedly*, as if you were serving the Lord, not people. . . (Ephesians 6:7).
- Slaves, you must always obey your earthly masters. *Try to please them at all times*, and not just when you think they are watching. Honor the Lord and *serve your masters with your whole heart.* Do your work willingly, as though you were serving the Lord himself, and not just your earthly master (Colossians 3:22-23).
- Each of you should use whatever gift you have received *to serve others*, as faithful stewards of God's grace in its various forms (First Peter 4:10).

One's daily work has five comparable components that demonstrate how one's work is rightfully *service to the Lord*, as shown in this diagram. It does not exclude evangelism but it is clearly far more than sharing the Gospel orally.

At the foundation, the endeavors of head, heart and hands enable individuals to *provide for their own sustenance*. God wants believers to care for themselves, as they may be able to do so, as seen in the following Scriptures.

- And our people should learn to earn what they require by leading an honest life and so *be self-supporting* (Titus 3:14, JBP).
- Try your best to live quietly, to mind your own business, and to work hard, just as we taught you to do. Then you will be respected by people who are not followers of the Lord, and *you won't have to depend on anyone* (First Thessalonians 4:11-12).
- . . . nor did we eat anyone's food without paying for it. On the contrary, we worked night and day, laboring and toiling so that *we would not be a burden to any of you* (Second Thessalonians 3:8).
- . . . *if you don't work, you don't eat*. . . (Second Thessalonians 3:10-11).

Second, daily work *serves family members* as a woman or man provides for the family's everyday needs.
- People who don't *take care of their relatives*, and especially their own families, have given up their faith. They are worse than someone who doesn't have faith in the Lord (First Timothy 5:8).
- If a woman who is a follower has any *widows in her family, she should help them*. . . (First Timothy 5:16).
- Jesus said, "But you let people get by without *helping their parents* when they should. You let them say that what they have has been offered to God. Is this any way to show respect to your parents? You ignore God's commands in order to follow your own teaching" (Matthew 15:5-6).

Third, honest work allows the breadwinner(s) to *have something to give away,* to the suffering and the destitute as well as to propagators of the Gospel such as missionaries, pastors

and other "Christian workers."
- ... Be honest and work hard, so you will have *something to give* to people in need (Ephesians 4:28).
- As the Scriptures say, "They share freely and *give generously to the poor. Their good deeds will be remembered forever*" (Second Corinthians 9:9).
- St. Paul writing to the believers at Corinth: "Who serves as a soldier at his own expense? Who plants a vineyard and does not eat its grapes? Who tends a flock and does not drink the milk? ... If we have sown spiritual seed among you, is it too much if we reap *a material harvest from you?* If others have this *right of support* from you, shouldn't we have it all the more? ... Don't you know that those who serve in the temple get their food from the temple, and that those who serve at the altar share in what is offered on the altar? In the same way, the Lord has commanded that *those who preach the gospel should receive their living from the gospel*" (First Corinthians 9:7, 11-14, NIV).

Fourth, the Christian at her or his daily labor acts as *leaven in the workplace,* providing:

enlightenment	forgiveness	gentleness
goodness	joy	optimism
orderliness	patience	pleasant speech
significance	truth	and *life*

— in places where the Good News is needed. Or, as Jesus declared,

You are like salt for everyone on earth. But if salt no longer tastes like salt, how can it make food salty? All it is good for is to be thrown out and walked on. You are like light for the whole world. ... *Make your light shine, so that others will see the good that you do and will praise your Father in heaven* (Matthew 5:14-16).

An exemplary life in the workplace speaks volumes to those who do not know God. An enthusiastic, competent worker is a witness to God's grace that goes beyond words. Additionally, within this context, personal words of encouragement, truth and calm via spoken word, text, e-mail, social media or telephone take on new meaning to those around her or him. Hence, a sincere witness to the Gospel's saving power may open doors for a Christian to share more in a natural way.

Fifth, perhaps a cornerstone of the mandate to work, *people daily serve the community and the world as benefactors* in such vocations as:

packer,	philosopher,	postal worker,
painter,	photographer,	potter,
paralegal,	physical therapist,	printer,
pastor,	physician,	probation officer,
pathologist,	physicist,	professor,
payroll clerk,	pilot,	programmer,
personal care staff,	planter,	proofreader,
personnel recruiter,	plumber,	psychologist,
pest controller,	poet,	pump operator,
pharmacist,	police officer,	purchasing agent,

and plenty more.

All are working in various ways and places, to the end that society functions in humane and just ways that bring great pleasure to God.

> ... a world we are called to live *for*. This world, Scripture proclaims, belongs to God, who then entrusted it to His image bearers. He created it good and loves it still, despite its brokenness and frustration. He has plans for it yet and

invites the redeemed to live redemptively, for its good and our flourishing, even as we live for Him.[4]

Conversely, God is *no* lover of:

addictions,	chaos,	darkness,
disease,	homelessness,	human trafficking,
hunger,	ignorance,	murder,
pain,	poverty,	slavery,
thievery,	warfare,	or other injustice.

Consequently, from packers to purchasing agents, from A to Z, *humans work alongside God to push back against God's enemies in the world.*

A Christian's daily work *is* ministry in and of itself, giving believers strong motivation to work heartily *to benefit themselves and others.*

A Maturing Christian:

➤ Loves God and Neighbor Through The Service of Christian Citizenship and Social Responsibility (Component 3).

The Bible insists that believers live as responsible members of society, using their God-given gifts and talents in their community and world to become exemplary citizens. Additionally, the Bible exhorts Christians to respect and obey civil authority, except in matters of conscience. As St. Paul wrote to Titus, "Remind the believers to submit to the government and its officers. They should be obedient, always ready to do what is good" (Titus 3:1, NLB). Individual believers are thus commanded to bring glory to God not only through their daily work but also in respect for the rule of law.

Moving beyond compliance, Christians serve their community; for example, as volunteers in and supporters of organizations and endeavors that promote human well-being and justice both locally and globally. In so doing, they spread the wholesomeness of God's kingdom. As Jesus eloquently expressed it, "Blessed are the peacemakers, for they will be called the children of God" (Matthew 5:9, NET). Likewise ancient Jewish prophets:

> "But let justice roll on like a river, *righteousness* like a never-failing stream!" (Amos 5:24, NIV). "This is what the Lord Almighty said: 'Administer true justice; *show mercy and compassion* to one another'" (Zechariah 7:9, NIV).

To summarize thus far, the service dimension of life for a Christian involves her/his participation in the workforce, as well as service in the community. Beyond that, an adult (and/or EMERGING-ADULT-*child*) believer shows love for God by being part of a local body of believers, where he/she may learn, worship, grow and serve, as follows.

A Maturing Christian:

➤ **Loves God and Neighbor Through Service With And Among The Family Of God** (Component 4).

God never intended Christian believers to walk the path of discipleship in a solo performance. Instead, God commanded Christ-followers to band together in local congregations for mutual edification and service to each other in the Christian community and in the world.

The plan outlined in the Bible consists of times for believers to gather for encouragement, for fellowship, for adoration, for learning and for mutual care of one another. Being empowered by these special times together and the Holy Spirit, individual Christians move out to serve God as they live, work and play in their communities, as well as reach out to their neighbors with Christ's love in its many forms. Romans 12:1 states, "Therefore, I urge you, brothers and sisters, in view of God's mercy, to *offer your bodies as a living sacrifice*, holy and pleasing to God — this is *your true and proper worship*" (NIV).

As a person becomes aware of their gifting and calling(s), he or she responds by using the talents God has given them in service, whether as a part of the congregation's ministries and/or in the world where they live and work. Maturity enables them to take greater responsibility for giving back to their Christian sisters and brothers in various ways, as well as working boldly for God's Kingdom in various just causes.

- My friends, you were chosen to be free. So don't use your freedom as an excuse to do anything you want. Use it as an opportunity to *serve each other with love* (Galatians 5:13).
- The *worship* that God wants is this: *caring for orphans or widows* who need help and keeping yourself free from the world's evil influence. This is the kind of *worship* that God accepts as pure and good (James 1:27, ERV).

Loving family, loving neighbors near and far, and loving other Christians is a daunting agenda, but the Bible mandates it. Yet the Christian Scriptures endorse one more goal for the maturing Christian.

A Maturing Christian:

➤ Cares for One's Self
(Component 5).

A responsible Christian adult takes care of self in its various dimensions: *physical, mental, social and devotional.*

Regarding physical well-being, proper diet, adequate exercise and health routines lead to appropriate care of "the

temple," as St. Paul describes it.
- You surely know that your body is *a temple where the Holy Spirit lives*. The Spirit is in you and is a gift from God. You are no longer your own. God paid a great price for you. So *use your body to honor God* (First Corinthians 6:19-20).
- As the saying goes, *"Exercise is good for your body..."* (First Timothy 4:8).

Mentally, a healthy intake of Bible truth helps the adult mind focus on "things above," whereas extensive exposure to secular thought-patterns is destructive to good character. As St. Paul reminds EMERGING-ADULTS-*children*, "And set your minds *and* keep them set on what is above (the higher things), not on the things that are on the earth" (Colossians 3:2, AMP). The Psalmist echoes, for those in an increasingly visual age, *"I will not look with approval on anything that is vile..."* (Psalm 101:3, NIV).

Coming to terms with one's place in life and society also leads to good mental health, yet it seems that many adults struggle in this area. The seeds for low self-esteem were sown when God cursed humankind due to their sin (Genesis 3). When a Christian believer comes to accept that she or he has been redeemed and is being conformed to the image of Christ, the path out of self-doubt is being marked out. As St. Paul put it,
- ... God sent his Son, ... to redeem those under the law, that *we might receive adoption to sonship*. Because you are his sons, God sent the Spirit of his Son into our hearts, the Spirit who calls out, "Abba, Father" (Galatians 4:4-6).
- And we know that in all things God works for the good of those who love him, who have been called *according to his purpose*. For those God foreknew he also predestined to be conformed to the image of his Son.... And those he predestined, he also called; those *he called*, he also justified; those he justified, he also glorified (Romans

8:28-30).

With Christian growth comes an awareness of God's bestowal of spiritual gifts on individual believers. An awakening consciousness of one's calling to serve in this world is intertwined with the life trajectory of a sensitive Christian. God instructs women and women to be involved in the world in which they live or will live according to God's endowments and opportunities and this becomes their calling.

Taking careful responsibility for personal mental health also includes such disciplines as learning how to be a good consumer of modern communication, such as the Internet, television, cell phones, and social media.

Lastly, and of equal importance, is the life of devotion, the development of the inner life that fuels the worship and service of the Bible believer. Thousands, perhaps millions, of books have been written to inspire and instruct Christians in the life of faith. Consequently, little needs to be added here, except to say that the soul of humankind seeks for the *shalom* that Jesus Christ offers.

> For it is by grace you have been saved, through faith—
> and this is not from yourselves, it is the gift of God— not
> by works, so that no one can boast. For we are God's
> handiwork, created in Christ Jesus to do good works,
> which God prepared in advance for us to do (Ephesians
> 2:8-10, NIV).

The *shalom* of Jesus is fostered by regular attention to personal prayer, Bible study, Scripture meditation, and participation in the life of the local body of believers.

In summary, growing up into Christ is a multi-faceted set of Biblical expectations that puts every Christian woman's and man's commitment to the test, and even more so for an EMERGING-ADULT-*child* who is seeking to attain adult maturity.

> **QUESTIONS TO PONDER** ◄

- How can a human being balance all five components of God's agenda for her or him as life pours forth in an unending stream of demands?

- How possible and/or important is it to maintain "balance" in one's life?

- What does it mean to "serve God" under the multiplex Biblical responsibilities for Christian men and women?

THE BIBLE's EXPECTATIONS OF **PARENTS** OF AN *EMERGING-ADULT-Child*

Because the young person is indeed moving into adulthood, her or his parents are called upon to make some serious adjustments in their *own* thinking and conduct. Within the Christian community, the parent(s) and the *EMERGING-ADULT-boy/girl* find themselves moving toward a brother/sister relationship, such as the parent may have with other members of the believing community. This paradigm shift may create a veritable family earthquake, especially as the youth vacillate between childishness and mature demeanor from day to day, even hour to hour. Realistically, and simultaneously, the parent(s) may be experiencing similar challenges to their own maturity!

The Biblical role for parents has been spelled out in a previous chapter — teaching and training in the Bible, modeling the Christian life and above all, loving. St. Paul's letter to his friends in first-century Corinth well expressed the realistic relationship between a parent and an *EMERGING-ADULT-child* and a parent.

- "I'm writing as a father to you, my children. *I love you and want you to grow up well*, not spoiled. . . . but there aren't many fathers willing to take the time and effort to help you *grow up*" (First Corinthians 4:14b-15, MSG).

When a parent desires a Biblically-based fraternal rapport with an EMERGING-WOMAN/MAN-*child*, she or he finds clear standards in the New Testament toward which to work. Parents-of-youth are thus informed regarding their responsibilities. *Believer-to-believer relationships* are charted by the following *Biblical commands*.

Love the EMERGING-ADULT-Child.

Whatever else a Christian parent may do, the command **to love** summarizes the Bible's teaching on what is expected when living with an EMERGING-ADULT-*child*, as expressed in the following Scriptures.

- Keep on *loving one another as brothers and sisters* (Hebrews 13:1, NIV).
- Jesus said, "A new command I give you: *Love one another*. As I have loved you, so you must love one another" (John 13:34, NIV).
- *Be devoted to one another in love. . .* (Romans 12:10, NIV).
- . . . *love one another deeply*, from the heart (First Peter 1:22, NIV).
- Stop being bitter and angry and mad at others. Don't yell at one another or curse each other or ever be rude (Ephesians 4:31).

Ideally, the love shown to an EMERGING-ADULT-*child* should not be qualitatively different than the affection parents show to their younger children. However, it can be problematic for parents when the EMERGING-ADULT-*boy*/

girl is in the childish process of testing limits or protesting against parental authority. Nevertheless, *love* is both the underlying and the overarching principle to follow.

Receive the EMERGING-ADULT-Child.

Often parents' love for the *EMERGING-ADULT-girl/boy* is mightily tested as the youth feels more and more independent from them (depending on cultural expectations).

Sometimes the *EMERGING-ADULT-child* may feel like a stranger within the family, or conversely, a parent may wonder what happened to their formerly-cooperative son or daughter. The unknown apostle wrote, "Be sure to *welcome strangers* into your home. By doing this, some people have welcomed angels as guests, without even knowing it" (Hebrews 13:2). What a challenge for Christian parents when their children seem like strangers to them!

The Bible instructs Christians to offer hospitality to strangers as well as to "one another." The Apostles instructed believers as follows.
- St. Paul wrote, "*Greet one another* with a holy kiss..." (Romans 16:16).
- St. Peter wrote, "*Offer hospitality to one another* without grumbling" (First Peter 4:9).

Jesus' parable of the Prodigal Son (Luke 15:11-32) demonstrates how to receive a wayward *emerging-adult-child*, but what about day-to-day living with a youth in the home? The Jesus principle was and is, "Open your heart to your *EMERGING-ADULT-girl/boy*." The behavior, demeanor and/or arguments from a child who is being immature and selfish have infuriated many a parent. Setting aside who is right and who may be wrong for the moment, what reception does the *EMERGING-ADULT-child* receive in the home? What atmosphere does the parent generate that allows for reconciliation, at least at the heart level? Is it chilly or warm?

As St. Paul expressed it, "Finally, brothers and sisters, rejoice! Strive for full restoration, encourage one another, be of one mind, *live in peace*. And the God of love and peace will be with you" (Second Corinthians 13:11, NIV).

Pray for the EMERGING-ADULT-Child.

All the prayers that Christian parents have ever offered for their children reflect their yearning for an unimpeded transition for their children into Christian maturity. But this expectation is often not met because of the unpredictable nature of humankind. Hence, the Bible's admonitions to pray are ones parents may find easiest to live up to, especially in times of parenting stress. "When all else fails, pray!" The Bible says *[emphases added]*:

- ...*praying at all times* in the Spirit, with all prayer and supplication. To that end keep alert with all perseverance, *making supplication for all the saints*... (Ephesians 6:18, ESV).
- If you have sinned, you should tell each other what you have done. Then you can *pray for one another*... (James 5:16, NIV).

Encourage the EMERGING-ADULT-Child.

Youth face many discouragements in their growth process. They may be frustrated by:
- Their physical appearance ("I wish I were taller").
- Their social standing ("No one likes me").
- Their school success or lack thereof ("I'm so stupid").
- Their family ("You are all so weird"), and/or
- Their inability to find employment ("I can't find work anywhere").
- If spiritually attuned, youth may begin to doubt

God's love and/or God's existence.

The Bible speaks to Christian parents as follows:

- Finally, brothers and sisters . . . *encourage one another*, be of one mind, live in peace (Second Corinthians 13:11-12, NIV).
- Therefore encourage one another and build each other up. . . (First Thessalonians 5:11, NIV).
- And let us consider how we may spur one another on toward love and good deeds . . . *encouraging one another*. . . (Hebrew 10:24-25, NIV).

Parents are excellently positioned to offer reassurance to disheartened youth, yet it is enormously difficult to do so without demeaning the seriousness of certain situations or offering superficial solutions. Yet it must be done.

Respect the EMERGING-ADULT-Child.

Perhaps the hardest shift a parent must make, particularly in adult-centered cultures, is coming to see the *EMERGING-MAN/WOMAN-child* as growing up **from** being under parental authority **into** becoming a person in his or her own right. The Bible obliges parents to listen to and respect the opinion of their *EMERGING-ADULT-girl/boy*, regardless of how irrelevant or juvenile they may seem to be. But "respect" does not require one to agree, simply to pay attention, in light of these New Testament passages.
- *Accept one another*, then, just as Christ accepted you, in order to bring praise to God (Romans 15:7).
- Be devoted to one another in love. *Honor one another* above yourselves (Romans 12:10).
- *Submit to one another* out of reverence for Christ (Ephesians 5:21).
- Finally, all of you, be like-minded, be sympathetic, love

one another, *be compassionate and humble* (First Peter 3:8).

Another form of respect is having high expectations for the youth. This allows them to take responsibility for their actions, such as doing their homework or saving money for a university education (if that is their goal). It is proper for parents to expect growth in maturity while tempering their hopes by knowledge of the youth's proclivity to make mistakes as they are learning.

Respect also includes giving the EMERGING-ADULT-*child* the freedom to fail. How can youth experience growth by learning from their mistakes, unless parents increasingly turn various decisions over to the EMERGING-ADULT-*girl/boy* to make? Often their painful failures when making poor choices teach more effectively than any parent lecture could do.

Closely related to the issue of respect is the way parental authority is exercised. When parents become fixated with the power of their position of supremacy, the following verses prescribe a way out; that is, personal humility.

- All of you, *clothe yourselves with humility toward one another*, because, "God opposes the proud but shows favor to the humble" (First Peter 5:5, NIV).
- You, my brothers and sisters . . . do not use your freedom to indulge the flesh; rather, *serve one another humbly in love* (Galatians 5:13).
- Live in harmony with one another. *Do not be proud*, but be willing to associate with people of low position. Do not be conceited (Romans 12:16).
- Then Jesus said to all the people: "If any of you want to be my followers, *you must forget about yourself*. You must take up your cross each day and follow me" (Luke 9:23).
- Fathers, *do not exasperate your children*; instead, bring them up in the training and instruction of the Lord (Ephesians 6:4, NIV).

When St. Paul decreed that men should be heads of their households, he did not mean them to lord it over their families. As expressed by one author,

> Rather, they exercised God-required authority as servant/leaders in their homes, and by their actions and affection evidenced that they loved their wives deeply . . . they put their wives and their children above their own interests.[6]

Forgive the EMERGING-ADULT-Child.

The ultimate "grace step" for parents is practicing the ultimate humility that admits to their own weaknesses and foibles, leading to both giving and requesting forgiveness. Some of the mistakes an EMERGING-MAN/WOMAN-child makes can be heinous, almost to the point of being unforgiveable. But the Bible clearly shows God's expectations.

- Be kind and compassionate to one another, *forgiving each other*, just as in Christ God forgave you (Ephesians 4:32).
- Bear with each other and *forgive one another* if any of you has a grievance against someone. Forgive as the Lord forgave you (Colossians 3:13).
- Therefore let us *stop passing judgment* on one another. Instead, make up your mind not to put any stumbling block or obstacle in the way of a brother or sister (Romans 14:13).

Coach the EMERGING-ADULT-Child.

Does the teaching aspect of parenting (see Deuteronomy 6:6-9) cease when a juvenile enters the EMERGING-MAN/WOMAN-child phase of life? Certainly not, though the relationship may become more collegial than previously. Parents are in the role of a coach as well as being a friend of

the *EMERGING-ADULT-boy/girl*.
St. Paul exhibits this rapport as he speaks of his relationship with his youthful disciple Timothy.
- "*I love him like a son...*" (First Corinthians 4:17).
- To Timothy: "... because of our faith, *you are like a son to me*. I pray that God our Father and our Lord Jesus Christ will be kind and merciful to you. May they bless you with peace" (First Timothy 1:2).

St. Paul, as an older man and more knowledgeable Christian believer, unmistakably mentored the younger man. Timothy was at St. Paul's side during some of his missionary journeys as well as co-authoring several of the Pauline Epistles.[7] Hence the Apostle instructed this young man to mentor others in Second Timothy 2:2.
- "And the things you have heard me say in the presence of many witnesses *entrust to reliable people* who will also be qualified to teach others (NIV).
- "Timothy...you have often heard me teach. Now I want you to tell these same things to *followers who can be trusted to tell others*" (CEV).

St. Paul wrote similarly to the younger Titus about mentoring:
"Titus, you must teach only what is correct. Tell the older men to have self-control and to be serious and sensible... . Tell the older women to behave. . . .They must teach what is proper, so the younger women will be loving wives and mothers" (Titus 2:1-4).

Likewise, dedicated Christian fathers and mothers undertake to disciple their children, up to and through their youth. What St. Paul told the Corinthian believers models the kind of challenge a Christian parent can present to the *EMERGING-ADULT-son/daughter*, "Keep your eyes open, hold tight to your convictions, give it all you've got, be resolute, and love without stopping" (First Corinthians 16:13-14,

MSG). Beyond that, given frequent tensions in families, wise parents and youth also seek out experienced Christian adults to aid in the mentoring process.

Parents who seek to guide their EMERGING-ADULT-boy/girl to maturity in Christ face a colossal task — to love, to pray for, to respect, to encourage, to forgive, to receive and to mentor — a mission that requires them by the power of the Holy Spirit to seek and do God's will with their child. Busy and overworked parents have precious little time to give to this effort, but the Bible demands nothing less.

The next chapters explain the role of the EMERGING-ADULT-child and additionally the role of the congregation as well as the *youthworkers* under the congregation's purview.

> ► QUESTIONS TO PONDER ◄
>
> - What can youthworkers do to carry the message about God's expectations to the parents of the EMERGING-ADULTS-children with whom they are working?
>
> - How can the youthworker help youth to see life from their parents' point of view?

NOTES

[1.] "Origins of the Bar/Bat Mitzvah," ReformJudiasm.org website.

[2] Jesus said, "Brothers and sisters will betray each other and have each other put to death. Parents will betray their own children, and children will turn against their parents and have them killed" (Mark 13:12).

[3] The material in the following section is gratefully adapted from *Your Work Matters to God*, by Doug Sherman and William Hendricks (Colorado Springs: Navpress, 1987), "Toward Claiming and Identifying Our Ministry in the Workplace," in *The Laity in Ministry*, by Richard R. Broholm (Newton Center, MA: The Robert K. Greenleaf Center, 1985), the writings of William H. Diehl, and numerous other sources.

[4] Warren Cole Smith and John Stonestreet, *Restoring All Things* (Grand

Rapids: Baker Books, 2015), 20.

[5] See also Romans 13:8; First Thessalonians 1:9; First Peter 3:8; First John 3:11, 23; 4:7, 11, 12; Second John 1:5.

[6] Mike Dowgiewicz, personal blog, February 24, 2015.

[7] Second Corinthians, Philippians, Colossians, First and Second Thessalonians and Philemon.

Chapter 11

Biblical Youth Ministry To/With The *"Emerging-Adult-Girl/Boy"*
ROLE OF YOUTH

What a great moment in a young person's life! She or he is presented with a certificate, a commission, a diploma, a qualification or a title, symbolizing completion of certain training. It represents considerable effort and time expended, a diligence that may never have been seen previously in his or her life. The individual is pleased, their family is delighted, their community thrilled by this achievement.

"But now what?" asks the young person, the family and friends. "What's next in the progression of life?"

In almost every culture, recognizing the gender of the youth being honored solves some of the query. Both males and females have certain expectations for their next step according to gender. If a young woman, the anticipation for her to marry is extremely strong in many cultures. A young woman who seriously pursues a non-conventional career often has to pay a price for her nonconformity. Similarly, a man may also ignore male norms, though it will cause him to become alienated from his culture of origin, for example, if he does "women's work" in the fields.

In the previous chapter, Biblical standards for adulthood were outlined and applied to the parents of youth. Now the focus is placed on the youth themselves, as they may aspire to grow up according to God's standards. This chapter highlights the responsibilities of the *EMERGING-WOMAN/ MAN-child* himself or herself in light of Biblical goals for maturity.

The Bible's Expectations of the Christian *EMERGING-ADULT-Boy/Girl*

The Bible's expectations for a *self-responsible Christian adult*, as described in Chapter 10, are high. God's objective is nothing less than personal maturity! Note the Apostle Paul's admonition addressed to believers in New Testament Corinth, "When we were children, we thought and reasoned as children do. But *when we grew up, we quit our childish ways*" (First Corinthians 13:11).

Growth toward maturity thus is the *desired outcome* for youth who are in the process of becoming adults. The goal for youth ministry is well captured by Colossians 1:28: "He is the one we proclaim, admonishing and teaching everyone with all wisdom, *so that we may present everyone fully mature in Christ*" (NIV). The answer to the question, "What is the goal for Biblical youth ministry?" is simply this — God expects youth *to grow up to be agents of Christ*, within their family, within their world and within their own person. As Apostles state,
- St. Peter wrote, "Be like newborn babies who are thirsty for the pure spiritual milk that will *help you grow* [up] . . ." (First Peter 2:2).
- St. Paul wrote, "Brothers and sisters, stop thinking like children. Be like babies as far as evil is concerned. But

be grown up in your thinking" (First Corinthians 14:20, NIRV).

It is *not* an option for the youthful Christian to remain mired in the dependent role of a girl or boy. However, the road ahead of them is unknown to them and perhaps to their parents, stepparent, grandparents and other mentors — it may have *many difficulties.*

Family background: Usually an *EMERGING-ADULT-boy/ girl* has a family of some sort, even if just biological. Because no parent is perfect, children grow up in environments that might be tinged by the sin of their parents, or deluged by parental evil or injured in some way by parental misbehavior and misguidance. To add to this morass, every child inherits a sin nature as a part of the human race. Sin, in whatever form, blocks the formation of Christian character in the *EMERGING-ADULT-child.*

Gender differential: One does not have to be a profound student of adolescence to realize that females mature more rapidly than males. This fact applies to all phases of development: physical, mental and social. Girls start to mature physically, on the whole, about two years before boys. One only needs to observe a mixed-gender group of twelve-year-olds to realize that many of the girls tower over many of the boys. A similar phenomenon occurs socially, so that girls are often attracted to boys a few years older than they are, because the females are relatively equal in maturity with the older boys. Conversely, *EMERGING-MEN-boys* feel more comfortable with younger girls — their female age peers are often threatening socially. Likewise, a class of *EMERGING-WOMEN-girls* is ready for more in-depth learning than boys of the same age. Putting girls and boys into the same instructional groups often means that the teaching proceeds tediously because the boys do not have the maturity to handle material that the girls are ready for.

Developmental differences among individuals: Each girl and boy moves into puberty with her or his individual development clock ticking. For example, much variation exists between females in terms of their first menstrual period. Some may experience it at age ten, whereas others might be as late as age sixteen. In any one age group of thirteen-year-olds, a few girls may have had a period for several years, a few may not experience it until much later, but by age thirteen most will have crossed that line. These ages are fluid according to cultural and health conditions, but the principle applies. The same is true among boys. Some achieve close to their adult height by age twelve, the majority probably not until age fourteen or fifteen, some as late as age eighteen. In any group of fifteen-year-olds, the maturity variations will be considerable.

Nevertheless, the girl or boy who is moving toward true adulthood desperately desires to grow up, with all its apparent privileges, yet he or she faces the unknown world ahead with considerable ambivalence. Because their parents, their Christian community and their youthworkers are banding together to guide them on life's path to adult-level responsibility, *youth are not alone in facing the difficulties of growing up!* Yet no one can force them to grow toward maturity — the process must be guided by their own decisions and deeds.

One must ask what Christian maturity might look like for today's *EMERGING-ADULT-child*. As set forth in the preceding chapter, the Bible teaches a *five-fold pathway to Christian maturity,* a vision that shows mature believers how to love God and neighbors, near and far.

But how able is a thirteen-year-old *EMERGING-ADULT-boy/ girl* in, for example, Zambia, to fulfill Biblical expectations of a mature Christian? Not without considerable effort. Not in Singapore, Guatemala, the U.S.A., Scotland, the Czech Republic, Canada or Vanuatu either! She or he has a weighty

"to-do-list."
- *Continuing to honor parents.*
- *Building responsible relationships with other family members.*
- *Serving God through daily work and/or study.*
- *Honoring God as a Christian activist.*
- *Serving God in devotion to the family of God.*
- *Caring for herself or himself.*

A careful reading of the Bible leads to the following distinct and imposing expectations to bring boys and girls to adult maturity.

➔ **Continue to honor parents.** An *EMERGING-MAN/WOMAN-child* continues to be under God's expectation that he or she will stay in the path given to them in the Ten Commandments, "Honor your father and your mother. . ." (Exodus 20:12). In traditional cultural settings, almost-unquestioning obedience may be expected from offspring until the death of the parent. A child is expected to obey without questions or backtalk, even when they become adults.

However, when Western cultural influences come in, confusion is created, raising the issue of when a child is released, if ever, from the Bible's directive to obey parents. In Westernizing cultures the idea of unquestioning lifelong obedience to parents by the *EMERGING-ADULT-child* often discarded by the time that person reaches her/his fourth decade. As the young adult becomes more self-sufficient, there will be a shift (at least internally) from *obedience* **to** parents — to continuing *respect for* and *deference to* their parents. Hopefully, Christian young adults continue to respect their parents throughout their lifetime, no matter what the culture dictates.

In addition to giving honor to parents, youth benefit from

realistically thinking through their family context. They come to recognize the failings of their parents, as well as grow in thanksgiving for God's sovereignty in placing them in a particular family. This self-examination allows parents and youth to come closer to a complementary relationship in future years.

→ **Prepare for life as a single or married person.** Standards presented in the Bible enable an *EMERGING-ADULT-child* to prepare himself or herself to ultimately enter marriage, according to God's will, and later to have children, also as God wills. By contrast, Western mass-media focuses on the romantic notion of "falling-in-love" that often appeals to both *EMERGING-ADULT* starry-eyed *females* and lusty *males*. Satan's lies about marriage seem so appealing.

However, the Bible defines marriage as a sacred relationship that requires deep intentionality and reverence. Every marriage needs to be built on a firm foundation of trust and fidelity. Hence the Bible expects high demands for chastity. In cultures that expect students to have secondary education and perhaps beyond, *EMERGING-WOMEN/MEN-children* are faced with a period of vexatious waiting for the appropriate time to form a new family with marriage followed by the birth of children. This is problematic because he or she is approaching physical sexual maturity, yet youth are restrained by societal norms to delay marriage for years, possibly many years. In effect, the extended time between puberty and culturally-approved marriage puts Biblical morality to the profoundest test, perhaps more so for young women than young men.

In a world where sexual restraint is almost unknown, the Christian *EMERGING-ADULT-girl/boy* is met by a Biblical call for sexual purity. One's culture may open the door, especially for boys, for promiscuity, use of pornography and exploitive sex. The resulting sexual impurity robs both the predator (often male) and the victim (usually female) of the virginity that ought to be brought to a marriage — or a life of celibacy. It matters not if the sexual expressions are illicit or consensual. Pressure is often placed predominantly on females to maintain any sexual standards, unfortunately.

In addition to chastity, the Christian youth faces the demands of integrity, and respect for sex as God designed, that is, heterosexual monogamous marriage as the proper environment for human families (see Genesis 2:18-25). As St. Paul instructed young Timothy, "Set an example for other followers . . . by *your* . . . *purity*" (First Timothy 4:12). Preserving one's self-respect and Christian faith in a sexually-permissive environment is a steep slope to climb. Additionally, females often face extremely frustrating circumstances in cultures where only a minority of young males sincerely follow Christ and participate in the Christian community.

Hence, a Christian youth's growing up process must include preparedness for a life of singleness and/or marriage through Biblical sexual restraint. In addition, a thoughtful *EMERGING-ADULT-child* can begin to build necessary maturity into her or his life by:
- Making careful decisions,
- Seeking the guidance of parents,
- Listening to older Christian mentors (such as youthworkers),
- Developing a keen devotional life,
- Acquiring a Biblical work ethic,
- Kindling a conscious desire to serve others and,
- Thus, determining to follow Jesus Christ in all he or she does.

The Bible's concern for families enlarges the scope of maturity to include the extended as well as immediate nuclear family.

→ **Build responsible relationships with family members.** The family was created by God to provide societal stability and perpetuation. The family institution also provides a practicum for spiritual development as both children and parent(s) move toward maturity. One's Christian faith is profoundly tested in the crucible of family life. The Biblical commands to love one another, forgive one another, respect one another and more are not easily obeyed in the intense relationships within a family. Yet it is a measure of Christian maturity.

A Christian *EMERGING-ADULT-boy/girl* must learn to get along maturely with siblings, grandparents and others in the extended family. Fewer shouting matches, reduced complaints, less frequent retaliations and not as much rivalry occur, as the Spirit of Christ produces fruit in an *EMERGING-MAN/WOMAN'S-child's* life. A maturing girl or boy hopefully becomes comfortable with existing family relationships. Moreover, a responsible Christian emerging-adult seeks to promote loving and forgiving interactions among family members.

However, the Bible's prescription for maturing in Christ includes more than being a maturing member of one's family of origin. Growing up also involves responsible action in wider society.

→ **Love God and Neighbor Through Service.** The Bible speaks out forcefully on ways Christians glorify God through a life given to service of humankind. Loving one's neighbor in mature fashion is shown in three ways.
- in hard work (school and/or otherwise),

- in Biblical activism in the community and world,
- in devotion to the Christian community.

How the *EMERGING-ADULT-boy/girl* reaches out to others in dedicated service is described below.

➤ **The Service of Work.** God blessed daily work from the very beginning of human existence, and God's approval continued in spite of the curse that Adam was given in which honest work was turned into tiring toil (see Genesis 3). Throughout the Bible God calls humankind to a life of God-directed service through productive labor.

To fulfill God's expectation for able adults to support themselves, some youth find jobs to help with family living costs. In many poor families, the *EMERGING-ADULT-child's* labor is probably crucial for his or her own survival, and the family's as well. Unfortunately throughout the world millions of youth, primarily males, are unemployed and struggle to subsist in spite of their migration to the world's swelling cities to find work. Only the meanest of jobs is available to them, if any at all. Ideally young men become apprentices for various occupations but these opportunities seem to be rare. Some females are fortunate to enter domestic service, perhaps overseas, whereas countless girls are drawn into sex trafficking, along with some young males.

For those who are jobless, serving God through daily work is more difficult, but not impossible. Diligently looking for work and/or volunteering to work might be an appropriate way to fulfill the mandate from Genesis 2:15, "The Lord God put the man in the Garden of Eden *to take care of it and to look after it.*" Sadly, by contrast, in Mexico, *ninis,* known by other names in other places, are a widespread phenomenon, especially among young men. A *nini* neither works nor goes to school, a potent mixture for social unrest.

Other *EMERGING-ADULTS-children* have the privilege of staying in school and receiving further schooling. The question arises about how they should obey God's command to work. An excellent way for Christ-following students is to apply themselves assiduously to study. This will help them attain suitable academic achievement that may equip them for wider employment and service opportunities later and/or scholarships for future study. Schooling is often the forte of females who thus find it easier to do schoolwork "as unto the Lord." For a variety of reasons, females seem to adapt well to the classroom environment, implying that males may need greater encouragement to make serious study a high priority in their lives.

Lastly, some students combine part-time employment with their schooling, for their own self-support, to aid their family and/or to save for educational expenses. This, too, receives God's commendation for daily work.

Here are some possibilities for service through employment during the years of emerging-adulthood.

EMERGING-MEN-*Boys* and EMERGING-WOMEN-*Girls* AT WORK

• Apprentice	• Janitor
• Bicycle repairer	• Landscaper
• Busboy	• Lifeguard
• Busker (street entertainer)	• Maid (*katulang, work-Mary*)
• Cashier	• Mechanic's helper
• Child care worker	• Nanny
• Cleaner	• Office assistant
• Clerk	• Receptionist
• Construction worker	• Retail clerk
• Cook	• Shelf stocker
• Dock worker	• Teachers' aide
• Driver	• Tout (solicitor of sales, peddler)
• Farm worker	• Vendor
• Filer	• Volunteer worker
• Fisherman	• Waitress/waiter
• Food service worker	
• Gardener	and doubtless others —
• Hawker/vendor	
• Intern	— working in various ways and places to serve God's wider purposes in society.

Each job listed above demands the full concentration of the youthful worker, as in Colossians 3:23-24.

> Whatever you do, put your whole heart and soul into it, as into work done for God, and not merely for men — knowing that your real reward, a heavenly one, will come from God, since you are actually employed by Christ, and not just by your earthly master. (JBP)

The Christian *EMERGING-ADULT-child* also provides light in places where the Good News is sorely needed, in the school, the shop, a restaurant, a retail store, the service trades or on the street. As Jesus eloquently expressed it,

> You [an *EMERGING-ADULT-child*] are like light for the whole world. A city built on top of a hill cannot be hidden, and no one would light a lamp and put it under a clay pot. A lamp is placed on a lampstand, where it can give light to everyone in the house. *Make your light shine, so that others will see the good that you do and will praise your Father in heaven* (Matthew 5:14-16).

Additionally, as St. Paul wrote to the believers in ancient Philippi,

> Do everything readily and cheerfully — no bickering, no second-guessing allowed! Go out into the world uncorrupted, *a breath of fresh air* in this squalid and polluted society. Provide people with a glimpse of good living and of the living God. *Carry the light-giving Message into the night* so I'll have good cause to be proud of you on the day that Christ returns (Philippians 2:14-16, MSG).

Moreover, when *EMERGING-ADULTS-girls/boys* work, they have the opportunity to learn how to use wisely whatever money they earn. That includes the concepts of saving as well as of giving generously to God and others. Work, then, allows the *EMERGING-ADULT-child* to have something to give, as they are able, to those in need, as God expects him or her to do. The pattern of financial stewardship as outlined in the Bible is important to develop during the years of youth. Learning about prudent financial management is especially important for *EMERGING-ADULTS-children* in affluent families and societies.

God's bountiful blessing upon youth's daily work, whether job or study or both, can give them strong motivation to work heartily to benefit their family as well as other people in their world.

➤ **The Service of Christian Community Activism.** The Bible calls youthful believers to live as responsible citizens, using God-given gifts and talents in social action in their community as well as in their school and job. The Bible exhorts young women and men to respect and obey civil authority, except in matters of conscience. As St. Paul expressed it to Titus, "Remind your people to recognize the power of those who rule and bear authority. They must obey the laws of the state and be prepared to render whatever good service they can" (Titus 3:1-2, JBP). Therefore, civil strife fomented largely by young adult males throughout the world must grieve the heart of God as their energies are wasted.

Christian youth activists serve their community as volunteers in, and supporters of, organizations and endeavors that promote justice and human rights. In so doing, they spread the wholesomeness of God's kingdom. They may have opportunity to work alone or alongside other youth and adults in group projects, mission trips, a gap-year term of service and the like.

Youth on the way to maturity develops a proper social conscience by:
- participating in school extra-curricular (or co-curricular) service activities, for example, student government, student publications.
- registering to vote, when and where applicable.
- doing national service (compulsory or otherwise).
- carrying out short-term missions (weeks to years, for example, *Take-Two*, an overseas two-year internship one U.S. mission offers to college graduates).

In summary, the service dimension of life for a Christian young woman or man involves her/his participation in the workplace and/or school, as well as service in the wider community. Beyond that, an *EMERGING-ADULT-boy/girl* shows love for God by being part of a local body of believers, where he/she may learn, worship, grow and serve.

➤ **Devotion to the Family of God.** Youthful believers have a significant service role to play in a congregation, just as a youngish Timothy was advised by the Apostle Paul, "Don't let anyone make fun of you, just because you are young. Set an example for other followers by what you say and do, as well as by your love, faith, and purity" (First Timothy 4:12).

God is at work grooming *EMERGING-MEN/WOMEN-boys/ girls* for leadership and influence within the family of God. In Ephesians 2:10, St. Paul stated, "For we are God's workmanship, created in Christ Jesus to do good works, which God prepared in advance for us to do." Young Christian men and women have been gifted by the Holy Spirit in various ways and therefore need opportunity to serve through the local church and/or parachurch organization(s), as they are able. As they use their gifts, they may become aware of God's call to service among the congregation, as well as in the world around them. So maturing Christian youth are reaching out to others and in so doing are discovering and practicing their spiritual gifts.

All the "one-another" passages in the New Testament presenting life among the congregation are also before them as challenges (see previous chapters).

Their devotion may be enhanced through group service projects sponsored by the local congregation in the local community or in the wider world. The challenge here for young believers is to serve their Christian brothers and sisters, whether in music, leading, helping, teaching or other openings, as suitable opportunities arise for them.

But growing into maturity includes even *more* than caring for one's family, working/studying, and being concerned for others in the world and sisters and brothers within the church body. The Bible presents one more goal for the *EMERGING-MAN/WOMAN-child* who would be mature in Christ.

→ **Care for one's self.** A responsible *EMERGING-ADULT-boy/girl* learns to take care of her or himself in its various dimensions: *physical, mental, devotional and social* (for *social*, see above).

Physical Health: Proper diet, adequate exercise and health routines lead to care of "the temple," as St. Paul describes it in First Corinthians 6:19-20.

> You surely know that *your body is a temple* where the Holy Spirit lives. The Spirit is in you and is a gift from God. You are no longer your own. God paid a great price for you. So use *your body to honor God*.

One of the great challenges for youth is the widespread use of artificial stimulants such as tobacco, alcohol, marijuana, cocaine and/or other harmful drugs. Tragically, it is the consumption of these toxic substances that appear to define "adulthood" in many societies. For example, hard alcohol is often described as "an adult beverage." Many youth are thereby attracted to experimenting with and often becoming addicted to these cravings. A Christian youth who desires to shun these deleterious habits faces serious temptations to follow the crowd.

Devotional health. Then there is the devotional dimension of life, that is, self-edification. The emerging-adult capabilities of boys and girls call for discipline that will stretch the capabilities of the soul. Using an American example, their prayer life may need to be upgraded, from a *"Now-I-lay-me-down-to-sleep"* bedtime prayer to a more mature approach of intercession and adoration.

Now also may come an awakening sense of God's calling on his/her life, in which or she learns to discern and obey God's will. Up to this point in life, they have had parental guidance to know God's will for their lives, but the *EMERGING-ADULT-girl/boy* must begin to do this on their own.

Mental/Psychological Health: A healthy intake of Bible truth helps the adult mind focus on life's realities, whereas extensive exposure to secular thought-patterns is destructive to good character. As St. Paul reminds *EMERGING-ADULTS-children,* ". . . set your minds *and* keep them set on what is above [the higher things], not on the things that are on the earth" (Colossians 3:2, AMP).

Beyond that, with *EMERGING-WOMEN's/MEN's-boys'/girls'* increasing capacity to do abstract thinking, they are becoming ready for learning Biblical history, theological truths and reflection, as might be encountered in some cultures in their confirmation classes. However, the earlier maturation of females gives them greater readiness for in-depth study and understanding. This fact suggests dividing instruction sessions by gender so that boys can be brought along at their own pace and so that, concomitantly, girls are not held back by the boys' lagging mental maturity.

During this period of maturation, a healthy *EMERGING-ADULT-child* will start to come to understand and accept herself or himself. He or she will begin to appreciate what Dr. Bobby Clinton terms, "sovereign foundations, the things you were born with—your heritage."[1] As *EMERGING-ADULTS-children* move toward self-acceptance, they discover how the hand of God has been working on their behalf, as

Egyptian Prime Minister Joseph realized when he told his brothers, "You intended to harm me, but God intended it for good to accomplish what is now being done...."[2]

Gender issues continue to arise, especially in societies where gender distinctives are being erased or at least there are erroneous attempts to do so. *EMERGING-MEN-boys* are often heavily influenced by the media and pressured by their peers to use their aroused sexual instincts to prove their masculinity. In some places, a misguided father might take his son to visit a prostitute as a form of initiation into manhood.[3] Young females may respond to male sexual advances to gain personal acceptance, not realizing that such trysts often mean little to the aggressor, leaving the *EMERGING-WOMAN-girl* defrauded and ultimately disillusioned when she awakens to reality.

Taking responsibility for personal mental health also includes certain disciplines such as learning how to be a good steward with modern communications, that is, the Internet, television, cell phones and social media.

Competitive sports often occupy the mind and time of an *EMERGING-ADULT-child,* predominantly *boys*, perhaps as organized by a school or informally. Participation in team sports is believed to develop physical fitness, mental alertness, teamwork and self-discipline among *EMERGING-ADULTS-children*. It is possible that pride, selfishness and dishonesty may also develop in the student athlete. Ideally a student-athlete would view himself or herself as serving the good of the school or community, by helping to develop a winning team. The temptation for the immature is to allow lesser motives take over his or her motivation.

In summary, growing up into Christ is a multi-faceted set of Biblical expectations that put every Christian woman's and man's commitment to the test, and even more so for those *Emerging-Adults-BOYS/GIRLS* seeking to attain adult status.

The challenge of First Corinthians 14:20-21 rings true for every *EMERGING-ADULT-child*.
How long before you grow up and use your head — your *adult* head? It's all right to have a childlike unfamiliarity with evil; a simple *no* is all that's needed there. But there's far more to saying *yes* to something. Only mature and well-exercised intelligence can save you from falling into gullibility" (MSG).

➤ QUESTIONS TO PONDER ◄

EMERGING-ADULT-children are moving toward adulthood, physically and hopefully in other ways as well.

- QUESTION: How can *EMERGING-ADULTS-children* be motivated to *take seriously the responsibility of growing up?*

- QUESTION: How can God's expectations for maturity outlined in this chapter be communicated to *EMERGING-ADULTS-children?*

- QUESTION: How can parents, youthworkers and congregational leaders facilitate healthy growth processes?

- QUESTION: How appropriate is it to use the term, *kids,* when speaking to or about *EMERGING-ADULTS-children?*

The next chapter presents possibilities for the way forward.

NOTES

[1] Paul Stanley and Bobby Clinton, *Connecting: The Mentoring Relationships You Need to Succeed.* (Colorado Springs: NavPress), 1992.
[2] Genesis 50:20 (NIV).
[3] As reported by several male students at Alliance Biblical Seminary (now Alliance Graduate School), Quezon City, the Philippines, variously in classes 1998-2006.

Chapter 12

Biblical Youth Ministry to and with the *EMERGING-ADULT-Child:*
THE CONGREGATION'S ROLE

Whose responsibility is it? Who is to shepherd, coax, invite, motivate and/or facilitate girls and boys from childhood to adulthood? According to the Bible, what responsibility does the congregation have?

> Youthworker: *"I don't know where to start. But how complex can this be, I mean it's youth ministry? Just go out and have fun with them! Yet, in spite of all the answers floating about, it still seems to be a HUGE mystery."*
>
> Parent: "You're the professional, you know about youth. You're not all that old yourself; you've just gone through all that trauma! How can YOU not 'get it'?"
>
> Youth: "Hey, why are you making this such a big deal? I'm doing pretty well on my own and my friends are basically happy with it all. We're having fun — or trying to. Besides, I've got lots of time to work on growing up. Just relax...."

Youthworker: *"Everyone, just be quiet, all right, please! ... Let me think. What's coming into focus is that as a youthworker I just might be redundant, you know, especially with all this evidence about the responsibility of Christian parents. Maybe I'm just not needed?"*

Parent: "Hold on – just one minute. I wonder if you have ever lived with one of these *EMERGING-ADULT-children?* Whatever the case, *youthworkers* usually know what to do with these *non-children-non-adults*, don't they?"

Youthworker: *"That's simply not true. What do I know, really? O.K., I've attended some seminars, read some books, you know, whatever I can find, looking for new ideas, the more exciting, the better. ... ☺"*

AND GOD SAID ... (May I paraphrase Myself?) "I expect parents to follow through in guiding any children I have given them until they reach maturity. When their offspring are very young, fathers and mothers care for them in every aspect of their being, insofar as they are able. Certain children need special ongoing attention, but most others gradually assume responsibility for their lives and well-being. That's the beginning of maturity. So as the years go by, the parent(s) turn over responsibility in increasing measure to their boys and girls. In short, the yoke of growth is shared early on, until the youth assumes the load for her or himself. Makes sense doesn't it?"

"But there are no perfect parents! Think about it, I'm Perfect – but my children Adam and Eve botched it up. As a result, to achieve full human maturity, children and their parents need to come to Me and admit their powerlessness, their helplessness and their sinfulness. I'm so pleased when they do. I can and do

> [God continuing] forgive them! But that doesn't make them perfect. Therefore, I give them other growing and established believers to come alongside, to empower, train and support them in being part of My family and serving others. That's what *people-power* is, what both youth and parents need to enable maturity. Then they can undertake the callings I have for them in the world. You-all need to be connected with people who will share the burden with you. Now do you understand?"

LATER ... [God continuing]

> *Youthworker, parent and youth* (in unison): "Another paradigm for youth ministry? Possibly an alternative way? A call to action in a clear direction? A renewal of old commitments? Who can know? Whatever the case, ANY change is demanding, even when prompted by the Bible. But who better to lead the assessment over a proposed paradigm for youth ministry than mature leaders of the congregation?"

In pursuing a Biblical motif for youth ministry, the congregation of believers is faced with the challenge of caring for and challenging their youthful members. That is in addition to the specific responsibilities for the development of maturing Christian women and men already outlined for the youth themselves and their parents.

THE BIBLE SAYS ...

The God-intended incubator and habitat for emerging young adults is within their family, even if stressed by poverty or disease, even if fractured by death or divorce or with troubles such as mental disorders, disabilities, addictions, homelessness and the like. Ideally, two Christian parents endeavor to fulfill God's commands to guide, train, teach and otherwise equip their children for serving God in their world (see Chapter 10). Many families realistically fall below this ideal, some may even fail miserably, but in God's plan they are able to rely on Christian sisters and brothers in the body of Christ for support in their parenting.

The New Testament stipulates that congregational leaders take the lead in assessing youth ministry in terms of its faithfulness to the Bible, in order to ensure that youth under the care of the congregation are well-served by their parents and other mentors.

- St. Paul to the Ephesian church leaders. *"Look after yourselves and everyone the Holy Spirit has placed in your care. Be like shepherds to God's church. . .* "(Acts 20:28a).
- St. Peter. "Church leaders, I am writing to encourage you. I too am a leader. . . . Just as shepherds watch over their sheep, *you must watch over everyone God has placed in your care.* Do it willingly in order to please God. . . . Let it be something you want to do. . . . Don't be bossy to *those people who are in your care,* but set an example for them" (First Peter 5:1-3).
- Epistle writer to believers. ". . . Your leaders . . . *are watching over you,* and they must answer to God. . . . Make them happy. Otherwise, they won't be able to help you at all" (Hebrews 13:17-18).

The issues raised in previous chapters lead to a further examination of a Biblical model for youth ministry. In short, *"As a congregation, how well are we doing to ensure that youth:*

- Are connected to the life of our congregation, receiving the love, acceptance and care they deserve?"
- Are being motivated and equipped to grow up into Christian women and men?"
- Are being trained for a life of service to and for Christ in the church and in their world?"
- Are learning how to connect basic Bible truth and Christian theology with daily life?"

More specifically, the senior leaders (elders) of congregations are charged with asking the questions and finding some answers to the youth ministry enigma, as spelled out below.

→ *To what extent do we, as a congregation, desire a multi-generational community? To what extent do we incorporate our youth into the life of our congregation?*

The Hebrew model (see Chapter 8) provides deliberate movement of the *EMERGING-MAN/WOMAN-child* into adult-level involvement in the life of the congregation. As martyr, theologian and unidentified youthworker Dietrich Bonhoeffer wrote, ". . . the church's ministry to the young is primarily about *encountering the living Word of God in the context of the whole church."* This is, of course, the desire of every pastor for the congregation.

So obvious answers to these questions are, "Yes, of course. Why would we want to exclude youth?" However, the question is, "To what extent. . . .?" As in many of the questions raised here, this one beggars facile solutions and requires ongoing vigilance to see it through. For example, American and Canadian churches have so long followed an age-graded system of instruction that it may be time for the pendulum to swing back toward intergenerational education. The prefix, *inter,* infers conversation, dialogue, interchange and mutual encouragement between persons of various ages.

This becomes a marvelous opportunity for reaching across age barriers and an acceptance of youth into the life of the Christian community, but it is a model not easily achieved, requiring considerable expertise and investment.

One flash point for some congregations is the musical genre(s) used for corporate worship services. Musical tastes vary much across the age spectrum, causing dilemmas for musicians and music directors alike. Music is probably only the "tip of the iceberg," in terms of issues that defy integration of youth with the children and other adults in the congregation.

Ideally, every Christian congregation desires to integrate EMERGING-MEN/WOMEN-*children* as believers-in-transition to adulthood, in such a way that no girl or boy feels isolated or abandoned by the congregation. Looking, then, at the *issue of body life* from other perspectives, some questions of implementation arise.

Foremost, how can we communicate to the EMERGING-ADULT-*boy/girl* that she or he is truly loved and accepted for who he or she is now and is becoming (an emerging peer), without becoming condescending?

→ *Related questions are:*

- EMERGING-ADULTS-*boys/girls* make many blunders in the maturation process. *An atmosphere of forgiveness* gives them the space and grace they need to grow in their faith and life. *"How can the love of Christ be shown to wayward youth, within the context of the body of Christ?"* The New Testament includes a marvelous story of a youth's restoration in the story of John Mark, who was rejected by St. Paul as a missionary helper, but probably rehabilitated by the ministry of the disciple, St. Barnabas (see Acts 15:37-39 and Second Timothy 4:11).

- "In what ways do we, or could we, challenge *the giftedness of our youth* within the context of Christian community? How well as a congregation do we facilitate the use of God's gifts in the lives of our *EMERGING-WOMEN/MEN-girls/boys*? To what degree do we provide service opportunities within congregational life for the *EMERGING-ADULTS-children* who are part of our body?"

Adult members of the congregation are expected to use their spiritual gifts to bless others, in teaching, in sharing, in giving, in serving, in helping and in proclaiming Truth. Qualified or eager *EMERGING-ADULT-boys/girls* may also deserve significant in-service roles in the body of Christ (appropriate to their level of maturity). Unfortunately, sometimes the expectation of service for the *EMERGING-MAN/WOMAN-boy/girl* within the congregational setting is limited to child-care as in *nursery duty* and/or music performance, for example, in a *youth praise band*. Many youth need opportunities to take responsibility beyond babysitting, musical expression and/or cameo appearances on the platform.

The Apostle Paul, writing to young Timothy, respected his character and gifting, even though he was young. "Don't let anyone make fun of you, just because you are young. Set an example for other followers by what you say and do, as well as by your love, faith, and purity" (First Timothy 4:12). Later St. Paul encouraged youthful Timothy to use his spiritual gifts. "So I ask you to make full use of the gift that God gave you when I placed my hands on you. Use it well" (Second Timothy 1:6).

One attempt to demonstrate acceptance of youth in some American congregations is an event often termed "Youth Sunday," at which time young men and women contribute to the church gathering through music, testimony and perhaps a sermon or devotional. As helpful as this experience might be for youthful participants, it may simply become a token acceptance of youth into the life of the believing community, rather than an earnest effort to find, develop and use the gifts and talents of youth to benefit the whole body on an ongoing basis.

- When appropriate, how can *mission trips or service projects* include qualified and mature E*MERGING-*A*DULTS-boys/girls* as part of an intergenerational mix?

Sometimes a congregation outgrows its meeting facilities and conducts multiple celebration-worship gatherings. In a worse case scenario youth are expected to participate in a *youth* celebration experience, apart from the rest of the worshipping community of adult believers. They are seemingly thrust aside instead of being included in the life of the adult Christian community. However, where physical space is limited, this may be a necessity, meaning congregational leaders must create other opportunities for mutual edification across generations.

E*MERGING-MEN/WOMEN-children,* as well *emerging-adults-*G*IRLS/BOYS,* want and need to be part of the local Body of Christ so they can move into Christian adulthood smoothly, while learning how to become contributing members now and in the future. The Bible instructs church leaders to ensure this is happening, for the benefit of all the members of the local body of Christ.

➔ *To what extent do we assert that growing youth need older, more mature Christian role models and mentors in addition to their home training?*

Lest these questions be carefully delegated to a

youthworker or church staff, the Bible points toward older believers taking the lead in discipleship responsibilities. A notable example is St. Barnabas who took a young Saul under wing and enabled him to become a premier leader in the early Christian church. Later, Saul/Paul followed his example in his mentorship of Timothy, Titus and others.

St. Paul's letter to a younger leader, St. Titus, encourages mature Christians to mentor, train, teach and guide youth toward full adulthood, particularly those who will provide same-gender guidance.

> [Titus], tell *the older men* to have self-control and to be serious and sensible. Their faith, love, and patience must never fail. Tell *the older women* to behave as those who love the Lord should. . . . *They must teach* what is proper, so *the younger women* will be loving wives and mothers. Each of *the younger women* must be sensible and kind, as well as a good homemaker, who puts her own husband first. . . . [You as a man] Tell *the young men* to have self-control in everything. Always set a good example for others. Be sincere and serious when *you teach* (2:2-7).

For example, in Filipino families, older siblings have considerable influence with younger ones. Hence some youthworkers perceive and present themselves as older brothers (*kuyas*) or older sisters (*ates*) in relationship to their youth ministry members, with focus on same gender interactions. This understanding is in contrast to the "buddy-buddy" ("I'll be your friend") approach sometimes used by immature youthworkers. It also seems to be in line with the New Testament model.

Accordingly congregational leaders/elders want to set appropriate models of maturity before EMERGING-ADULTS-*boys/girls*. When youthworkers are being selected (and/or hired) on behalf of the fellowship, the following questions are suggested in an examination of the types of persons who

should be recruited.
- What diversity of models is exhibited to youth in terms of age, gender and marital status? What is the balance exhibited in the youth leadership staff between:
  ➢ Male *and* female leaders?
  ➢ Married *and* single individuals?
  ➢ Young *and* "old" (as in "over 40") persons?

- To what extent do potential youthworkers strive to exemplify Christian maturity and stability?

- How much life experience do members of the youth ministry team have?

➔ *To what extent are we committed to leading youth into a maturing Christian adulthood? How can we affirm an EMERGING-WOMAN/MAN-girl/boy in the distinctives of Christian womanhood and manhood.*

This two-part question is needed for a congregation to crystallize their goal(s) of youth ministry. The first concerns the ultimate destination hoped for each girl and boy targeted by youth ministry. The second focuses on gender issues.

First, sometimes the goal(s) of *youth ministry* is expressed in reaching boys and girls for Christ, then retaining them in the church or other youth program with basic discipleship training and probably many "fun happenings." Does this go far enough? Probably not.

As proposed earlier, the goal is nothing short of facilitating a healthy passage of boys and girls *into* CHRISTIAN ADULTHOOD which will allow them to change the world(s) they live in, now and in the future. This requires a steadfast pressing toward the mark of *Christian maturity* for each boy or girl, by means of parental guidance and congregational encouragement, and also by effective Biblical teaching. A congregation must ask themselves, "Are we content with anything less than this for our youth ministry?" The attainment of the goal might seem demanding or even elusive, but the Bible calls for Christians to grow up — and for the more mature to show the way to the less mature, i.e., youth ministry.

The Bible encourages EMERGING-ADULTS-*girls/boys* to be becoming the Christian women or men God wants them to be, following the pattern that Jesus set for the youth growth process, as found in Luke 2:52, "Jesus continued to grow in body and mind; he grew also in the love of God and of those who knew him" (JBP). The Biblical expectations for parents and youth to undertake with their EMERGING-MEN/WOMEN-*children* (as expressed in Chapters 10 and 11) also guide congregational leaders in their consideration of their role in facilitating the EMERGING-ADULT-*child* into Christian maturity. "To what extent do we challenge EMERGING-MEN/WOMEN-*boys/girls* to grow up?" One wonders if the widespread use of the American terminology, *kid,* is appropriate to describe the EMERGING-MAN/WOMAN-*child* in youth ministry!

A second related question is the role of gender in human development. In many cultures, the journey to adulthood is markedly different for female and male children. Every culture distinguishes between female and male humankind. At a normal birth, a person's gender is made known, if not identified before birth through amniocentesis or ultrasound. As a result of God's creation molding (Genesis 2), a child finds his or her path of life to be defined by childbearing, at the very least. Only females can produce offspring! Hence, in many cultures, a female's expected destiny includes marriage followed by motherhood.

Almost universally, female children are guided toward future roles as wife and mother, whereas male children are prepared to be able to provide for a future family. God's reproductive plan normatively calls, though not exclusively, for women and men to marry, have children, then care for their progeny, within the sanctity of the marriage of one man and one woman for as long as they both shall live. As set forth in Genesis,

> Then the Lord God said, "It is not good that the man should be alone; I will make him a helper fit for him." . . . But for Adam there was not found a helper fit for him. . . . And the rib that the Lord God had taken from the man he made into a woman and brought her to the man. Then the man said. "This at last is bone of my bones and flesh of my flesh; she shall be called Woman, because she was taken out of Man." Therefore a man shall leave his father and his mother and hold fast to his wife, and they shall become one flesh (2:18, ESV).

At the core is this question about gender: "To what extent do we affirm the differences of men and women as presented in Genesis 1-2 and elsewhere in the Bible?" The congregation's commitment to God's creation of male *and* female is being challenged today in Western cultures. Genesis provides God's clear expectation.

> Then God said, "Let us make man in our image, after our likeness. And let them have dominion over the fish of the sea and over the birds of the heavens and over the livestock and over all the earth and over every creeping thing that creeps on the earth." So God created man in his own image, in the image of God he created him; male and female he created them (1:26-27, ESV).

As the Biblical base of Western cultures erodes, the task of twenty-first-century youthworkers becomes extremely significant. Worldwide popular culture opens the door for gender blurring and the practice of homosexuality, though not in traditional Africa. Therefore, God's people need to be clear about God's definitions of male and female and God's expectations for their relationships.[2]

The blurring of gender identity in some cultures via homosexuality or surgically altered physiology does not call for congregations to be gender-blind. In fact, in face of sexual aberrations (as presented by St. Paul in his letter to the Romans), Bible believers are constrained to confront the lies of Satan about sex and marriage as presented in the media.

Congregations often respond to this reality in adult programming, for example, "men's Bible study," "women's support group," "women's missionary society," or "men's fellowship." But when considering youth ministry, what happens to the Christian commitment to Biblical sexuality and marriage? A Bible-based congregation needs to prepare a resounding response to the lies about singleness and marriage being propagated in today's world, so youth will be adequately taught according to Biblical standards.

Some consequent questions:

- How can we affirm each child's place in the home, school, church and community as providentially *female* or *male*? Instruction on gender appropriate behavior is necessary. EMERGING-ADULTS-*children* who have contact with Western-based media and/or the Internet are being shaped into sexual values and attitudes absolutely antithetical to the Bible. A relativistic basis for morality flies in the face of Biblical certainty, so youth are left wondering what is the right thing to do in all dimensions of morality.
- How can a congregation best enable their boys to become uniquely Christian men and their girls uniquely Christian women?

- How courageous can we be in structuring our teaching activities for EMERGING-ADULTS-*boys/girls*, in such a way that each gender is adequately served at their own level of maturity? For example, girls begin their adolescent growth spurt and maturity-development about two years before boys, on the average [there are many exceptions]. Separating Bible classes, discipleship groups, and/or confirmation classes, for example, by gender contributes to greater in-depth learning, especially when the EMERGING-MEN-*boys* are taught and/or discipled by maturing Christian men.
- What opportunities do young men and women have to build close-knit same-gender relationships? If most youth ministry is carried out coeducationally, what will happen to the distinct needs of boys and girls for single-gender fellowship and discipling?[2] When genders are consistently mixed in social situations, the atmosphere is simply not conducive for the tight-knit bonds such as are formed on an all-boys or all-girls athletic team. Positively stated, EMERGING-MEN-*boys* bond well with other males in the congregation through manly activities. Likewise most girls with feminine interests like a shopping trip, for example, instead of rough-and-tough *futbol*.

  In the Philippines, same gender groups, called *barkadas,* form during secondary school years — and these relationships continue long into adulthood. Why not encourage gender-specific Christian peer groups as part of congregational life. [This does not exclude a menu of options for coeducational approaches.] Today's world calls for distinctly Biblical manhood training and womanhood training, separately and equally, but not identically, given the different roles secular cultures provide for males and females.
- Correspondingly, what parallel wholesome occasions

exist for youth to socialize in coeducational settings?

A cloud may loom on the horizon during these considerations about gender as a part of youth ministry. In short, "We can't find men in our congregation to work with our boys and young men!"

Two answers to this dilemma are proposed, built around other questions:

1. "What is lacking in our ministry to men that we have so few qualified for youth leadership?" Some congregations likely need to develop better sensitivity to boys and men. How this might be done is best devised locally.
2. "What examples do we have from the Bible when men are not available?" In the Old Testament, Deborah was called by God to step into leadership when no male was present for the task at hand. Likewise the first congregation in Europe was co-founded by St. Paul and a business*woman*, Lydia. Often, women, especially mothers, have influenced and do influence young men in positive ways, but the Biblical ideal seems to be a male-bond such as St. Barnabas and St. Paul experienced.

➔ *To what extent do we believe that the Christian family is the primary means for guiding youth into productive Christian adulthood? To what extent do we empower, train and support parents of* EMERGING-ADULTS-*children in their strategic role in the "growing up" process?*

A congregation serious about youth ministry will want to broaden its adult equipping ministries to include parenting issues, if not being done so already. Parents, both Christian and otherwise, need help from the Christian community in knowing how to guide children, especially during the years of adolescence. They also need resources provided to enable them to better fulfill God's goals for them as parents. A congregation that decides to focus on family-helpful ministries arranges for resources, program and personnel to present effective answers to parents and their youth.

→ *To what extent do we have a sense of urgency for manhood and womanhood preparation because our youth may leave our purview at the end of secondary school?*

One of the realities for many congregations is the geographical loss of EMERGING-MEN/WOMEN-*children* about the time of their leaving secondary school or sooner. In many cases, youth leave their home environs and migrate to cities or abroad to seek and perhaps find employment, not only for themselves but also for support of family members left behind in their village, town or small city. In other situations, youth leave for further education in other places, often not to return to their home of origin when schooling is finished because of a lack of job opportunities there.

A congregation committed to the development of Christian *adults* is then faced with an almost impossible situation. Western cultures may foster an extended period of education or other dependence upon parents, often catching the parent, EMERGING-WOMEN/MEN-*children* and the congregation by surprise when the young adult leaves. "It all happened so fast," a parent may assert. Parents may wish they had a longer time to closely steer a youth's progress toward maturity — and in fact they do, even if from afar, because youth often desire their parents' approval as they are maturing.

Likewise a congregation may be caught by surprise, not anticipating the maturation that must be encouraged over a few short years. When there are amorphous goals for youth ministry, the congregation may fall short of stretching the *Emerging-Woman/Man-girl/boy* intellectually, socially and spiritually. This can be seen in programs that seem to major on promoting events and "happenings" rather than maturity-building. Meanwhile, time goes on, youth disappear, especially young men, and the maturing process is deferred to other influences, that is, work place, university campus, military service or unemployment.

When an appropriate urgency is recognized, steps may be taken to accelerate the process. For example, some congregations depend on catechism classes to open the door for youth to greater understandings of Christianity, a wonderful first step. However, if what follows an initial catechetical training is an agenda consisting of "relevant topics" and/or a *potpourri* of devotional thoughts delivered by a sincere youthworker, it is falling short of what can be achieved by an advanced Biblical/theological curriculum. The challenge for the congregation is to expect the *Emerging-Adult-boy/girl* to wrestle with significant theological issues — and ensure that this is happening. The challenge for the youthworker is to teach the substance of God's Word so that it is interesting and relevant.

A related example is the result of shortchanging youth intellectually. During earlier years, children of the church hear much-repeated Bible stories, but often what is retained may be disconnected and unrelated, except perhaps knowing that the Bible narrative begins with, "In the beginning God created the heavens and the earth" (Genesis 1:1). But as youth gain greater ability in abstract thinking, they are ready for solid instruction in Biblical chronology, church doctrine and church history. Thus, more careful attention to a curriculum of "youth maturation" encourages an enriched diet of teaching and learning during the *Emerging-Men/Women-children* years. It is reasonable to expect that youth receive a quality and depth of Bible and theological instruction equivalent, if not superior, to that received by adults in the congregation.

Consequently, Christian youth ministry achieves its God-given goals when the preparation for maturing adulthood philosophy permeates it from top to bottom. It also provides a focused urgency appropriate to the end-of-secondary-school deadline.

"What an order! We can't go through with it," might be the response of some congregations. Yet a deep respect for Bible truth compels the Christian community to pursue the implications above and contemplate the questions below.

> ➤ **QUESTIONS FOR CONGREGATIONAL LEADERS TO PONDER** ◄
>
> *Where Do We Start? Or, More Specifically:*
>
> - In what ways might we stimulate our congregation to follow a Biblical approach to youth ministry that may be countercultural?
>
> - How well does our church body facilitate the individual growth of children and youth, both female and male?
>
> - How well do we communicate to the *EMERGING-ADULT-child* the full extent of the Bible's expectations for them as they are growing up?
>
> - To what extent does the "youth ministry" of our congregation focus on:
>
>   - Individual mentoring and discipling, boys with men, girls with women?

> - Inductive and in-depth Bible study and teaching?
> - Service, in the school/community and in the church-fellowship?

But what about our faithful youthworker(s)? What's their place in the ministry? Chapter 13 explains this more fully.

NOTES

[1] Andrew Root, "Stop Worrying About the Millennials" (*Christianity Today*, January/February 2015, Volume 59, No. 1), 36.

[2] Some babies are born with chromosonal, hormonal and/or developmental problems that make sex identification problematic. For example, ambiguous genitalia is a rare condition in which the external genitals are not clearly male or female at birth. Between 0.1% and 0.2% of live births are of ambiguous nature, requiring across-the-board sensitivity by physicians, parents, pastors, teachers and youthworkers. Also, chromosone variations, such as Klinefelter or Turner Syndrome, may create gender issues that may not be discovered into later in childhood, even into puberty. Persons with either Klinefelter or Turner Syndrome are sexually sterile and should be cared for by endrocrinologists.

[3] In the author's experience, what actually happens is that when youth ministry bends toward a feminine world, the result is a sharp falling away of the participation of male youth as the years pass. It is so common a phenomenon that it is surprising so little concern is expressed about it in youth ministry literature. D.C.J.

Chapter 13

Biblical Youth Ministry to and with the *"EMERGING-WOMAN/ MAN-Child"* ROLE OF THE YOUTHWORKER

What responsibility does the YOUTHWORKER have to shepherd, coax, invite, motivate and/or facilitate girls and boys from childhood to adulthood? What does the Bible say?

Elder: "That's 'serious stuff' [in the preceding chapters]! What do you make of all that?"

Youthworker: *"Well, you mean all those Bible references and inferences? Almost too much for me — you know, I have to prepare for a youth meeting tonight!"*

Elder: "Just give me a minute, please? All those questions are hard to swallow, don't you think?"

Youthworker*: "Yeah, well, so much theorizing! How can I make time for that? I've got a youth retreat to put together, and fast!"*

> *Elder:* "You are busy, that's for sure. Personally, I have never regarded youth ministry as much more than getting the Gospel to youth while making sure it was lots of *fun*." [In American vernacular, fun means the hilarious, exuberant, ludicrous, nonsensical, comical, farcical, lively, silly and playful.]
>
> Youthworker: *"Really? It's more than that, as you know. We try to teach the Bible diligently, though with seventy-five fidgety middle-schoolers looking me in the face every Wednesday night, it's not easy."*
>
> *Elder* "*Yes, the Bible!* That is supposed to be the foundation of our ministry, and you'd agree. But it's scary to look at what might be an alternative paradigm."
>
> Youthworker: *"I'm willing if you are. Let's go for it, but not now — I've got to run."*

QUESTIONS FOR YOUTHWORKERS TO PONDER
Regarding the Ministry to and with the *"EMERGING-ADULT-Boy/Girl"*

An earnest *youthworker* faces another paradigm with great trepidation. Possibly it shakes the foundations of all that she or he has done in youth ministry. Or, on the other hand, it may articulate concerns the *youthworker* has entertained for a long time, yet not known how to express. Whatever the case, a Biblical approach to youth ministry, as interpreted through the eyes of impending adulthood, is worthy of earnest pursuit.

To summarize the previous pages from the perspective of a *youthworker*, revisit the following overarching questions:

- "To what extent are youth being motivated and equipped to grow up into Christian women and men?"

  - "To what extent are youth learning how to connect basic Bible truth and Christian theology with daily life?"

  - "To what extent are EMERGING-MEN/WOMEN-children being trained for a life of service to and for Christ in the Christian community and in their world?"

- "To what extent do youthworkers believe that the Christian family is the primary means for guiding youth into productive Christian adulthood?"

- "To what extent are EMERGING-ADULTS-boys/girls connected to the life of our congregation and receiving the love, acceptance and care they deserve?"

Who can answer these questions? A good starting point is consultation with parents. Other useful thoughts can be gathered from the congregation's church elders and staff. Moreover, everyone in the congregation who deals with youth on an ongoing basis has worthwhile insights. The most mature of the EMERGING-ADULT-girl/boy community also have input to make. Lastly, the insights from the Holy Spirit help to shed light on answers.[1]

Whatever conclusions are reached, it is helpful to evaluate one's youth ministry more specifically by asking the following questions.

1. In what ways can *youthworkers* motivate and equip youth to be growing into gradually-maturing CHRISTIAN MEN AND WOMEN?

a. "To what extent is *guiding youth to adulthood* a conscious goal in all we do? To what extent is our time and effort spent on substantial issues that move toward that goal?"
b. "In what ways do we challenge youth to 'grow up'?"[2]
c. "How can the composition of our *youthworker* cadre provide a variety of Christian adult role models for youth?"
   (1) Gender mix? Where are vibrant Christian men to show EMERGING-MEN-*boys* that it is possible to follow Christ and not lose one's masculinity?
   (2) Age groups? What's wrong with being over 40? A little gray hair (or even a lot!) may help to exhibit what *maturity in Christ* looks like.
   (3) Marital status? Ought not EMERGING-WOMEN-*girls* come to realize that it is possible to be single *and* fulfilled? Likewise, ought not models of Christian marriage be presented as an alternative to the romantic and exploitive notions of secular society?
d. "How committed are we to the Biblical concept of God's creation of male and female as well as the divine institution of one-man/one-woman marriage? Where does this show up in our teaching? To what extent is this an ongoing emphasis?"
e. "How satisfactorily are our boys taught at their level of maturity, especially during the early years of adolescence? Our girls?" [SUGGESTION: Girls on the whole are maturing faster than boys and therefore are ready for substantive learning at a younger age. This is often true until the latter years of secondary school, or even later.]
f. "How can we make it normative for our *emerging-men-BOYS* to be taught and directed by our maturing Christian men? Our GIRLS by maturing Christian women?"

g. "What opportunities exist for *EMERGING-ADULTS-children* in our fellowship to build close-knit social clusters of males-only and females-only?"
h. "What occasions are there in our congregation for *EMERGING-ADULTS-boys/girls* to participate in healthy coeducational activities and events?"
i. "What opportunities exist for individual mentoring and discipleship, boys with Christian men, girls with Christian women?"
j. "In what ways do we recognize the multifaceted nature of the lives of *EMERGING-ADULTS-girls/boys*, realizing they are not only *'students'* but also children in a family, hopefully church members, possibly participants in extra-curricular activities, possibly part-time employees? How might we help them to become helpful and conscientious servants of God in each environment in which they find themselves?"

2. How can *youthworkers* enable a better integration of *EMERGING-MEN/WOMEN-children* with the body life and ministry of the wider congregation?
   a. "In what ways are the gifts and talents of our youth being employed as channels of blessing to the wider congregation? How can this be improved?"
   b. "If *Youth Sunday* is part of our congregational tradition, how can it be used more effectively to integrate the body of Christ?"
   c. "How can our *EMERGING-ADULTS-boys/girls* and other adults work together in more assimilated fashion in service and outreach in the community and to the world?"
   d. "If youth have separate worship services in our congregation, how can this age segregation be muted, overcome or changed?"

3. To what extent do *youthworkers* believe that the Christian family is the primary means for guiding youth into productive Christian adulthood? To what extent are parents of *EMERGING-ADULTS-children* being empowered, trained and supported in their strategic role in the "growing up" process? What is being done to support parents who seek to be Biblically-obedient.
   a. "To what extent do we rigorously stand with parents in affirming to youth the principle of respect for parents and obedience to them? Do we teach it unashamedly and consistently?"
   b. "In what ways do we seek the input from and the cooperation of parents in youth ministry, aside from their probable roles in providing transportation, refreshments, being a disciplinarian, etc.?"
   c. "How can parents participate more fully in supportive prayer underpinning for our youth ministry?"
   d. "What opportunities are there in our youth ministry for:
      1) Parents to learn how to understand their growing children so they can better communicate with each other? Also about cultural influences on youth?"
      2) Youth to acquire some grasp of what their parents face in life and come to honor them?"
      3) Youth to be exposed to healthy marriages as ideals for themselves?"
      4) Parents to be encouraged to be responsible for, yet not unreasonably overbearing with, their adolescent children?"
      5) Families in oppressively authoritarian cultures become Biblically counter-cultural?"
   e. "What is the ideal relationship for *youthworkers* to seek to build with parents whose life and values are seemingly non-Christian?"
   f. "How can families living in adult-centered, authoritarian cultures become Biblically counter-cultural in

relating to their *EMERGING-ADULTS-children?"*

g. "How can we serve as effective go-betweens for youth and their parents? How can we build bridges of trusting relationships?"

4. "To what extent do *youthworkers* have a sense of urgency for manhood and womanhood preparation because their youth may leave their purview at the end of secondary school?

5. "To what extent are youth learning how to connect basic Bible truth and Christian theology with daily life, now and in their future?"
   a. "To what extent do our programs focus on *maturity-building* at their core and focus, in contrast to activities-for-activities sake?"
   b. "In what ways does our teaching ministry enable an *EMERGING-MAN/WOMAN-child* to develop an expanding understanding of the basic content of the Bible and its themes? Do we treat them like ADULTS or babies?" [Cf., "You need to be taught the simplest things about what God has said. You need milk instead of solid food. People who live on milk are like babies who don't really know what is right." Hebrews 5:12b-13]
   c. "What opportunities do our *EMERGING-ADULTS-girls/boys* have to dig deeper into theology, church history and faith?

Youthworker: *"Whew! All these questions I'm supposed to ponder. I didn't know this was going to require rethinking almost everything I've ever done."*

Maestro de iniciación: "What can I say? It is what it is. Seems like a commitment to Biblical Truth calls for some active response."

> *Youthworker:* "I am committed, but I simply didn't know. So where do I go from here?"
>
> *Maestro de iniciación:* "You can do it; I know it. Read on to Part III to get some pointers on next steps."
>
> *Youthworker:* "Will you go with me? I feel like I really need a mentor now!"
>
> *Maestro de iniciación:* "You know my answer. Let's GO!"

SPECIAL SECTION TO EMERGING-ADULT YOUTHWORKERS

Some congregations assign some of the youngest of their adult membership and professional staff to be the official *youthworkers*. The chief justification for these decisions is the unproven assumption that "twenty-something-year-olds" will be best able to relate to youth. Unfortunately, many young adult *youthworkers* still struggle with their own maturity issues, perhaps causing them to interact uncomfortably with their parent constituency. Perhaps more importantly, they may be deficient at setting a model of maturity for the youth under their direction.

> "How can some of us *youthworkers*, perhaps barely out of adolescence ourselves, overcome the disadvantages that come with our own personal life inexperience?"

NOTES

[1] "Holy hunches!" in American parlance.

[2] A related semantic question specifically for Americans is: "How appropriate is it to use the term, *kids*, when speaking to or about EMERGING-ADULTS-children?"

PART III –

CHANGING THE WORLD

Chapter 14

A PATH THROUGH ADOLESCENCE

Youthworkers are confronted with a daunting challenge — helping parents and other interested parties pilot their children from childhood to a Christian adulthood. Because the modern world is filled with ambiguities about what constitutes maturity, parents and adolescents alike find it extremely difficult to find their way.

A strong temptation exists, to look wistfully back to Bible times and traditional cultures when crossing over into adulthood was so well defined. But modernity marches on. There seems to be no way to stop the press of commercialism, the demand for more education and/or the push to conform to media images. Both youth and their parents are affected by this, though differently. Parents from a traditional village setting may be baffled by the changes their youth are undergoing. Meanwhile, the youth seem to flow along with whatever and whoever is trendy. Oftimes Christian youth programs seem to get caught up in whatever seems up-to-date, sometimes shattering cultural boundaries.

In traditional settings, when village children leave for their respective male or female initiations, the whole community is buzzing with excitement. No longer will these girls or boys frolic around the edges of adult happenings, nor be found nearby to assist in daily tasks with mother or father. When they return from initiation ceremonies, these young men and women will start working, getting married and setting up households, communing with adults, and worshipping/celebrating with the clan; in short, living as adults, grown-ups.

In so doing, they must first leave childhood behind, then undergo the perils and thrills of their training during initiation and lastly cross the threshold into adulthood. All of this can take place in days, weeks or months — and then it is over. *Voilà,* no adolescent upheavals to worry anyone — adulthood achieved!

In Westernized and Westernizing cultures, however, the process becomes extremely complicated and confusing. The three turning points are often hazy and ambiguous, and in some cases may not occur at all. To complicate things further, almost every adult retains some *childishness,* that is, immaturity and/or self-centeredness, in their being. While the preservation of child*likeness* is important for adult life, child*ishness* leads to broken relationships, divorce, criminal behavior, addictions and similar shortcomings. Attaining full maturity is an ephemeral goal, but worth striving for. As St. Paul expressed it,

> I have not yet reached my goal, and I am not perfect. But Christ has taken hold of me. So I keep on running and struggling to take hold of the prize. My friends, I don't feel that I have already arrived. But I forget what is behind, and I struggle for what is ahead. I run toward the goal, so that I can win the prize of being called to heaven. This is the prize that God offers because of what Christ Jesus has done (Philippians 4:12-14).

Moreover, the overt process of maturation may take years to complete, from the onset of puberty until an individual reaches age 30, possibly. This long extension of financial dependence on parents often occurs when any graduate school education is factored in. Meanwhile, the tension exists,

- "Am I an adult — or not?"
- "May I still amuse myself in childish and irresponsible pursuits, for example, intoxicating liquor parties — or must I settle down and work?"
- "Do I need to grow up when everything around me shows me otherwise? Is sexual accountability part of maturity, even if scoffed at by contemporary Western culture?"

Parents, youthworkers, teachers and the public at large look on, as baffled as the youth.

> Youthworker: *"Hey, let's just stop right here. My head is swimming with the murkiness of it all. But I do want to minister to youth along the whole passage to adulthood!"*
>
> *Maestro de iniciación:* "Mine, too. And murky it is, also mysterious and ill-defined. But it's more understandable if you think of it in terms of *three turning points*, with a vast plateau of *ambiguities in between*."
>
> Youthworker: *"You mean we can try to measure maturity development as part of youth ministry?"*
>
> *Maestro de iniciación:* "Maybe not measure but at least make better sense of what is going on with adolescents in the modern world."
>
> Youthworker: *"I'm all for that. Bring it on. I'm listening for all it's worth!"*

In an attempt to untangle the conundrum of adolescence, a division into *three phases* paralleling traditional initiations offers some clarification.

- First, *leaving the village* for initiation.
- Second, *success in initiation*, receiving the necessary preparation for adulthood, including wise parental guidance, formal education (in the Western and Westernizing world), and possibly vocational training. Optimally, care from a Christian congregation with its attendant youth and young adult ministries will be included.
- Lastly, *returning to the village*, passing over the threshold into well-developed maturity for functioning effectively as a person, family member, worker, community member and child of God.

PHASE ONE, LEAVING CHILDHOOD

Every culture has expectations for children. Exasperated parents may say to an adolescent acting immaturely, "Don't be so childish." Both the youth and the parents subconsciously acknowledge what is considered "childish" and what is not.

The question to be raised — what attitudes and actions are typical of children in a given culture? If playing with toys is considered childish, then the emerging adolescent will soon abandon them; for example, a girl would not play with her dolls any longer (though she might embellish her university dorm bed with a few — but *not* as *toys*). A teenage boy in the Western world will have abandoned his *Lego* blocks — or at least not let his friends know that he plays with them.

If asked when a child exits babyhood, one might answer, "When he or she is able to feed himself or herself." Or, at a later date, "When she or he is able to get dressed in the morning without help." But the departure from *childhood* perhaps is less clear-cut, at least for males. Girls have no choice when it comes time to move up — their bodies tell them. They may in their hearts still desire to climb trees, or swim naked on a Scandinavian beach, or play with dolls, but menstruation warns them that those days are drawing to a close.

Little boys find puberty coming to them gradually — a hair or two here, a squeaking of the voice there, the growing allure of girls. The sexual awakening may be a surprise or welcomed, but it comes in any case. Boys seem to have a harder time giving up their toys, physically and symbolically.

Whatever the case, parents know that a child is transitioning to adolescence when she or he responds to a protective admonition, "I'm not a baby!"

In many cultural situations, the exit from childhood involves not only a rejection of childhood behavior, but also the adoption of another culture. For example, a child growing up in Latin America is likely to want to speak and use Spanish or Portuguese, the prestige languages, rather than the indigenous idiom of their parents. This phenomenon is the despair of Bible translators who labor intensively for years to prepare a Bible in the indigenous tongue, only to have the younger generation rejecting the dialect as inferior. Moreover, the prestige language is usually the language of the classroom, so a young person who desires to advance educationally must master it, rather than their mother tongue. Furthermore, other tribal ways may be put aside, in favor of urban clothing styles, worldly aspirations, trendy music and electronic gadgets. The young person moving to the city often feels that to live in traditional ways represents naïveté and banality. Hence, youth may more or less turn their back on their origins in their desire to adopt urban, i.e., Westernized ways and/or language. They may need help from their youthworkers in understanding both the culture into which they are moving and their special status as, in effect, "third-culture kids," not in actuality belonging to either their old way of life or their new one.

In nations such the United States, Canada, Australia, and the United Kingdom, a token of the departure from childhood might be the possession of their first house-key. This tells the child that the parents believe he or she is responsible to be left alone at home. Another symbol, depending on the family, is receiving one's own cell/mobil phone to use. The entrance to American middle school is often a signal of the transition, though boys are slower to find much maturity.

In countries where secondary schools are not available in rural areas, the time when a student moves away from the village farm to a town or city dorm is definitely a "good-bye" to childhood.

Some religious traditions recognize a ceremony like *bar mitzvah* or *confirmation* as the equivalent to leaving childhood. However, one might question doctrinally-heavy Christian confirmation classes when the lack of brain development of young adolescents leads to incomplete understanding of credal concepts. Moreover, in certain denominational settings, *confirmation* may be seen as graduation from church school or other religious instruction, undermining the work needing to be done intellectually and spiritually during adolescence.

Perhaps there are ways parents can assist their child to see the need to move ahead in life by helping them say "good-bye" to childhood. Increased responsibility may be given to the child, commensurate with their age. Giving tangible and useful help to the family may be one way to achieve this. Conceivably it is time, in affluent homes, to sort through unused children's clothing and belongings and donate them to a local charity. It is a challenging task for parents to adjust to the idea that their offspring is now an *emerging-adult-*C*hild* (see Chapter 9) but it must be done.

Likewise, the local congregation may be able to make available mature women and men who will become "caring adults" for blossoming adolescents. Possibly, a transition ceremony to recognize "graduation" from childhood could enhance the boy's or girl's awareness that they are entering a new stage of life with attendant privileges AND responsibilities. If movement to Phase Two requires a physical move (for example, to a more advanced school in a distant city), the congregation might plan a "sending away" celebration, wishing the new student success in their further preparation.

> Youthworker: *"Wait! Don't go any further. I need to think about this."*
>
> *Maestro de iniciación:* "You want to re-examine your own maturity?"
>
> Youthworker: *"Not exactly. But I will if you will."*
>
> *Maestro de iniciación:* "Let's do it together! Want to look at the agenda for growing up in Chapter 1 or in Chapter 10?"
>
> Youthworker: *"Why not both? We can learn from the process."*
>
> *Maestro de iniciación:* "Here we go. In Chapter 1 we are being asked:
> - To what extent do you and I value *social interdependence?*
> - To what extent are you and I *economically competent?*
> - To what extent do you and I have *healthy family interdependence?*
> - To what extent do you and I *participate in the life of the Christian community?*

- To what extent do you and I contribute to *the civic dimensions* of society, locally, nationally, globally?
- In what ways are you and I *healthy personally?*"

Youthworker: *"This may take us some time. Maybe we should look at the other checklist?"*

Maestro de iniciación: "Why not? The list in Chapter 10 isn't so different. What about our proficiency in the following:
- Building and maintaining healthy *family* relationships?
- Serving God and our neighbor in *daily work*?
- Honoring God through *community service*?
- Ministering in and among a *Christian congregation*?
- Caring for one's *self?*"

Youthworker: *"That's enough! It scares me, because I have much to work on personally. But also because we are faced with helping parents empower their children for these issues. How do we do that?"*

Maestro de iniciación: "Additionally, we must put together a training scheme that will enable the *emerging-adult-CHILD* to make some progress toward maturity."

Youthworker: *"Don't you think this maturity emphasis is a little severe for a young adolescent? I mean, it's demanding for me. Why shouldn't we just let them have some* fun *at this stage?"*

Maestro de iniciación: "We have *no time*. They are probably leaving in just a few years. There's an urgency here, don't you see?"

> Youthworker: *"Suppose I don't want to see it? It's frightening to think about. But, O.K., I give up! So let's plunge deeper into the still-to-be-explored depths of adolescence."*

PHASE TWO, A COMMITMENT TO CHRISTIAN ADULT LIFESTYLE

At a certain point, youth must take a further step toward their eventual maturity. Given the promiscuity fervently promoted through Western media, *emerging-adults-children* quickly absorb the message that sexual savvy is the true measure of being grown up. Sadly, they are captivated by sexual indulgence due to their easy access to internet sites, social media and television in many parts of the world. They are deceived to think the following are steps toward adulthood:
- First crush and flirtation
- First date
- First kiss
- Mutual masturbation
- Oral sex
- Losing one's virginity
- Fathering or birthing a child.

What a mockery of the Bible's standards for sexual purity! How tragic! What a challenge for parents and youthworkers to tackle! More than the wisdom of Solomon and/or an annual talk on sex will be needed to offset this tide of moral pollution around the globe! Maturity certainly requires more than sexual so-called sophistication.

Other false measures of adulthood, such as underage drinking and/or alcohol abuse, illicit drug use, smoking or carrying a gun, invite adolescent involvement. These erroneous symbols of maturity ensnare many EMERGING-ADULTS-*boys/girls*. When peer pressure is factored in, the appeal of these false paths of adulthood is enormous. It is only natural that youth want to prove themselves! But are there not safer transitions to maturity?

Rather, at the heart of the issue, the *emerging-adult-CHILD* must shift gears and make a determination to *grow up*. Here are some possible forms this move toward true adulthood might take:

- A pledge to maintain sexual purity.
- A promise to finish secondary school. For example, out of ten children who enter Grade 1 in the Philippines, only three will finish high school.
- Updating one's previous commitment to Christ as a product of a maturing faith rather than simply a childhood decision.
- A new commitment to concentrate on scholastic studies.
- A decision to embark on military service.
- A plan to advance to a university education.
- A resolution to interact responsibly with their parents.
- Embarking on rigorous preparation for a specific career.
- A combination of these.

In each case, the young person is saying, "I no longer want to be an *emerging-adult-CHILD*, but rather an EMERGING-ADULT-*child*." The youthful person is coming to the place where they begin to understand their inner personhood and are able to articulate it to others, that is, in the words of a designer of a 21st-century humanistic rite-of-passage, "to know where you stand, what you value, what you desire, what you tolerate and what you don't. . . ."[1]

In order to do this, the adolescent will need careful and

wise guidance from their parents and elders, as well as a willingness to accept instruction.

Some ethnic/religious/social groups acknowledge this step toward adulthood with celebrations or other recognitions. Unfortunately, many of these seem to have only vague grounding in the steps to maturity they originally represented. Here are some:

- *Sweet Sixteen* birthday party — or 18th or 20th birthday!
- Debutante balls; senior prom; cotillion.
- Earning a driving license (one of the few concrete gauges for adult status in affluent societies — in some cases, owning a car).
- Getting a job.
- Enlisting in military service.
- Joining through hazing into a university fraternity, sorority or other group.
- Leaving home to matriculate at a distant university.
- Graduation from secondary school (often with a subsequent party). For example, *Australian Schoolies Week*, a graduation festival celebrated by Year 12 school leavers.
- *Confirmation* in middle teen years that affords the participants opportunity to receive the Christian faith more authentically than when conducted at an earlier age.

In considering these attempts to measure progress toward maturity, one realizes that a youth's conscious decision to move in that direction is more of an individual matter. If that is the case, an *EMERGING-ADULT-child's* participation in communal events, such as graduation, confirmation and senior proms, becomes fairly meaningless, unless it is accompanied by personal authenticity.

However, a group recognition may be helpful in publicly confirming the fact that the obligations of adult life are being faced and accepted, as is the intention of the final step of *confirmation*, that is, to join the church as an adult member. In traditional initiations, the successful initiates declare their allegiance to the community upon their return — and the community welcomes them back. A group confessional of some sort may build the comraderie supportive of follow-through on one's individual commitment, along with the reinforcement of the congregation. How to combine sincere personal commitments with group affirmation is something for youthworkers to wrestle through.

Whatever the case, an *EMERGING-ADULT-boy/girl* is ushered into the final stages, perhaps over many years, from commitment to fruition. During this stage, in addition to grappling with the stiff demands of emerging maturity, some intensely-personal questions may arise. According to one experienced youthworker these are:[2]

- Who am I beneath my social *persona*?
- What is life about, beyond learning a skill, getting a job, establishing a primary relationship, or raising a family?
- What unique . . . gift do I bring to the . . . human community [and to the family of God]?
- What, for me, is the difference
  ➢ between sex and romance,
  ➢ between survival and living,
  ➢ between a social network and true community,
  ➢ between school and real learning,
  ➢ between a job and soulwork [a calling]?
- What is death . . . honor, consciousness, the universe, soul, spirit?

To these must be added,
- What does it mean to be fully Christian in the world?
- What is God's will for me and my life. "But more than anything else, put God's work first and do what

he wants. Then the other things will be yours as well" (Matthew 6:33).
- How can I serve and love others through my life?
  - ➢ When I was hungry, you gave me something to eat, and when I was thirsty, you gave me something to drink. When I was a stranger, you welcomed me, and when I was naked, you gave me clothes to wear. When I was sick, you took care of me, and when I was in jail, you visited me (Matthew 25:35-36).
  - ➢ You are like salt for everyone on earth. But if salt no longer tastes like salt, how can it make food salty? All it is good for is to be thrown out and walked on. You are like light for the whole world. A city built on top of a hill cannot be hidden, and no one would light a lamp and put it under a clay pot. A lamp is placed on a lampstand, where it can give light to everyone in the house (Matthew 5:13-15).

PHASE THREE, CROSSING THE THRESHOLD INTO ADULTHOOD

"Have I arrived?" This is a reasonable question for an EMERGING-ADULT-girl/boy to ask as the long road through adolescence to adulthood seems to be ending. Unfortunately, the directional signs along this road are very confusing, even within a single culture. In the United States, someone who reaches the age of 18 may legally vote, serve in the military, drink beer and wine (but not whiskey), get married without parents' permission (though not true in all states). However, sometimes younger teens may be charged with an "adult crime." In child custody cases, children of reasonable age may testify, as determined by a judge, concerning their wishes. So when is a child old enough to make that adult-

type decision? To add to the confusion, children may stay on their parents' health coverage until age twenty-six, according to U.S. Federal Law.

Persons at age 18 may buy cigarettes in many U.S. states, but not in all. In contrast, in many European nations, persons of any age may buy cigarettes. But in Japan, it is illegal to smoke a cigarette before the age of 20. Concurrently, Western visual mass media presents smoking as a mature activity. Is there any wonder youth find the achievement of adult status so elusive?

As another example of ambiguity, the age when an "adult" can donate blood varies across the globe. In Europe, some countries allow 17-year-olds to give blood, but others require age 18. Outside Europe, the lower limits vary from 15 to 18. In the U.S., a youth must be at least 17 years old to donate, but some states allow a younger age.[3]

The world of further education also proves elusive. For example, in the United States one hundred years ago, a person completing a high school education was highly regarded. Later a university degree became a more notable achievement. Currently, a Master's degree is the coin of the realm in the Western world. The bar to be crossed into adulthood gets raised higher and higher. Students are often thrust into financial dependence on their parents long after they are otherwise able to care for themselves.

Beyond education is the work world. When a graduate enters the work force, the expectation is that she or he will soon find a "real" job. In some parts of the world, for example, India and Africa, "real" means a white-collar, and/or a desk job. In fact, in the U.S.A. a young person with a degree who ends up in blue-collar work is regarded with some disparagement. The *EMERGING-ADULT* worker whose call is outside the norm faces questions about their maturity level. Likewise, in many parts of the world, a single woman is regarded as not entirely "grown up" and often exiled to the youth department in the church. Also, a married woman without a child is sometimes perceived as not quite "grown up," encouraging couples, in the Philippines for example, to have a baby within the first year of marriage.

Getting older by itself does not cause us to mature psychologically. Adolescence is not at all confined to our teen years. And adulthood cannot be meaningfully defined as what happens in our twenties or when we fulfill certain responsibilities, such as holding down a job, financial independence, or raising a family. Rather, an adult is someone who understands why he *[sic]* is here on Earth, why he was born, and is offering his unique contribution to the . . . world.[4]

ACCEPTANCE INTO THE ADULT WORLD

Traditional initiations feted newly-minted adults with dancing, feasting and for-adults-only fellowship. Such events cemented the self-image of the young adults that they were indeed now fully mature in the eyes of the community. They basked in that recognition and reincorporation into village life. They knew they had crossed the threshold into adulthood and so did their new peers.

What this means in various cultural settings in the twenty-first century must be carefully hammered out by those who desire to receive *young adults* with their new identity.

> ➤ QUESTIONS TO PONDER LATER ◄
>
> • What parallels to traditional village celebrations for new adults exist for young adults in the Christian congregation?

> - How can emerging adults be genuinely and deeply affirmed as members of the body of Christ? Is a swearing-in-ceremony for church membership sufficient? Perhaps. Might adult believers baptism be another landmark of faith for emerging adults?
>
> - What other ways exist to encourage *EMERGING-ADULTS* as they mature, to acknowledge their change of status, from one phase to another?
>
> - How can individual growth decisions made by an *EMERGING-ADULT* be honored corporately without manipulating premature and/or insincere results?

CONCERNED FOLKS

Moving youth toward God's goal of becoming mature in every way requires intense and earnest effort by all parties concerned: the young person, the parent(s), the youthworkers, exemplars of the congregation and society as a whole.

- Little growth occurs unless the *EMERGING-ADULT-CHILD* undertakes for themselves the concept of preparing themselves for adulthood. Opportunities need to be given for growing children to accept the challenge of increasing responsibility. The process is much aided by eliciting youth's enthusiastic response. But *emerging-adults-boys/girls* should be forewarned, "You will clash with youth culture around you." In so doing, they become the salt and light that Jesus desires (Matthew 5:13-16).

- Parents have God-given responsibility and opportunity to guide and mold the lives of children in their care. They are often upended when the youth's need for Western-style individuation bumps up against their ideas of parental authority. Christian parents need all the encouragement, training and support they can get.

- Youthworkers and congregational leaders want to be available as models for youth as boys and girls may find the growing-up process to be baffling and sometimes utterly frustrating.

- Contemporary Western society seems conflicted about its desires for youth. On the one hand, amazingly optimistic expectations are placed on upcoming generations. A sentiment oft spoken at graduation ceremonies goes like this, "You can be anything you want to be." This is certainly a falsehood, but it is widely believed, even though the Bible communicates the truth about humankind, that is, all are flawed and helpless without God. On the other hand, Western culture seeks to degrade youth by enticing them into materialism, sexual exploitation and hedonistic use of dangerous substances, all for the sake of material profit. Honestly, Christian parents cannot expect Western secular society to contribute much that is positive to the growth of children.

> Youthworker: *"HELP! HELP! I'm confused, overwhelmed. This problem is much bigger than me and my work."*
>
> ***Maestro de iniciación:*** "You are no doubt correct, BUT — but — God has called you to bring youth not only into a life of Christian discipleship but also into Biblical maturity. Do you accept that?"

> Youthworker: *"HELP! I can't fight against God's will. But inadequate am I, to raise these issues with parents and seek to address myself? I am almost totally disheartened."*
>
> **Maestro de iniciación:** "You got the message all right! We are not able, but God working through his Holy Spirit is."
>
> Youthworker: *"You want me to turn my life and my will over to the care of God and let God work through me in youth ministry? I am WILLING."*
>
> **Maestro de iniciación:** "Praise God. Let's trust the Lord to guide us in every phase of youth ministry, my friend."
>
> Youthworker: *"Yes, and let's enlist others. Of course, the parents of youth and congregational elders."*

FOCI FOR PARENTS AND YOUTHWORKERS

Some foci are necessary at this point, lest youthworkers sink into the sea of generalizations, vague paradigms or spiritualized notions — or parents drown in hopelessness and melancholy. The way out can be summarized as follows:

1. God desires to oversee the process of girls' and boys' development, because God loves every one of them, no matter how mature or immature. God also is ready through his *Holy Spirit* to guide parents, church leaders and youthworkers, no matter how mature or immature, into the assuredness of being in God's will for the emerging adults in their care.

2. The falsehoods of Western secular society can best be confronted by Truth, "I am the Way, the Truth and the Life," said *Jesus*.

3. *Truth* can be brought to bear upon youth, explicitly and implicitly.

   a. *Positive role models* are the most powerful influence on *emerging-adults*. As fathers and mothers and/or Christian men and women show youth what it means to be grown up, the Word becomes flesh as personal relationships flourish between the generations. The Word of God brings Light to lives, subtly but powerfully, especially when youth feel accepted, understood, trusted and secure in their interactions with their same-gender role models.

   b. The *explicit teaching of the Bible* shows youth what God's expectations are for them as *emerging adults*. Additionally, youth need to be taught "the whole counsel of God" ("I have told you everything God wants you to know," avers St. Paul in Acts 20:27). Careful attention must be given to the teaching curricula for youth, so they are equipped to respond when explaining their Christian faith. As St. Peter expresses it, "Always be ready to give an answer when someone asks you about your hope" (First Peter 3:15). Youth need to be challenged with one of St. Paul's warnings to Corinthian Christians: "My friends, stop thinking like children. Think like mature people. . ." (First Corinthians 14:20).[5] Perhaps more time should be given to plain teaching of Bible content to those youth who are ready for the meat of the Word.

Unfortunately, so many youth seem to have little appetite for robust teaching, as St. Paul wrote:
> You are like babies as far as your faith in Christ is concerned. So I had to treat you like babies and feed you milk. You could not take solid food, and you still cannot, because you are not yet spiritual (First Corinthians 3:1-3).

Honestly, no easy answer exists when ennui about the Bible sets in among immature youth. In some cases, the lack of interest is a reflection of poorly planned or presented Bible teaching. That can often be remedied with effort on the part of the teacher (see Chapter 17).

Concurrently, youthworkers may wish to focus special attention on those who are hungry for more of Christian Scripture, while also providing a more modest diet for those youth who are not ready for it.

Youthworker: *"What an order! I can't go through with it, can I?"*

Maestro de iniciación: "You don't have to be perfect! You have been called of God into youth ministry! Remember what St. Paul wrote, "Whatever I have, wherever I am, *I can make it through anything* in the One who makes me who I am" (MESSAGE).

Youthworker: *"By faith, I accept. But I still would like some actual examples. . . ."*

NOTES

[1] *The Journey from Childhood to Adulthood: The Importance and Limitations of Rites of Passage*, Bill Plotkin. Based on *Nature & the Human Soul: Cultivating Wholeness and Community in a Fragmented World*. (Novato, CA: New World Library, 2008).
[2] Plotkin.
[3] Source: World Health Organization.
[4] Plotkin.
[5] "How long before you grow up and use your head — your *adult* head? It's all right to have a childlike unfamiliarity with evil; a simple *no* is all that's needed there. But there's far more to saying *yes* to something. Only mature and well-exercised intelligence can save you from falling into gullibility" (First Corinthians 14:20, *The Message*).

Chapter 15

NOW WHERE DO WE GO?

When great rivers come together, the effect is breathtaking! Consider some possibilities:
- The Darling and the Murray Rivers connecting in New South Wales.
- The Marikina River linking with the Pasig River in Metro Manila (astounding at flood times).
- The Missouri River joining the Mississippi River.
- The Neckar River flowing into the Rhine at Mannheim, Germany.
- The Onyx River emptying into Lake Vanda, Antarctica!
- The Ubangi River meeting the Zaire (Congo) River in central Africa.
- The Ucayali River flowing into the Amazon River in eastern Peru.
- The Yalong River running into the Chang (Yangtze) River.

Thus the threads of this book come together, as two important streams of investigation draw to a close.
- The Biblical Foundations of Christian Youth Ministry.
- The Cultural Foundations of Youth Ministry.

Serious inquiry has been made into what is explicitly taught in the Bible, as well as into cultural factors growing out of God's general revelation to humankind. These rivers of thought emanate from the Almighty as God's will has been revealed down through the history of humankind. They combine in this chapter, to find the truths that undergird a youth ministry that can be truly Christian *and* culturally relevant from root to fruit.

Certain universal themes emerge to guide youthworkers in every cultural setting. Returning to the conclusions of the previous chapter, youthworkers need to evaluate and perhaps upgrade their goals and programs, and further than that, create paradigms for youth ministry that will be absolutely and authentically indigenous out of their national, tribal, cultural, regional and/or religious settings. Several fundamental convictions, or non-negotiables, are at the heart of Christian youth ministry.

Conviction #1 — APPREHENDING GOD

At the core of youth development is knowing God — coming to know God through learning the Bible, through perceiving God in nature (general revelation), through recognizing individuals who reflect a godly nature in their lifestyles and, in some cases, a direct mystical perception of God. A boy or girl who sincerely seeks to become aware of God, the mighty Creator of the universe and its Sustainer, may look within, as in Eastern religion, but with limited results, according to the Bible. Any inner light is necessarily clouded by the nature of humankind, as the prophet Jeremiah wrote, "The heart is deceitful above all things. And it is extremely sick; who can understand it fully *and* know its secret motives?" (Jeremiah 17:9, AMP).

In traditional observances, boys are taught about tribal creation stories, how to reverence their gods and how to appease them. These traditions sprang up from their ancestors' perceptions of the natural world, but their ideas of God were inescapably distorted, as St. Paul testified in Romans 1:19-23.

> They know everything that can be known about God, because God has shown it all to them. God's eternal power and character cannot be seen. But from the beginning of creation, *God has shown what these are like by all he has made*. That's why those people don't have any excuse. *They know about God*, but they don't honor him or even thank him. . . . They don't worship the glorious and eternal God. *Instead, they worship idols* that are made to look like humans who cannot live forever, and like birds, animals, and reptiles.

In practice, so much of initiation instruction was tied into false religious beliefs that ". . . many African [Christian] pastors today cannot imagine an initiation ceremony that is not completely pagan."[1] Early missionaries in African usually tried to squash the practice of initiation. They were often successful in stopping the ceremonies, but an unintended distressing cultural result was denying boys the right to become men.

Spirituality was also an integral part of initiation for American Indians, as reflected in a statement of Dr. Charles Alexander Eastman, a nineteenth-century Santee Sioux.

> From childhood I was consciously trained to be . . . in the broadest sense a public servant. After arriving at a reverent sense of the pervading presence of the *Spirit and Giver of Life*, and a deep consciousness of the brotherhood of man, the first thing for me to accomplish was to adapt myself perfectly to natural things — in other words, to *harmonize myself with nature*. . . . I must have faith and patience; I must learn self-control and be able to maintain silence. . . . a true Indian always shares whatever he may possess."[2]

A study of traditional initiation ceremonies reveals the

universality of religious teachings and expression. Even in the secular national holiday in Japan, Coming-of-Age Day, honorees are expected to spend time in dutiful worship to a deity of their choice.

Designers of contemporary rites of passage also acknowledge the need for spiritual direction. For example, Mary Lewis, in *HERSTORY, Black Female Rites of Passage*, declares that spirituality is essential in the development of a whole, proud person. She also asserts the need for a storyline of grace to permeate the ritual. It helps girls from difficult settings to survive and ". . . combat against sometimes tremendous odds and beat them."[4]

Contemporary expressions of initiation usually include ethical, if not religious, training because knowing right from wrong and good from bad is an important part of being mature. Growing out of that is the spirit of service that such programs seek to develop within their participants. This too has religious rootage.

A prerequisite, therefore, for youth ministry is an apprehension of God. The starting point for seeking God's insight is, of course, the Bible (see Chapters 8-13), where God reveals Truth through the Holy Spirit. Divine insight is best achieved when seeking heavenly guidance, whether it is parents, children, youth, youthworkers and/or others. "If any of you need wisdom, you should ask God, and it will be given to you. God is generous and won't correct you for asking," the Apostle James recommended (James 1:5).

Conviction #2 — A SINGULAR PURPOSE: Attainment of Maturity

The whole impetus behind youth ministry is facilitating girls and boys to grow up to be responsible Christian women and men. This represents a step beyond such important vital goals as evangelism or even Christian discipleship of youth.

A focus on helping youth reach adulthood makes it possible to evaluate all other objectives and programs successfully and realistically. When a youthworker's concern is attainment of "the product" rather than simply the process, greater progress toward maturity will be evident in the lives of youth.

Even though Western-world adolescence is a very long process, with years turning into decades perhaps, those years pass rapidly. As far as parents are concerned, they may seem impatient for their offspring to take on adult obligations, yet may not be eager at heart for their sons or daughters to leave the family of origin. They are often basically conflicted.

As far as many local congregations are concerned, usually their influence is undercut when the EMERGING-ADULT-child leaves for jobs, schools or military assignments elsewhere, probably sometime after finishing secondary school. So in those situations, a program of personal development for adolescents must of necessity be compressed into half-a-dozen years.

For Christian believers, youth ministry becomes a matter of urgency of moving toward maturation, because a focus on maturation runs counter-culturally in the Western world in which youthful irresponsibility is almost encouraged. Hence, the need to be fixed on a singular goal of moving toward Christian adult servanthood is fundamental.

Conviction #3 — A RESPECT FOR GENDER DIFFERENCES

The New Testament makes it clear, ultimately, that basic gender classifications are obliterated under the Lordship of Christ. St. Paul states unequivocally, "Faith in Christ Jesus is what makes each of you *equal with each other,* whether you are a Jew or a Greek, a slave or a free person, *a man or a woma*n" (Galatians 3:28). Yet the family roles of husband, wife and child were repeatedly affirmed by St. Paul. He evidently did not view individuals as genderless. In fact, both his letters to the congregations at Ephesus and Colosse spell out how Christian families are to live together (cf. First Peter, chapter 3). So gender matters! God does not intend us to view humankind in unisex ways, that is, ignoring distinctions of gender. Society respects such differences with regard to physical qualifications for certain jobs, usually with regard to lavatory facilities (though not in Europe), and division for certain contact sports, for example, with separate Olympic and World Cup men's and women's competitions in *fútbol, ibhola, calico, Fußball, fotbal, sokker, voetbal, soka, putbol, futebol* (U.S.=soccer).

Western types of education include both single-gender schools, colleges and universities and also coeducational institutions. Christian congregations likewise approach church life in different ways. In some traditions, men and women sit separately in congregational gatherings. In some parish classes, both adults and children are taught in gender-divided groups. Some Christian camps are exclusively for one gender or the other. But in Christian ministry to adolescents, mixed gender groupings *(coed)* seem to predominate.

In examining both historic and contemporary rites of passage programs, the direction seems to favor substantial separation of the genders, having men prepare boys for manhood, women groom girls for womanhood. In light of the distinct needs, interests and maturation rates of adolescent females and males, Christian youthworkers will want to consider different and separated methodologies for boys and girls, in which male-on-male mentoring is highlighted, likewise female-on-female

Conviction #4 — PARENT INVOLVEMENT

The parents of youth are not only the primary formers of their children's values through their example, but they are also responsible to attend to the value formation of these boys and girls. This is not to say the children are the property of their parents, but God gives mothers and fathers the responsibility of rearing children properly (see Chapters 8-10). As such they too must embrace the conviction that youth need to be prepared and guided into adult maturity. It would be unthinkable for any but an impoverished parent to send a child out the door without the means to feed oneself — that might lead to the child's starvation and demise. In like manner, youth should be ready to thrive in the adult world when they have passed through adolescence. With that understanding in place, youthworkers can seek to motivate and prepare parents for the precious task of guiding their youthful boys and girls.

Parents, therefore, have vital roles in contributing to whatever programmatic expressions are developed by congregational leaders and youthworkers. At the minimum parents need to treat the passages of their children as truly significant, not just more dull ceremonial affairs or another thing they are supposed to do and take part in simply because they are expected to do so. Actually, parents can prepare their daughters and sons by talking about the growing-up process from the time they are little, thus preparing them for the challenges ahead of them of:

(1) leaving childhood,
(2) receiving mentoring from teachers, youthworkers, pastors, and others through adolescence,
(3) graduating into responsible adulthood.

Additionally, the parents' faith convictions need to be passed along. More specifically, as adolescence looms on the horizon, it will be fitting to plan father/son or mother/daughter talks to discuss the principles of Biblical faith, their personal views on other weighty matters and their advice on being a Christian woman or man.[5] As recommended by the

Psalmist, "One generation commends your works to another; they tell of your mighty acts" (NIV).

An interesting parallel is found in the Sioux Indian tradition. A boy's father would constantly ask him questions about natural phenomena, to see if he could identify certain plants, animal tracks, weather patterns and so on. As one man recalled it,

> When I left the teepee in the morning, he would say: "Hakadah, look closely to everything you see" and at evening, on my return, he used often to catechize me for an hour or so. "On which side of the trees is the lighter-colored bark? On which side do they have most regular branches?" It was his custom to let me name all the new birds that I had seen during the day. I would name them according to the color or the shape of the bill or their song or the appearance and locality of the nest — in fact, anything about the bird that impressed me as characteristic. I made many ridiculous errors, I must admit. He then usually informed me of the correct name. Occasionally I made a hit and this he would warmly commend.[6]

So, what happens in various cultures, in the providence of God, conforms to the Bible's expectations for parental involvement. This participation is especially important with respect to sexual morality in societies in which Biblical standards for youth are considered obscurantist and embarrassing.

Conviction #5 — MATURE LEADERS FOR YOUTH MINISTRY

God's revealed Truth directs the flow of Christian youth ministry toward dependence upon esteemed women to be role models and mentors for adolescent girls — and upon men above reproach to be that for boys. However, such a conclusion does not rule out persons of any age and maturity from contributing to Christian youth ministry according to their gifts and passion. In fact, youth ministry that provides adolescents with a wider spectrum of role models is propelled by a "ministry team" composed of people who represent a cross section of the body of Christ. This principle derives from the study both of the Bible and human culture.

An ideal youth ministry team might be made up of at least one each:

- *A married couple* (with a marriage centered on Christ and untroubled).

  Modern society proposes such skewed perspectives on marriage that an adolescent, especially from a broken home, is easily swayed by some of the *Western world's false notions,* such as:
  ➤ No one believes in sexual purity any more.
  ➤ Stay single, be a pleasure-seeker as long as possible.
  ➤ Marriage only lasts as long as it is convenient and pleasant for me.
  ➤ Fidelity in marriage is not fashionable.
  ➤ Sexual promiscuity will not affect my marriage.
  ➤ Using pornography is a victimless offence.
  Thus, a Christian couple will help to expose some of these lies through their example. The longer the couple has been married, the more robustly their Biblical beliefs will be displayed.

- *A vibrant Christian man.*

  Emerging-men/women-boys/girls desperately need a man in leadership to demonstrate that it is possible to follow Christ and not lose one's masculinity. Young women long to know a man with honorable intentions and close relationship with God, perhaps subconscious but nonetheless a real desire. Boys, on the other hand, with so many men neglecting or deserting their families, desperately need an available father-figure who lives the Christ-life before them. This issue is exacerbated when boys glance around congregational meetings and discover females predominate in number and influence. Hence, a Christian man's presence in a leadership role seems absolutely essential for the youth ministry team.

- *A person in the reflective years* (life review stage, see Chapter 8).

What is being proposed here runs counter to a popular conception that older adults, perhaps those over thirty or even sixty, simply do not have the energy to participate in youth activities. The underlying widespread assumption here is that the ideal youth leader is young, energetic and able to engage with youth in their vigorous activities. But who is better suited to manifest the fruit of a life of obedience to Christ than someone who has walked the path of life a long time? This is especially true for youth whose parents' walk with God is immature or questionable.

- *A single female, old enough to be comfortable as an unmarried person.*

Some church and/or cultural traditions unfortunately consign single people to "not-really-an-adult" status. This custom projects to adolescent girls that they must get married in order to be accepted and respected as an adult. Given the fact that most Christian congregations have fewer males than females, EMERGING-WOMEN-

girls face an intense dilemma. "If I want to become an acknowledged woman, I may have to marry, even a non-Christian man. If I want to stay true to my faith and Biblical standards, I may end up unmarried." Hence, it is ideal when adolescent girls are given a healthy unmarried female role model. Hopefully, some single woman (or women) in the congregation will receive the call to work with youth.

- *Someone with gray hair* (or its equivalent).

Being over thirty-years-old is *not* detrimental to youth ministry. A little gray hair is helpful to make one look distinguished, but a youthworker with life experience is priceless. The maturity that is presented by this person provides the steadiness of which youth have such a need and helps parents to be more communicative with a person whom they can trust.

- *Maestro de Iniciación,* someone who takes leadership of the team.

As suggested above, when a team approach to youth ministry is feasible, one person must oversee the people and the programs for youth. As an orchestra director, he or she will seek to build relationships with parents, with leaders and with the youth. This person needs to be a respected leader, corresponding to an *elder* in a tribal initiation or in a Christian congregation. A *maestro* strategizes the ministry, leads the youth ministry team as well as interfaces with youth. Last and certainly not least, the *maestro* recruits adult team members who will work together to challenge *emerging-adult-children* to grow up, ideally to develop a balanced team approach.

- *A parent of an adolescent.*

    Perhaps one of the above categories will fit this expectation, that is, that a parent be involved in youth leadership. Indeed, some parent-child combinations will not be viable, but others may work well in the same group. This father and/or mother sometimes provides a role model of parenting that a child from another home may find vital to their own character development.

Conviction #5 — PROGRAMS BUILT ON TIME-HONORED CULTURAL FOUNDATIONS

As tribal initiation ceremonies evolved centuries ago over many generations, they were endorsed by the whole community not only because of reverence for tradition but also because they functioned to maintain highly-valued stability in that culture. In short, initiation worked to produce productive adults.

In today's world, except in rare cases, Westernized ways clamor for the attention of youth, even among the most traditional people-groups. Missionary interventions and government schools create counterforces against the old ways. For example, traditional medicine often conflicts with modern health practices. National leaders, because of their close association with Western missionaries, may have unconsciously imbibed (or consciously imitated) Western ways, thus losing touch in some ways with their cultural roots. When youth migrate to urban centers, cultural tensions are intensified as they copy Western ways, but cherish family traditions simultaneously.

For example, a T'boli youth on Mindanao Island in the Philippines is at heart T'boli, not Australian, Arab, American or, for that matter, Filipino! For that reason, Bible translators believe in getting the Bible into the 'heart language' of the people. Likewise, the cultural underpinning of youth cannot be disrespected if one desires to get to the hearts of *emerging-adult-children*. Sometimes so much of the host culture is marginalized, at least in church settings, that youthworkers may need to re-imagine Christian ministry possibilities that are supportive of the distinctive outlooks, traditions and coping mechanisms of the people "back-home" and not inconsistent with Biblical teaching.

Another point of tension between Western and other cultures is the degree of importance that is placed on the individual. American and similar democratic societies endow the individual person with entitlements and freedom of choice. On the other hand, Asian, African and native American civilizations have long focused on the corporate good as being of greater consequence.

Evangelicals have struggled with this collision of cultures because historically Western-based evangelism has been targeted at individuals, rather than at groups, even though the Bible has examples of collective responses to the Gospel. Christian youthworkers can respect group-oriented ethos in their evangelistic approach, but this may probably require more attention to family groups than youthworkers have traditionally given.

Is it possible for an expatriate to find the cultural foundations that count and integrate such into their thinking and ministry? Perhaps yes, perhaps no. On the one hand, an outsider may have insights into the culture that the indigenous people cannot perceive, just as a fish cannot "see" water because it lives in it. On the other hand, a national may sense more accurately the pulse of the culture because they grew up in it. A solution is not easy to find, though bi-cultural teamwork promises to produce the best results.

Youthworkers will be most successful when they blend the teachings of the Bible with the customs of the people when compatible, without destroying the integrity of either.

Not a task for the weak and weary!

A Checklist for Those Not Fainthearted

Lord God, I/we want to apply these convictions to our youth ministry, wholeheartedly, but we must honestly confess our weaknesses before You. Here's my self-evaluation:

To what extent do *I sincerely believe* in a youth ministry that (check one column for each item):

	VERY MUCH	SOME	A LITTLE	DON'T KNOW
Seeks the power and glory of God?				
Has the building of maturity as its singular purpose?				
Has respect for gender differences?				
Seeks authentic involvement of parents?				
Enlists mature leaders?				
Builds on valid time-honored cultural foundations?				

NOTES

[1] Personal letter from Gregg Yarian, veteran American missionary in Togo, January 10, 2016.
[2] Brett and Kate McKay, "Lessons from the Sioux in How to Turn a Boy Into a Man," *The Art of Manliness*," October 2, 2015.
[3] Mary C. Lewis, *HERSTORY, Black Female Rites of Passage*, (Chicago: African American Images, 1988), 65.
[4] Lewis, 64.
[5] Brett and Kate McKay, "Coming of Age: The Importance of Male Rites of Passage."
[6] Brett and Kate McKay, "Lessons from the Sioux in How to Turn a Boy into a Man."

Chapter 16

DEVELOPING UNIQUE COMING-OF-AGE CEREMONIES

Initiation ceremonies may seem incongruous to the modern world, perhaps even archaic to adolescents who long to be accepted as well to be fashionable. Yet there is something to be said for adapting concepts from traditional cultures and infusing them with authentic modern-day meaning. Various groups, both secular and religious, have created contemporary rites to use with youth in the Western world, that is, with males and females experiencing extended adolescence.

Composing one's own rubric for use in a specific youth ministry setting may be daunting, but even more so is the mission of convincing parents, congregational leaders AND youth to accept and honor it. Possibly any plan so devised might be optional, restricted to youth and their parents who are willing to accept the challenge of growing up. Whatever the case, a Biblical contemporary coming-of-age program for youth has many attractive possibilities.

A prerequisite question looms over any consideration of initiation event or events. That is the question of timing, "When is the appropriate time to pass the child into adulthood?" In the traditional world, it was not a question.

When the child reached physical maturity, that is, puberty, it was obvious to indigenous peoples that the individual was ready to cross over into adulthood, even though the young adult's physique would continue to develop for a few more years.

In the Westernizing world, the crossover is not nearly as simple as in traditional times, in fact, it is incredibly complex with adolescence polluting young lives for years and years, in a no-man's land (or no-woman's land) between leaving childhood and truly growing up. Hence, no single event, program, observance or ceremony seems adequate to address all the issues and changes in adolescence.

However by contrast, many children are thrust into adult-level responsibilities at a young age to enable the family to survive, providing childcare, physical labor or even income through begging and/or other demeaning activities. For children of poverty, leaving childhood is accomplished early and without fanfare. In spite of their material neediness, they may wish to play like other children, but adulthood is thrust upon them, involuntarily. They have been denied anything that approximates childhood, and hence they appreciate the loving care of Christian adults and congregations who reach out to and serve them.

Keeping in mind that millions of children fall into the former category, what about the affluent who may have lived beyond the grasp of poverty for their whole lives?

The path described in Chapter 14 is a good starting point in devising a configuration of what might be considered forms of initiation for today's youth. Confidently, a studied approach to maturation will produce adults instead of overgrown children.

THRESHOLDS TO DISTINGUISH

Early Adolescence, A Time to Leave

Adios, good-bye, totsiens, paalam na, adieu, búcsú, caio, kwaheri, Auf Widersehen — Farewell to childhood. However one may say it, childhood is about to finish as puberty arrives. Leaving it all behind is almost impossible for an *emerging-adult-CHILD*, though they may long for the time when they are no longer feeling like a social isolate, an awkward fool, a bumbling juvenile. They believe that being grown up will not only give them societal ease, but also deliver some coveted privileges, like drinking alcohol, having sex and the like. So there is an eagerness to get on with life. However, the *emerging-adult-CHILD* also desires continued indulgence by parents, a life that may be marked by convenience and comfort if the family is affluent at least to some degree.

The pattern for female farewells-to-childhood is largely individual, often marked by interpretation by a mother, sister or other female relative about the unusual thing that is happening to her body. Not every parent may be comfortable introducing their daughter to her new life, except perhaps helping her with bodily basics. Other women who serve as mentors can help to bridge the gap. Maturity is so much more than a changing body. The need for personal responsibility kicks into high gear in order for a girl to reach adequate womanhood. Exiting childhood means turning her back on childish pursuits, actions, words and idleness.

> A significant shift is required to move from girl to woman and if older women assist in this shift, and create an event to mark this, it is less likely for a girl to grow up into a woman-child and more likely for her to become a grown woman of vision.[1]

For this, there may need to be a period of mourning that might be shared with other girls of the same age, as they pass the threshold out of childhood.

For males, the configuration is different because their entry is not nearly so clear, and it usually happens a couple years later than their female age peers. The phrase, "Boys will be boys,"[2] characterizes some of the foolishness that males manifest as they enter adolescence. Fathers, when available, can help their sons across the threshold, but the example and counsel of other men is almost mandatory. Hence, it is logical to consider a group experience (or experiences) in which responsible Christian men lead boys into work that guides them toward maturity. In Kenya, an experimental program ascertained that connectedness to significant community members was fostered through facilitated experiences with men and boys.[3]

In the USA, Canada and other places, the threshold into *emerging-adulthood* is probably most easily marked by entry into "middle school," roughly ages 11/12-14. In other countries it may be known as "junior high school, intermediate school, *jung hakgyo*, secondary school, *Sixième a Troisème*, upper primary, middle lower school, *Secundaria, 3th ciclo*, Basic Cycle, etc.," depending on the structure of the educational system.

Mid-adolescence, A Time to Commit

Decisions made in childhood and early adolescent years are often adjusted, upgraded or, in ruinous fashion, set aside. This change of direction or determination to continue on course toward maturity as defined by the Bible may occur as the EMERGING-ADULT-*child* leaves the shelter of hometown and school, moving into the work world, the military or higher education. Some congregations recognize this transition already, asking individual members to promise to pray especially for someone of those moving away.

As indicated in the previous chapter, the ideal move toward full maturity is to make a commitment to a Biblical adult lifestyle. Parents may put pressure on adolescents to do this, as well as youthworkers, but a manipulated response is valueless. It is not possible to program a preordained response at this point, but opportunities to make a vow in an adult manner should be available. A contemplative retreat for graduates might provide the unhurried atmosphere for reflection and decision. Some congregations, depending on their tradition, might suggest adult-believer-baptism for the EMERGING-ADULT-child to mark this step.

Chapter 14 spells out possible directions and/or facets of this recommitment to "growing up."

Neophyte Adult, A Time to Pass Into Emerging Maturity

If the measurement for entering adolescence is uncertain, it is even more so to determine when a man or a woman leaves the stage of EMERGING-ADULT-child. Since the Bible describes maturity as a lifelong pursuit of being a responsible person, moving over the threshold to maturity is illusive, especially when societal norms, for example, define adulthood in terms of marriage, childbearing or vocational achievement. But simply earning a diploma, or getting married, or having a baby does not an adult make.

In terms of family relationships, ideally the neophyte would find increasing deference from their parents. In some cultures, setting up a separate place of residence and caring for one's personal needs signifies adult accomplishment. When this is not appropriate or possible, mutual respect is engendered when the young adult is responsible financially and contributes to family maintenance.

For the believer, acceptance as a fully-participating

member of the congregation is one marker that arises gradually yet meaningfully. What kinds of ceremonies would be appropriate for this transition seems elusive, since few people can claim that they have "officially graduated" into maturity. However, there may be some culturally-appropriate recognitions that could be explored and utilized.

PROGRAMS TO CONSIDER, A Time to Innovate?

Initiation experiences can be a catalyst that propels an adolescent youth into adulthood. A distillation of both traditional and contemporary replications of these reveals the rationale, the content, the methodology and the timing of such curricula.

Rationale

An initiation episode (or episodes) potentially benefits families, youth, their congregations and their world. In traditional societies, initiation offered them the occasion of seeing the world as they knew it and to prosper in it. In a sense the new men and women shaped in this fashion offered hope and joy, as all affected constituencies benefitted.

First, initiation gave *families* anticipation that the careful training parents had given the child would be crowned both by the tutelage of respected elders and the achievement of a worthy target by their child. Bringing another responsible adult into the community would be a source of family pride. Initiation experiences may also encourage parents to release the child into the world. In an overly-protective society, parents may need this nudge to open some doors of freedom for their child, which in turn unlocks the possibilities of learning by trial and error.[4]

Other values for the family include supplementary sex education (assuming that to be an essential element of the initiation). Also, the child's broader understanding of what it means to be a family member will enhance family life.

Second, initiation experiences bring great benefit to *the individual boy or girl*, depending on the nature and content involved. Just the psychological movement of one's sense of self, from child to EMERGING ADULT may have the effect of force-feeding the growing-up process. As long as a girl or a boy thinks of themselves as youngsters or children (*"kids"*), their rootless behavior may be disposed toward immaturity. The opposite may also be true. One's expectations of oneself often govern behavior. Therefore, if responsibility is increased as a result of initiation, the youth has the privilege of handling himself or herself responsibly.

Another yield from an initiation process that depends on established adults as individual and/or group mentors is connection across the generations. According to one author, to adolescents the adult world can be ". . . unreachable, unapproachable, and certainly unsupportive."[5] The relationships potentially developed between mentors and individual boys or girls help to dispel this barrier to the communication necessary for maturation to take place.

Assuming that initiation-related training is relevant to real life as an adult, the boy or girl is able to capture helpful skills and insights about real life, as opposed to the fantasy worlds of romance in novels, movies, *telenovelas* and pornography. Somewhat boldly educational institutions promise to inculcate attitudes and skills to equip EMERGING-ADULT-*children* for what lies ahead.

To the extent that Biblical teachings and values are transmitted, to that extent will the initiate absorb and make real their personal faith and ethical commitments. Their walk with Christ will be enhanced by a reduction in egocentrism, a dangerous temptation for any adult, as they learn and experience more about service (see Chapter 11). Lastly, the individual benefits from increased self-esteem as the *EMERGING-ADULT* status comes to their consciousness.

Third, as the initiation activity progresses as it should, the adolescent thinks increasingly about their role in *service to the community and then on to the world*. The seed of being a world-changer can be nurtured as youth realize how they can contribute their gifts, abilities and energies in bringing life, redemption, justice, and mercy to needy people near and far. The community also benefits from the opportunity to pass along revered traditions and convictions, building unity with local, national and universal principles.

Finally, everyone benefits from the emergence of young adults out of the shadows of adolescence, into a world of responsible service. The future of the community depends upon developing healthy women and men as opposed to juvenile adults.

Sequencing

Initiation involves a three-fold pattern, as explained and illustrated earlier. In each case, there is a leaving, a time for training and enrichment, followed by a return to normal life. It has been described as a dying, a birthing process (bringing forth a more mature person) and rebirth (though not in the sense of doctrinal regeneration[6]) for life in the congregation, community and world.

Necessary Components

Common threads exist in various versions of historic and contemporary initiation. Each should be considered for usage in various ways as appropriate for the age of the participants and resources available.

First and foremost, *leadership* of the experience(s). Having experienced women and men to coach and disciple youthful girls and boys is a theme running deep in this investigation. How sensible it is to have adults who are well on their way to maturity in life (see Chapter 11) to interact with youth and exhibit Christian character before them. Yet conventional wisdom throws up imagined generational barriers and turns to unseasoned young adults for leadership of youth. A contemporary program for boys aims to have a leadership configuration in which each man takes responsibility for five boys whom he will coach to aid them in giving birth to greater maturity. Each "elder" acts ". . . as surrogate uncle, teacher, counselor, wilderness guide, vocational guidance counselor, personal friend, or superior officer, according to what is needed at the moment."[7] Ideally, this takes place in an environment in which youth can grow.

Second, a period and/or place of *seclusion* or *sequestration* seems to be required to allow initiates to focus on the rigorous physical, mental and devotional dimensions usually needed in an atmosphere of growth. Some programs include a time of solitude (minutes, hours, could be days) so personal reflection becomes part of the process. Some Biblical precedents of isolation come to mind easily: John the Baptist living in the wilderness, Elijah by the Brook Cherith, Moses tending sheep for forty years in Horeb, Jesus being tempted in the desert and more. Being separated from everyday life, they are likely to be open to personal change and come away in some ways a new person. NOTE: The usage of cameras, mobile/cell phones and audio devices will normally be prohibited for the period of sequestration.

Third, instruction is a vital component of any initiation. This dimension is anything but merriment, laughter and whoopee. The principle stated by Jim Rayburn, founder of Young Life Campaign, "It's a sin to bore a kid *[sic]*. . . ," is still valid. But categorically youth need to learn (1) practical information about life, for example, goal-setting or sex education, and (2) about Biblical/ethical truth, such as the difference between right and wrong. Chapter 17 includes some suggestions for how to make learning consequential, as contrasted with juvenile diversion.

A *fourth* element to be built-in is the development of a *Biblical service outlook* on life. A Native American (Sioux) man expresses a Christian ideal in reporting about his initiation.

> Every boy, from the very beginning of his training, is an embryo public servant. He puts into daily practice the lessons that in this way become part of himself. There are no salaries, no "tips," no prizes to work for. He takes his pay in the recognition of the community and the consciousness of unselfish service.[8]

The form of service can be fitted to the group and the opportunities available. The goal is to enable youth to think beyond themselves and instead respect other people and the world around them. Some congregations have encouraged each youth and mentor to do a social action or social service project together, or help to organize a service project that all participating youth and mentors do together.

A *fifth* element frequently used in initiation events is *risk,* either real or apparent. A ropes course, for example, when properly supervised, looks far more risky than it actually is. But the value to the participant to overcome fear is great.[9] When Jesus sent out his disciples by two's to spread the Good News, he knew that his Father would keep them from all harm, but his followers did not have that assurance. Some risk will be experienced as an individual, but at other times it becomes a group team-building event.

Finally, it is helpful for everyone to savor a culminating episode with the group. Participants can reflect upon insights they have received concerning their own maturity and celebrate their progress with the group. Some may wish to share with the group, either orally or in some other form of communication like a song, a poem, or a reading. Individually, the EMERGING-ADULT-*child* may be encouraged to develop a journal about his or her convictions and abilities. A photo album might also be put together by a designated photographer because personal electronic tech devices are not permitted.

Also, a public ceremonial event to which parents and significant others are invited adds to the climax. Some ceremonial features to be considered are:
- Collection of childhood toys, including electronic gadgets, and donating them to charity.
- As a group, singing a song of Christian commitment.
- Gathering unsuitable children's clothes and delivering them to others who can wear them.
- A campfire service.
- Writing out, with or without parental assistance, a personal commitment plan and publicly signing it.
- Presentation of student-designed skit or skits, representing the farewell to days of "being a baby."
- Amassing an album of then/now photos, including a visual record of the ceremony.

The next turning point is leaving early adolescence toward a time of mature commitments. Some ceremonial possibilities are:
- Recognition of graduation from secondary school.
- Commissioning for a youth mission trip.
- Upgraded version(s) of some of the above.

The passage is enhanced when parents, mentors and others are invited to witness and/or participate in the ceremony or ceremonies.

Suggestion for Implementation

When the blending of the various components in appropriate proportions is done with the guidance of the Holy Spirit, a Biblically harmonious initiation promises to touch the lives of EMERGING-MEN/WOMEN-*children* and that of their mentors. With regard to an outline, one present-day planner reported, "We committed ourselves to a loose structure, design and vision that we hoped would enable us to test certain ideas and principles but leave much scope for discovery."[10] That advice is a helpful starting point in formulating an indigenous plan.

A strategy that includes yearly check-points has potential merit. This program format allows the *emerging-adult-child* to engage in dialogue with parent(s) and/or youthworker and/or both, as his or her progress toward maturity is measured. When a public dimension is added, care should be given to maintain the authenticity of the ongoing commitment of the *emerging-adult-child* so the ceremony does not become an empty benchmark.

A Final Word of CAUTION

Youthworkers with experience in developing initiation experiences warn that ceremonial events, in themselves, have less meaning than what happens in the youth ministry *between* the events. It may be easy for youth, their parents and youthworkers to get swept up in the intensity or the scope or the beauty or the excitement of the various occasions for celebrating personal growth of the EMERGING-ADULT-*girl/boy*, and these observances are definitely important.

But there is no substitute for the Christian parent who takes seriously the responsibility to prepare their boy or girl for adult life and does so diligently, year after year, as the children are released into the responsibilities of maturity.

Likewise, the youthworker continues to ply his or her abilities among youth, day by day, week by week, month by month, year by year. As the Bible speaks,
- I have observed something else under the sun. The fastest runner doesn't always win the race, and the

strongest warrior doesn't always win the battle. The wise sometimes go hungry, and the skillful are not necessarily wealthy. And those who are educated don't always lead successful lives" (Ecclesiastes 9:11, NLT).
- Therefore, since we are surrounded by such a huge crowd of witnesses to the life of faith, let us strip off every weight that slows us down, especially the sin that so easily trips us up. And let us run with endurance the race God has set before us (Hebrews 12:1, NLT).
- But the one who endures to the end will be saved (Mark 13:13b, NLT).

The time between the rituals is the most important part — teaching, training, mentoring, grooming, coaching, counseling and in every way possible so that youth will grow up to change the world!

NOTES

[1] Kim McCabe, *Rites for Girls, Mothers Supporting Daughters As They Come of Age* (Word Press, 2011-2016).

[2] This term came from a Latin proverb, translated as "Children [boys] are children [boys] and do childish things." In English it was first recorded in 1589 (*The American Heritage® Dictionary of Idioms*, Christine Ammer, Houghton Mifflin Harcourt Publishing Company, 1992, 1997, 2003). All rights reserved.

[3] Muhia Karianjahi, *Connectedness to Community in a Contemporary Church-based Adolescent Rites of Passage Program in Nairobi* (unpublished Ph.D dissertation, Biola University, La Mirada, CA, 2013.

[4] *Focus on the Family* (Colorado Springs, CO: USA) suggests a book to guide father/son activities for a family rite-of-passage: *Raising a Modern-Day Knight*, by Robert Lewis (see bibliography).

[5] Louise Carus Mahdi, Nancy Geyer Christopher, and Michael Meade, *Crossroads, the Quest for Contemporary Rites of Passage* (Chicago, IL: Open Court, 1996), 410.

[6] St. John 3:3, "Jesus replied, 'Very truly I tell you, no one can see the kingdom of God unless they are born again.'"

[7] Steven Foster, "Passage into Manhood," (*Gender*,Spring 1987, copyright by Context *Institute*), 50.

[8] McKay, "Charles Eastman: Lessons from the Sioux in How to Turn a Boy Into a Man," *The Art of Manliness*.

[9] **CAUTION:** More is required than simply having youth to physically finish a ropes course. Afterward, youth need to be debriefed on their feelings and character development.

[10] Mahdi, et. al., *Crossroads, 405*.

Chapter 17
OTHER QUESTIONS CONSIDERED

> Youthworker: *"I really get it now! There's much to be done. But a distressing question lurks in the back of my mind."*
>
> *Maestro de iniciación:* "I think I may know what you may be thinking! So tell me. You've had enough theory, right?"
>
> Youthworker: *"YES. I still have the youth to deal with. What do I do?"*
>
> *Maestro de iniciación:* "A superb question. You are asking, 'How does all of this play out in specific plans, programs and activities?'"
>
> Youthworker: *"You've got it! Just tell me what to do!"*

The practicalities of youth ministry demand some attention, yet volumes have been written, countless conferences have been held and many careers have been built on ideas, designs, programs, schemes and the brainstorms of earnest creative people in youth ministry. But youthworkers must carefully discern which of the many proposals moving about are consistent with a ministry that shows the way for youth to grow to Christian maturity. Consequently, earlier chapters have raised a multitude of questions for reflection, with few practical techniques included.

This book suggests a fresh paradigm for international youth ministry, so it is directed toward those who are brave enough to pioneer, to experiment, to test and, if need be, fail in efforts to bring *emerging-adult-children* into growing Christian maturity in their own culture. Consequently, the door is hopefully left wide open for trial and error, by which youth, parents, youthworkers and congregations may learn. The guidance of the Holy Spirit, the sincere efforts of *maestros de iniciación* and other congregational leaders *will* eventuate in a generation of growing young men and women who will, on the behalf of the Kingdom of God, change the world for the better through evangelism and social justice efforts.

Now, what are a few of these "other questions" to be addressed?

PERSUADING THE CONGREGATION?

When an alternative paradigm of youth ministry is initiated, questions will naturally be asked of the *maestro de iniciación*. But it is impossible to implement a growth-centered model for youth ministry without the full cooperation of congregational (or organizational) leadership. It may take some time to enlist the support necessary from elders or other congregational leaders to move ahead. Once there is the realization and acceptance of the notion that the primary focus of local youth ministry is on end-product results, that is, *developing maturing young adults,* some openness to new approaches may appear. Ideally, elders will identify with St. Paul who wrote to the Corinthians, "... we won't be in the way or get in the way of your growing up" (Second Corinthians 2:19b, MSG).

When there is sufficient backing for change, or at least a willingness to attempt something different, the congregation/ organization and their leadership will want to examine the questions posed in Chapters 9-14, in collaboration with the *maestro* and other youthworkers.

Next, parents of adolescents can be enlisted to consider the transition of their children into adulthood. They will likely become strong allies of the proposal because in their hearts they know it is right and proper. More than anyone else involved, they desire to see their young sons and daughters become *Christian men and women* who will impact the world for Christ. Moreover, they will want to know their role in the growth-to-adulthood paradigm, since it is central to all that happens.

Lastly, adolescent youth, depending on their level of maturity, must be brought into the process. It is *their* lives which are at stake and they need to face the responsibility of growing up, right from the start of adolescence. Early adolescent boys will be least likely to understand what is at stake, but they will eventually mature enough to take hold of their responsibilities, too.

HAVING *FUN* YET?

What is the place of "fun" in a program focused on an *emerging-adult* Biblical paradigm of Christian maturity? It may seem obvious at first glance to ask the question, "But isn't youth ministry supposed to be fun?" How is it possible for a youthworker to keep the interest of restless adolescents without "fun," unless Bible study, worship, outings, etc. are "fun." It all depends....

In English, the word "fun" has many meanings—hilarity,

exuberance, entertainment, play, absurdity, amusement, joking, laughing and/or wit. In other languages, "fun" is described as: *divertidos,*[1] *Lustig,*[2] *saya,*[3] *plezier,*[4] *zábava,*[5] *prêt,*[6] *niém vul, furaha* [happiness].[8] [9]Must youth ministry always be based on or enhanced by entertaining silliness as "fun"? Is "fun" always "fun"?

The *Contemporary English Version* suggests a definition of "fun" as frivolity. Quoting the Old Testament sage,
I said to myself, "*Have fun* and enjoy yourself!" But this didn't make sense. Laughing and *having fun is crazy.* What good does it do? I wanted to find out what was best for us during the short time we have on this earth. So I decided to make myself *happy* with wine and find out what it means to be foolish... (Ecclesiastes 2:2-3).

But St. Peter proposed another perspective tinged with sinfulness,
... They think it is *fun* to have wild parties during the day. They are immoral, and the meals they eat with you are spoiled by the shameful and selfish way they carry on (Second Peter 2:13).

Is "fun" more than frivolity, a diversion, a distraction, giddiness and humor? And how should "fun" be implemented in Christian youth ministry? To enhance the attractiveness of a program? As a hook to capture interest?

At the root of this issue is a nonbiblical worldview underlying Western civilization. The philosophy of Plato, promulgated four hundred years before Christ, is an antecedent to today's view that existence is two-fold, in ordinary language, sacred and secular. Judaism and the Bible reject this widespread formulation, but it continues to haunt Christianity. Hence, the religious and entertainment worlds would seem to exist in separate spheres. With that perspective, praying is spiritual and playing sports is secular. Inductive Bible study is sober and subdued, but Bible quizzing[10] may be regarded as exciting. Religious activities in youth ministry are then relegated to the spiritual realm while "fun" events or program elements are considered secular.

Youth ministry easily accepts this thinking, at least at the practical level. Many millions of times youthworkers around the world have barked out these words, "Settle down now — this is the *serious part* of the program"? *[Umayos kayo. Ito ay seryosong bahagi ng programa.[11]]* A common understanding seems to be, "This is the spiritual stuff so you need to *listen* — it is 'serious'; your eternal destiny depends upon it."

Because adolescents are so full of life, youthworkers often assume that programs focused on the devotional and/or cognitive will automatically be spurned. The temptation is to turn to "fun" as a palliative. In fact, many youthworkers will freely admit that games, humor or stunts are simply "bait," enticement to "get them in" or to arouse their interest. In this scenario, there is little realization of the underlying inference that anything "spiritual" is dull, boring and uninteresting and will therefore be distained by *emerging-adult-children*. One concludes that a "fun-based" progam appeals to the adolescents' reluctance to growing up and/or to the childishness so often observed, certainly in affluent youth. So the "fun" becomes in effect a bribe[12] — and the Truth of the Gospel is denigrated as a result. Moreover, it is an insult to adolescent intelligence to assume *emerging-adult-children* are more the latter (children) than the former (emerging adults).

How can the element of "fun" be used, but not as bait, hook or a gimmick designed to increase attendance/interest?[13]

A solution emerges if one broadens the concept of "fun." An informed definition of "fun" includes adjectives such as "pleasurable, enjoyable, satisfying, rewarding, gratifying, heart-warming and pleasing (because 'it meets my needs').''

"Fun" is not therefore necessarily always the humorous, the mindless, the ridiculous and so on. In fact, when a broader concept of "fun" is employed, Bible study can be "fun" when it meets one's heart needs, volleyball can be "fun" when it is part of joyous recreaction, likewise worship can be "fun" if it is heart-warming. In short, *Christian youth ministry ought to be "fun" all the time,* even in the reflective, sedate and quiet times, in the sense that the deepest needs of adolescents are being met, whether intellectual, physical, social or devotional. Does this mean playfulness is "out" and solemnity and gravity are "in"? Not at all, nor do these need to be woodenly balanced. The issue is, "What is the underlying purpose of any event/activity/class?" Appropriate methodology grows out of purpose. Sometimes hilarity is called for, other times not. But *it ALL can be "fun"* in the broadest sense of the word.

When *every* aspect of youth ministry is *powered by purpose*, it can then be said that the whole program is "serious," meaning related to goals and objectives, in this case, the maturation of youth. This purposeful dimension demands careful planning and preparation, in short, it is serious. Every element of youth ministry is, therefore, ideally marked as being *both "serious" and "fun."* "Fun" because youthworkers want to help teens have "satisfying experiences" and also "serious" because it is *all* related to Jesus Christ (spiritual). For instance, even a challenging wilderness trek can ultimately be "fun" for youth, though the process may include hardship, exhaustion and perhaps fear.

A better question to ask instead of, "Having fun yet?" is, "How can our program, curriculum, activities, classes, discipleship and whatever else we do, help build greater maturity into adolescents?" When that mission is being accomplished, questions about "fun" fade into the background as *every aspect* of youth ministry becomes both *fun and serious*. Instead the question can be, "Are we having serious-fun?"

TEACHING THE BIBLE TO YOUTH?

Certainly the teaching of the Bible deserves a central place in Christian youth ministry. *Emerging-adult-children* need to rely on God's Truth to understand how to live, today, tomorrow and forever. They must come to trust in the Bible to define their destinies in life, now and in the hereafter. Adolescence is a propitious time of life to discover and apply God's truths, even if they have not been exposed to these principles by their parents or elsewhere previously. Every Christian youthworker will heartily agree.

As a result of these insights, many *questions* rise to the top.
- What is it that *emerging-men/women-boys/girls* need to learn to have a maturing relationship with God?
- When should Bible truths be taught and/or learned? What information and at what ages?
- Who is responsible to see that God's Word is taught firmly, deeply, consistently and effectively?
- What role does a youthworker have in the preceding issues?
- How can youthworkers teach the Bible in a way that not only holds adolescents' interest but also becomes integrated into their lives?

Recently a seasoned youthworker wrote about an experience he had as a guest teacher a group of American youth.

> Looking over the various options of subject matter from the curriculum company we [the congregation] use, I was appalled! Sunday school curricula, in my opinion, has gigantically "dumbed-down" the content, most likely

because good old-fashioned Bible study must appear to be far too "robust" (and likely doesn't sell well either!). It ought to be called "pablum *[drivel]* for teens." I wonder if most of the fifteen or so teens in the class probably have grown used to such spiritual "junk food" *[not nutritious]* because that's all that's been offered.[14]

The writer's assessment of the problem was threefold:
1) The written curriculum seemed unsuitable.
2) The youth exhibited immaturity, apparently only ready for the milk of the Word, not the meat as described by St. Paul,
   - My friends, you are acting like the people of this world. That's why I could not speak to you as spiritual people. You are like babies as far as your faith in Christ is concerned. So I had to treat you like babies and feed you milk. You could not take solid food, and you still cannot because you are not yet spiritual (First Corinthians 3:1-3a).
   - In the *New International Version,* "not yet spiritual" is translated, "Are you not acting like mere humans?" Or like worldly youth?
3) The youth may have had and/or now have ineffective teachers who have reduced learner expectations for Bible instruction.

How accurate this one man's critique is in terms of current Bible teaching styles around the world is unknown, but it presents an issue probably not uncommon. Teaching the Bible should not be a haphazard or insubstantial activity within youth ministry. Or, better put, learning God's Word ought to be regarded as a resolute endeavor among youth, their parents and youthworkers.

Serious questions exist about Bible instruction for parents, congregations and youthworkers. These are not minor issues. Note the following concerns expressed in the Bible.

1) The prophet Hosea sadly writes, "My people are dying *for lack of knowledge...* (Hosea 4:6).[15] He is referring to the nation of Israel, but these words may possibly be applied to the lowered level of Bible erudition among adolescents. The paucity of grasp of Bible content may be due to home background, poor teaching at younger ages, youth's general immaturity and/or lack of commitment to grow and/or clumsy Bible teaching by youthworkers, perhaps too much levity and/or perhaps less than purposeful.

2) St. Paul instructs the leaders of the Ephesian believers to build up the body of Christ,
"... to mature manhood ... so that *we may no longer be children*, tossed to and fro by the waves and carried about by every wind of doctrine, by human cunning, by craftiness in deceitful schemes" (Ephesians 4:13-14, ESV). Or as paraphrased in *The Message*, we may become "... fully mature adults, fully developed within and without, fully alive like Christ."

As parents and youthworkers work to build maturity in the lives of youth, it is their obligation to bring them to the place of being able to handle substantive Biblical teaching and in fact to be eager to learn more. In short, Biblical education should not be considered an insignificant enterprise within the life of a congregation.

3) The Apostle Peter urges believers to exercise personal responsibility, "For this very reason, make every effort to *supplement your faith* with virtue, and virtue with *knowledge*, and knowledge with self-control, and self-control with steadfastness, and steadfastness with godliness..." (Second Peter 1:5-6, ESV). Or as stated

in CEV, "Do your best to *improve your faith*. You can do this by adding goodness, *understanding*. . . ." *Emerging-adult-children* have the major stake in their own Christian growth, whether they realize it or not. It is not inappropriate, therefore, to expect them to rise to this kind of challenge, given by parents and/ or youthworkers.

4) A lengthy challenge from the Book of Proverbs urges youth and others to seek wisdom through learning:
> These are the proverbs of King Solomon of Israel. . . Proverbs will *teach you wisdom* and self-control and *how to understand* sayings with deep meanings. *You will learn* what is right and honest and fair. From these, an ordinary person can learn to be smart, and *young people can gain knowledge and good sense*. If you are already wise, you will become even wiser. And if you are smart, you will learn to understand (Proverbs 1:1-5).

The question for youth is this. *To what extent am I or are we ready to accept responsibility as an emerging adult for my/our Biblical education?* The question for parents, congregations and youthworkers is this. *In what ways can we realistically challenge the emerging adult to wrestle with demanding Biblical and theological issues?* Neither of these questions comes with a simple answer.

Professor James E. Cote, in *Arrested Adulthood: The Changing Nature of Maturity and Identity*,[16] posits the argument that adolescents are not growing up because many adults have not done so! How realistic is it to expect early adolescents to step up and take responsibility for their learning about Christianity when their parents may only be sipping the milk of the Word of God? That is an issue for another book.

Fundamentally, the responsibility that an *emerging-adult-CHILD* will take for learning rests on several calculations.

First, are parents willing to prayerfully, responsibly and gradually hand over responsibility to the growing adolescent? If a parent, for example, closely superintends the boy's or girl's completion of schoolwork from day to day, the expectation for the child to be ready to dig into Bible learning for themselves may not be high.

Second, if a congregation is satisfied with:
- A milky-level curriculum, and/or
- Dry lecturers as teachers and/or
- Unpredictable devotional talks by a youthworker, in place of serious inquiry of the Bible, youth will soon learn to adopt lower aspirations for themselves.

Professor of youth ministry Thomas Bergler writes about it this way:

> As they [youth] listen to years of simplified messages that emphasize an emotional relationship with Jesus *over intellectual content,* teenagers learn that a *well-articulated belief system* is unimportant. . . . This feel-good faith works because it appeals to teenage desires for fun and belonging. It casts a wide net by *dumbing down* Christianity to the lowest common denominator of adolescent cognitive development and religious motivation.[17]

To whatever extent this one man's opinion is true, it offers a tragic commentary on contemporary youth ministry. Youth should demand more, but taking the path of childish immaturity is easier for them, especially when youthworkers may have low expectations for *the kids*.The problem is compounded when not-quite-matured adults are in leadership. As an ancient proverb declares, "A river cannot rise higher than its source."

The challenge for youthworkers, then, is, *"In what ways can we teach the core data and doctrines of God's Word so that they are interesting and relevant to youth?"* To fulfill this charge, a youthworker must seek to personally master Bible content, doctrine and theology. This does not necessarily require a seminary education, but it does call for diligent personal study. Additionally, a youthworker needs to become skilled in the art of teaching. Many books and resources are available to an individual who seriously desires to master the science and art of the teaching-learning process. Lastly, the real test of commitment for the youthworker is this. "Will you carefully and effectively *TEACH the Bible, TEACH the Bible, TEACH the Bible?"* Anything less is defaulting on what youth need as they emerge into manhood and womanhood.

The Apostle Paul is very clear when coaching his disciple Timothy. " . . *Proclaim the message*; be persistent whether the time is favorable or unfavorable; convince, rebuke, and encourage, *with the utmost patience in teaching"* (Second Timothy 4:2, NRSV).

ARE YOUTH EVER *FULLY MATURE IN CHRIST?*

"Maturity" is an elusive goal, in spite of all the evaluations that might be made of it. One may wonder, "Are adults ever *fully mature in Christ"*? The Bible teaches that the Christian life is a long journey of obedience and service to God, as expressed in one's daily life activities. The great Apostle Paul admits that he is still striving toward the goal, even though he also admits that he has run a good race. Perhaps living with this seeming contradiction is part of being mature. A Christian may be fully engaged in a life of service, yet still so permeated with the sinful nature that causes her or him to kneel humbly at the cross every day, seeking the Holy Spirit's infusion for power and guidance.

Perhaps there is something such as being "fully mature" for whatever stage of life someone is in. Or better put, *becoming* fully mature, to emphasize the process of sanctification and growth. Hence an adolescent has the potential to be on the road to maturity by following Jesus and the Bible consistent with his or her circumstances.

Are these goals too lofty? The answer lies in the adolescent's, the parent's and the youthworker's hearts. Certainly God has great goals for each one.

DEALING WITH LARGE GROUPS?

A practical issue faced by some youthworkers will be the tension existing between the disicpleship/mentoring of individuals, versus the large group approach to Bible teaching and activities. Often the youth minister is overwhelmed by the impossibility of facilitating *emerging-adult-children* in their journey toward maturity when she or he is faced with a large group.

This is particularly pronounced when a larger congregation is able to hire a part-time or full-time youth pastor who is in consequence expected to turn out both remarkable programs for, and growing attendance by, *emerging-adult-children*. The congregation vaguely hopes that the students will come away with lives on fire for Christ, a comprehension of worship, a knowledge of the Bible, a desire to serve God throughout life wherever they are and, last but not least, loyalty to the local church.

Frequently in a larger congregation activities are designed primarily for coeducational participation, as in the oft-applied designation, "youth GROUP." Many times the programs are staged with sparkling chatter and loud music. The youth minister is expected to capture the sometimes-wandering attention of adolescents as well as develop within them a fervor for Jesus and/or the Bible, possibly leading to some conversions. But time and again the youth minister finds it difficult to enlist experienced Christians outside the under-thirty-crowd to mentor youth individually, possibly because the congregation feels that they have delegated their responsibility to a paid staff.

> Youthworker: *"There you go again! I'm feeling depressed now."*
>
> **Maestro de iniciación:** "You despair of getting help?"
>
> Youthworker: *"Well, I know God is with me. But I'm still overwhelmed."*
>
> **Maestro de iniciación:** "Are these insuperable obstacles?
>
> Youthworker: *"O.K., you're right. It's not impossible in Christ. Just tell me what to do!"*

No one wants to minimize the challenge of being a paid youthworker. But the situation is not without hope. The Bible simply instructs youthworkers to be faithful in what they have been charged with doing and leave the results in God's hands. For example, St. Paul wrote to the believers in ancient Corinth,

- "Now it is required that those who have been given a trust must prove faithful" (First Corinthians 4:2, NIV).
- "For if the readiness is there, it is acceptable according to what a person has, not according to what he does not have" (Second Corinthians 8:12, NIV).

But what a lonely task! Better to pray for helpers by recruiting a team with Biblical objectives and do together what one cannot do individually.

CHANGING THE WORLD?

Does it sound grandiose, "changing the world"?

Perhaps it is. Jesus' imperative to his disciples as recorded in Acts 1:8 also seems quixotic! "But the Holy Spirit will come upon you and give you power. Then you will tell everyone about me in Jerusalem, in all Judea, in Samaria, and *everywhere in the world.*"

Emerging-adults-children, their parents and youthworkers *are* able, with the aid of the Holy Spirit, to make a difference! Envisioning Christian women and men penetrating their spheres of influence anywhere in the world is an achievable dream — it can and must be done for the glory of God. Amen.

NOTES

[1] Spanish.
[2] German.
[3] Filipino.
[4] Dutch.
[5] Czech.
[6] Afrikaans.
[7] Vietnamese.
[8] Swahili.
[9] Did the author have "fun" digging up these other translations? You can be sure he did!
[10] Thankfully, long passed away from the youth ministry scene — hopefully. D.C.J.
[11] Filipino/Tagalog.
[12] *Bribe* = to persuade someone to act in one's favor, typically dishonestly, by an inducement of some kind.
[13] Brian H. Cosby, *Giving Up Gimmicks: Reclaiming Youth Minstry from an Entertainment Culture* (Philipsburg, NJ: P and R Publishing House, 2012).
[14] Personal e-mail from veteran youthworker, Ronald H. Rynd, January 13, 2016.
[15] J.B. Phillips, *Four Prophets* (New York: The Macmillan Company, 1963), 34.
[16] James E. Cote, *Arrested Adulthood: The Changing Nature of Maturity and Identity* (New York: NYU Press, 2000).
[17] "When Are We Going to Grow Up? The Juvenilization of American Christianity," by Thomas E. Bergler (*Christianity Today*, June 8, 2012. Vol. 56, No. 6). 18ff.

AFTERWORD

New vistas are open today to youth, parents and youthworkers who are willing. Finding effective means for ministry to adolescents requires patience and creativity. This is especially true in societies in which youth are growing up into physical adulthood, but are still caught up in the irresponsibility and childishness of emotional immaturity.

Two futures rapidly confront adolescents, their parents and their youthworkers. One is the calendar that brings legal adulthood, as defined culturally, to the fore. The other future is the world, starting with the people next door,
- The people in the next compound or farm,
- The people down the road,
- The people in the next village, town or city, and
- The anonymous millions on the planet —

— each one with personal issues, perhaps spiritual emptiness or physical needs such as food, shelter and medical care, educational/psychological opportunities and finally freedom to pursue their lives with liberty from oppression. ". . . humans are to bring glory to God by living for the good of the world."[1]

As citizens of the world, Christians are sent to spend their lives in service to the peoples of the world in a myriad of meaningful ways.

Who will respond to God's call?

Who will, by the power of the Holy Spirit, prepare this and coming generations?

NOTES

[1] Warren Cole Smith and John Stonestreet, *Restoring All Things* (Grand Rapids: Baker Books, 2015), 22.

BIBLIOGRAPHY

Ambrose, Dub and Walt Mueller. *Ministry to Families with Teenagers*. Loveland, CO: Group Books, 1988.
Asante, Molefi Kete, and Ama Mazama, eds. *Encyclopedia of African Religion*. Los Angeles: SAGE, 2009.
Australian Aboriginal Culture. Canberra: Australian Government, 1989.
Berkhof, Henry. *Systematic Theology*. Grand Rapids: Wm. B. Eerdmans, 1996.
Borton-deTrevino, Elizabeth. *My Heart Lies South*. Bathgate, ND: Bethlehem Books, Ignatius Press, 2000.
Broholm, Richard R. "Toward Claiming and Identifying Our Ministry in the Workplace." *The Laity in Ministry*. Newton Center, MA: The Robert K. Greenleaf Center, 1985.
Carlson, Sherri. Letter to the author. 9 Dec. 2015.
Chagnon, Napoleon A. *Yanomamo*. San Diego: Harcourt Brace Jovanovich, 1992.
Conteh, Prince Sorie. *Traditionalists, Muslims, and Christians in Africa: InterreligiousEncounters and Dialogue*. Cambria, 2009.
Delaney, C. H. "Rites of Passage in Adolescence." *Adolescence* 30 (1995): 891-897.
DeVries, Mark. *Family-Based Youth Ministry*. Downers Grove, IL: InterVarsity Press, 1994.
Dowdy, Homer E. *Christ's Witch-Doctor*. Gresham, OR: Vision House, 1994.

Dowgiewicz, Mike. Personal blog. 24 Feb. 2015.

Dumont, Jean-Paul. *Visayan Vignettes, Ethnographic Traces of a Philippine Island*. Chicago: University of Chicago Press, 1992.

Eliade, Mircea, ed. *The Encyclopedia of Religion*. Macmillan, 1987.

Encyclopedia of Papua and New Guinea. Melbourne University Press, 2015.

Frazer, James George. *The Golden Bough*. 3rd Edition. London: Macmillan, 1926.

Griffin-Pierce, Trudy. *Earth Is My Mother, Sky Is My Father*. Albuquerque: University of New Mexico Press, 1992.

Gwynne, S.C. *Empire of the Summer Moon*. NY: Simon and Shuster, 2010.

Hall, G. Stanley. *Adolescence: Its Psychology and Its Relations to Physiology, Anthropology, Sociology, Sex, Crime, Religion, and Education* (Vols. I & II). New York: D. Appleton & Co., 1904.

Hill, Paul, Jr. *Coming of Age: African American Male Rites-of-Passage*. Chicago, IL: African American Images, 1992.

Howard, J. Grant. "Biblical Perspectives on the Church and Home." Unpublished Paper. Western Conservative Baptist Seminary.

Hyams, Edward, and George Ordish. *The Last of the Incas*. NY: Barnes and Noble, 1963.

Karras, Ruth Mazo. *From Boys to Men: Formation of Masculinity in Late Medieval Europe*. Philadelphia: University of Pennsylvania Press, 2003.

Keller, Dr. Timothy. "What is Common Grace." Redeemer City to City, 2003.

Keneally, Thomas. *The Chant of Jimmie Blacksmith*. NY: Viking, 1972.

King, Philip J., and Lawrence E. Stager. *Life in Ancient Israel*. Louisville, KY: Westminster John Knox Press, 2001.

Klopper, Sandra. *Ceremonies.* African Heritage Series. Cape Town: Struik, 2001.
Lewis, M. Paul, Gary F. Simons, and Charles D. Fennig, eds. *Ethnologue: Languages of the World.* 18th edition. Dallas, TX: SIL International, 2015.
Lewis, Mary C. *Herstory: Black Female Rites of Passage.* Chicago, IL: African American Images, 1988.
Lewis, Robert. *Raising a Modern-Day Knight.* Colorado Springs, CO: Focus on the Family, 2007.
Mahdi, Louise Carus, Nancy Geyer Christopher, and Michael Meade. *Crossroads, the Quest for Contemporary Rites of Passage.* Chicago, IL: Open Court, 1996.
Mahdi, Louise Carus, Steven Foster, and Meredith Little, eds. *Betwixt & Between: Patterns of Masculine and Feminine Initiation.* LaSalle, IL: Open Court, 1987.
Malina, Robert M., Claude Bouchard, and Oded Bar-Or. *Growth, Maturation and Physical Activity.* U.K.: Human Kinetics, 2004.
Mandela, Nelson. *Long Walk to Freedom.* New York/Boston: Little, Brown and Company, 1994.
Mckay, Brett, and Kate McKay. *Art of Manliness.* Artofmanliness.com. 9 Nov. 2008. http://www.artofmanliness.com/2008/11/09/.
Modi, Jivanji Jamshedji. *Education Among the Ancient Iranians.* Bombay: Times Press, 1905.
Mundhirī, 'Abd al-'Azīm ibn 'Abd al-Qawī, and Muslim ibn al-Ḥajjāj al-Qushayrī. *The Translation of the Meanings of Summarized Sahih Muslim.* Riyadh, Saudi Arabia: Darussalam, 2000.
Ong, Tony. "Reflection Paper #2.. Foundations of Youth Ministry course. Alliance Biblical Seminary. Quezon City, the Philippines. 12 July 2001.
Plotkin, Bill. *The Journey from Childhood to Adulthood: The Importance and Limitations of Rites of Passage.* Novato, CA: New World Library, 2008.

Popovic, Mislav. "Coming of Age Ceremonies in China" Traditionscustoms.com 2012. http://traditionscustoms.com/coming-of-age/coming-of-age-ceremonies-china.

Richards, Larry O. *Youth Ministry: Its Renewal in the Local Church (Revised Edition)*. Grand Rapids, MI: Zondervan Publishing House, 1985.

Roces, Alfredo, and Grace Roces. *Culture Shock – Philippines*. Portland, OR: Graphic Arts Center, 1985.

Sherman, Doug, and William Hendricks. *Your Work Matters to God*. Colorado Springs: NavPress, 1987.

Shoko, Tabona. "Komba: Girls' Initiation Rite and Inculturation Among the VaRemba of Zimbabwe." Published Paper. Department of Religious Studies, University of Zimbabwe, Harare, Zimbabwe.

Soga-Ang, Segundo, Filipino youthworker from Paracelis, Mountain Province, Luzon. Interview. "Foundations of Youth Ministry" course. Alliance Biblical Seminary. Quezon City, the Philippines. April 1997.

Stanley, Paul, and Bobby Clinton. *Connecting: The Mentoring Relationships You Need to Succeed*. Colorado Springs: NavPress, 1992.

Stephenson, Bret. *From Boys to Men*. Rochester, VT: Park Street Press, 2006.

Tadiar, Neferti X.M. *Things Fall Away: Philippine Historical Experience and the Makings of Globalization*. Durham and London: Duke University Press, 2009.

Turner, Victor. *The Ritual Process: Structure and Anti-Structure*. New York: Aldine de Gruyter, 1969, 1995.

Van Gennep, Arnold. *The Rites of Passage*. Trans. Monika B. Vizedom and Gabriella L. Caffee. Chicago: The University of Chicago Press, 1908/reprinted 1960.

Wilson, Laurence Lee. *Ilongot Life and Legends*. Southeast Asia Institute, 1947.

Yarian, Gregg. Letter to the author. 10 January 2016.

Youth ministry classes and/or seminar participants. Armenia, Canada, Mexico, Philippines, Singapore, USA.

APPENDICES

APPENDIX A, Traditional Female Transitions to Adulthood

- **With the *Yanamano,*** a jungle tribe in the Amazon Basin, a gender differential is obvious. "The distinction between male and female status develops early in the socialization process."[1] "Perhaps the most conspicuous and most important of these are the distinctions . . . that each sex goes through in growing to adulthood. . . ."[2]

Female children assume responsibilities in the household long before their brothers are obliged to perform domestic tasks. At an early age, girls are expected to tend their young brothers and sisters and help their mothers with such chores as cooking, hauling water, and collecting firewood. By the time girls have reached puberty, they have learned that their world is decidedly less attractive that than of their brothers.

. . . .

. . . the males marry later than the females do, so these boys are really young men, and the girls they are interested in are much younger, often just children. . . . The girl does not start living with her husband until after she has had her first menstrual period, although she may have been officially married for several years.

. . . .

323

A girl's childhood ends sooner than a boy's. Her game of playing house fades imperceptively into a constant responsibility to help her mother. By the time a girl is ten years old, she has become an economic asset to her mother and spends much of her time working. Boys, by contrast, spend hours playing together, and many manage to prolong their childhoods into their late teens and early twenties—by which time a girl will have married and may have a child or two.

....

A girl's transition to womanhood is obvious because of its physiological manifestations.

....

At first menses, *Yanomamo* girls are confined to their homes. . . . Their old cotton garments are discarded and replaces by new ones. . . . During this week of confinement, the girl is fed sparingly by her relatives and the food must be eaten with a stick, as she is not allowed to come into contact with it in any other fashion. . . . After her puberty confinement, a girl usually takes up residence with her promised husband and begins her life as a married woman.[3]

- **An example from the Philippines.** The Ilongot have their teeth filed when they are in their middle teens. Wilson[4] presents a vivid picture of how this is done.

A group of her boyfriends will rally round a girl in her house and hold her down tight while one cuts her teeth down — no matter how much she screams from the excruciating pain. After the operation, one lad will take a pencil-sized twig from a guava tree or the stem of a batac plant, heat it in the fire, and rub the warm bark on the teeth: thus, stopping the blood and easing the pain.[5]

APPENDIX B. Descriptions of Filipino *Tuli*

Newspaper accounts reveal the cultural expectation of both Filipino boys and men.

- By the time they [Filipino boys] leave elementary school, they will have to answer a serious query: "Tuli ka na ba?" (Are you already circumcised?) Their response will most likely have a profound effect on their self-esteem as they enter their teenage years, for in the macho Filipino society, every boy is expected to be circumcised before he becomes *a man*.[6]

- Today on reaching puberty, the boy starts to wear long pants and he is usually circumcised. . . . The boy goes with his friends to someone in the barrio or neighbourhood who is known to do the job — often the town barber. It is performed in private, with a razor or sharp bolo. . . . The rite makes the boy a man. He learns about sex though his peers. Circumcision . . . is more a macho act. Filipinos question derisively the manhood of someone who has not been circumcised with the derogatory term *supot*."[7]

- They used to soak themselves in cold and icy springs or salty beaches until they quiver to the bones for that once in a lifetime rite of passage. Nobody bothered to explain why, but for the boys of summer, this ritual serves as an anesthetic. After all, there are no surgical knives for the pain and no antiseptics for the cut. The quivering will dull the pain and minimize the flow of blood. No disinfectant and povidone-iodine solutions to prevent infection. For the boys, it was the old fashion *[sic]* young guava shoots chewed then spit on the slit of the foreskin that serves as roadside antiseptic. Yes, those were the days when pubescent boys in very loose T-shirts sans underwear nervously form the beeline for their turn to the annual summer ritual also known as circumcision. Those were the rude days when elderly uncles or grandpas initiated them into manhood. With homemade knives crafted by your neighborhood blacksmiths (are they still around?) serving as the only "surgical" instrument. The pointed tip of the razor-sharp knife is inserted into the foreskin of the penis and hammered by a wrist-size branch instantly cutting an incision (traditionally called *pukpok*). The sight is ghastly to some. For others, it's a fulfillment of a promise and entry into the *"brotherhood of men."* After all, no Filipino kid *[boy]* wants to be teased *"supot"* or uncircumcised.

....

Modern science and wider access to health care are however now affording kids painless incisions with antibiotics and antiseptic to boot when they go home. But elsewhere it is still the old fashion *[sic]* way. Now, go jump into the river![8]

APPENDIX C — Description of Filipina *Debut*

The following report appeared in a Manila newspaper.[9]

> K.M.R. formally joined *adult society* recently with a grand debutante's party at the storied X.X. Golf and Country Club. . KMR, a high-school senior . . . is the only daughter of . . . M.R.

....

> Instead of a cotillion [a dance with 9 couples], there was a lively (and often touching) presentation of 18 treasures, 18 moments and 18 roses to the debutante. Presenters were KMR's close chums from school and a slew *[sic]* of loving *titos* [uncles], *titas* [aunts] and cousins.

....

> The celebrator's sprightly grandfather . . . was the bubbly debutante's first dance.

> Her next dances were with her titos. . . .

In the "debut" tradition, each new dance partner gives the debutante a rose, until she carries 17. (It is an honor to be chosen to dance in the cotillion.) The last dance and rose come from a young man who serves as her escort.

This rite of passage includes 18 brief well-wishing greetings by parents and friends (just 18, each one holding a candle), more dancing, lavish refreshments and gift-giving.

Appendix D—*Creating a Rite of Passage in Your Family*, as quoted from the website cited below

One need not be a member of a religious community to undergo a rite of passage into manhood. A family is a very small community unto itself, and parents may create unique familial ceremonies in which sons are inducted into manhood. The options for such a ceremony are limited only by your creativity. Consider drawing up a list of tasks your son must learn to perform himself. When he has mastered all of these skills, throw him a celebration in which you present him with a medallion of some sort to commemorate the occasion. Or take him on a long backpacking trip in which he is responsible for making the fire, setting up camp, navigating, cooking food, etc. Along the way impart all the manly wisdom you have gleaned from life experience. Or you might want to take an extended father/son road trip.

To increase the "separation" required of a rite of passage, consider sending your son on a service trip to a foreign country or on a trip guided by an organization like Outward Bound. Enrolling your son in Boy Scouts is another great option. The Scouts have built in "rites of passage" that increase boys' skills, responsibilities, and feelings of competence. Whichever avenue you choose, the important thing is to imbue the process with great significance. Don't be cheesy *[sic]* about it, be sincere. And treat your son differently when the process is complete, giving him both greater respect and greater responsibility."[10]

Author's Note: *With recent changes in the policies of the Boy Scouts of America organization, some Christian parents may want to investigate the approach and programs of Christian Service Brigade (In USA, P.O. Box 1010, Hamburg, NY 14075, office@csbministries.org; in Canada, 1000 Stormont St., Ottawa, Ontario, K2C 0M. canada@csbministries.org). The use of "junior leaders" (secondary school students) within their adolescent curriculum promotes a sense of responsibility that contributes to maturation. These young leaders have authentic discipling opportunities with their peers within the scope of the stated program and for that reason, it is commendable. D.C.J.*

NOTES

[1] Napoleon A. Chagnon, *Yanamamo* (San Diego: Harcourt Brace Jovanovich, 1992), 150.
[2] Chagnon, 144.
[3] Chagnon, 151.
[4] Laurence Lee Wilson, *Ilongot Life and Legends*, Southeast Asia Institute, 1947.
[5] Teresita R. Infante, *Initiation into Adulthood*, Kasal.com.
[6] Ricardo T. Pamintuan, "'Tuli' or not 'tuli' (or the boyhood rites of summer)," *Philippine Star*, March 20, 2012.
[7] Alfredo and Grace Roces, *Culture Shock—Philippines*. (Portland, OR: Graphic Arts Center Publishing Company, 1985), 172.
[8] Edwin G. Espejoon, "The Boys of Summer Philippine Style," (*MindaNews*/14 May 2012). http://www.mindanews.com/feature/2012/05/15/the-boys-of-summer-philippine-style/.
[9] "Debutante cooks up her coming-of-age party." *Philippine Daily Inquirer*, May 23, 2004.
[10] http://www.artofmanliness.com/2008/11/09/coming-of-age-the-importance-of-male-rites-of-passage/.

INDEX

Aborigines, ... 76-78
Adolescence, definition of, ... 22, 27-28, 30-32, 112-114, 152-153, 291
Africa, ... 58-70, 84, 92, 105, 113, 274
Ambiguity, ... 31, 85, 112, 151, 254-256, 265-268
Analytical Model, ... 117-128
Apache Nation 110
Apprehending God, ... 276-278
Apprenticeship, ... 80-82
Asia, ... 72-74, 91, 108-110
Australia, ... 76-78, 259, 264, 275
Authority of parents, ... 137
Barkada, ... 34-35, 237, 259
Bar-mitzvah, ... 140-141, 180, 259
Becoming a man, ... 70
Bible teaching, ... 118, 134
Bible's expectations, ... 49, 161, 179-203, 209-222, 235, 272-273
Bonhoeffer, Dietrich, ... 228
Canada, ... 82-84, 94, 208, 229, 259
Catechism, ... 240
Christian growth 180-195
Changing the world, ... 22, 56, 100, 297, 310-318
Childishness, .. 158, 179, 196-197, 255-257, 313, 320

China, ... 72-73, 109, 129, 225
Circumcision, ... 60-61, 67-68, 94, 105
Citizenship, Christian, ... 191-192
Clitoricdectomy 94-95
Coeducation 86, 172, 207, 220, 237-238, 246-247, 280
Comanche Nation 83
Community activism, ... 213, 217-218
Confirmation, ... 82, 85, 99, 206, 220, 259, 264
Congregation's role moving youth toward adulthood, ... 224-242, 305
Correction, ... 119, 167
Creator/God,... 52-53, 124-125, 130
Curriculum, ... 241, 249, 310-315
Daily work, service of, ... 185-191
Daniel and companions, ... 86-88
Debut, ... 90, 317, 329-330
Denmark, 80-82, 106-107, 256-258
Developmental differences, ... 159-160, 208-209, 246
Discipline, ... 166
Elka, ... 22-29, 118, 134
Emerging-adult-child, parental acceptance of, ... 197-198
Emerging-adult-child, parental coaching of, ... 202-203

329

Emerging-adult-child, parental encouragement of, ... 199-200
Emerging-adult-child, parental forgiveness of 201-202
Emerging-adult-child, parental respect for, ... 200-201
Erikson, Erik, ... 144, 146, 156
Europe, ... 80-81, 105-108
Family life education, ... 119, 125, 239, 248
Female Genital Mutilation (FGM), ... 84-95, 105
Fun, ... 271
Gap year, ... 107-108, 217
Gender roles, ... 26, 234-235
Gender-specific preparation, ... 26-28, 42, 86, 121-123
General revelation, 51-52, 56, 103, 117, 124-125
Germany 106-107
Giftedness of youth, ... 230, 247
Goals of youth ministry, .. 118-120, 127, 181-195, 206-207, 241
Group, youth 316
Hebrew manhood growth stages, Boyhood, ... 135-140
  Emerging manhood, . 140-142
  Enhanced manhood, .. 142-144
  Generative manhood, . 144-145
  Life-review manhood, . 145-147
Hebrew womanhood growth stages, ... 149-157
  Barrenness, ... 149-152, 157
Holy Spirit, 43, 49, 157, 203- 218, 271, 278, 301, 315, 317, 321
Hope, ... 49-50, 271-272, 318
Howard, J. Grant, ... 153-154, 157, 160
I am a man, ... 60
Immature adults, ... 172, 284, 297, 313, 315

Incas, ... 75
India, ... 74-74, 109
Initiation, ... 22-25, 30-31, 53, 58-68, 116-128, 277-278, 293-301
Iran 86
Italy, ... 112-113
Japan, ... 74, 109, 278
Jesus, 138, 140-141, 155-156, 165, 182, 195, 198, 268, 272, 317
Jugendweihe, ... 106-107
Keller, Timothy, ... 52
Kenya 293
Kid, ... 234, 251, 296, 314
Korea, ... 110
Latin America 258
Leaders of youth, ... 282-286
Leaving childhood, ... 257-262, 292-293
Loving the Neighbor, ... 113-114, 212-213
Maestro de iniciación, .. 29, 41-42, 99, 120
Malaysia 99
Male socialization, ... 27
Mandela. Nelson, ... 58-63, 118
Matura, ... 108
Mature women 96-98, 110, 121-122, 150-151, 259
Measures of adulthood, false, 219, 262-263
Measures of adulthood, valid 260-261
Menstruation, 28, 90-94, 121-123, 292
Mentoring, .. 95-100, 202-203, 232
Mexico, ... 111, 213-214
Modeling, . 145, 168, 246, 297-298
Modernity, ... 254
Moses, ... 120, 135, 137, 139, 142
Mother Earth, ... 91, 111

Muslim, ... 95, 99, 101, 111

Native Americans... 82-84, 90, 99, 110, 277, 292
Navajo Nation, ... 90, 99
New Guinea, ... 78-80
North America, ... 82-85, 110
Norway 107
Oceania (see also Philippines), ... 78-81
O.F.W., ... 35-36
Parent involvement, ... 196-204, 280-282
Parent's role moving youth toward adulthood, ... 28, 119, 137-139, 163-164, 225-226
Peru 75, 275
Philippines, Republic of the 30-43, 95, 226, 232, 237, 263, 268-269, 275, 286, 328-329
Play, ... 28, 118, 120, 136-137
Proverbs, 120, 138, 161, 185-186, 313
Questions to Ponder, ... 42, 76, 85-86, 97, 114-115, 145, 170-175, 195, 204, 222, 224, 226, 228, 232, 236-242, 244-250, 268-269, 310, 313-314
Quinceaña, ... 40, 78, 90, 98, 110
Readiness for adulhood, ... 120
Respect for elders.... 105, 123-124
Responsibility of parents,.119-121
Role models, ... 114, 272, 283
Same-gender relationships, ... 121
Scarification, ... 65-66, 92
Seclusion,....54, 59-63, 92-94, 298
Seijin-no-hi, ... 109
Service outlook on life, ... 299
Service, family of God,.. 192-103, 218-219
Sex, purposes of, ... 125, 182-183

Singleness, ... 37, 246, 267-268, 284-285
Social media, ... 35, 40
South America,.. 22-25, 74-76, 91, 93
South Africa 58-63, 65-66, 105
Sports, ... 118, 120
Teaching the Bible, ...310-315
Teaching, ... 164-165
Ten Commandments, ...125, 161, 209
Tension between traditional culture and modernity, ...69, 103-105, 110-113, 116, 123-124, 209-210, 254, 258-259, 270
Tuli, ... 31, 328-329
Twenty-somethings,.98, 172, 224, 250
United Kingdom 107-108, 259
U.S.A. 82-84, 129, 148, 220, 229, 251, 259
Urgency in youth ministry, ... 249
Videregående, ... 107
Wai Wai people, ... 22, 27
Walkabout, ... 77-78
Youth, ... 152-153, 273, 278, 288
Youth Sunday, ... 231, 247
Youthworkers' role moving youth toward adulthood, ... 42
Zambia 97-98, 101-102, 208
Zimbabwe, ... 56, 96, 98-100